T0284761

IRANIAN WRITERS UNCENSORED

OTHER WORKS BY SHIVA RAHBARAN

The Paradox of Freedom:
A Study of the Life and Writings of Nicholas Mosley

Nicholas Mosley's Life and Art: A Biography in Six Interviews

IRANIAN WRITERS UNCENSORED

Freedom, Democracy, and
the Word in Contemporary Iran

SHIVA RAHBARAN

Translated by Nilou Mobasser

DALKEY ARCHIVE PRESS
CHAMPAIGN / DUBLIN / LONDON

Originally published in Persian as *Jayegah-e Sokhan* by Kitab-i Arzan, Kista, 2004
Copyright © 2004, 2012 by Shiva Rahbaran
Translation copyright © 2012 by Nilou Mobasser
First edition, 2012
All rights reserved

Library of Congress Cataloging-in-Publication Data

Rahbaran, Shiva, 1970-
 [Jaygah-i sukhan. English]
 Iranian writers uncensored : freedom, democracy and the word in contemporary Iran / Shiva
Rahbaran ; translated by Nilou Mobasser. -- 1st ed.
  p. cm.
 ISBN 978-1-56478-688-3 (pbk. : alk. paper)
 1. Authors, Iranian--20th century--Interviews. 2. Authors, Persian--Iran--Interviews. 3. Persian literature--20th century--History and criticism 4. Politics and literature--Iran--History--
20th century. 5. Politics and literature--Iran--History--21st century. 6. Iran--Politics and gov-
ernment--1979-1997. 7. Iran--Politics and government--1997- I. Mobasser, Nilou. II. Title.
 PK6415.5.R3413 2012
 891'.5509004--dc23
                              2011029773

Partially funded by a grant from the Illinois Arts Council, a state agency, and by the University
of Illinois at Urbana-Champaign

www.dalkeyarchive.com

Cover: design and composition by Laura Adamczyk, illustration by Nicholas Motte
Printed on permanent/durable acid-free paper and bound in the United States of America

INTRODUCTION

> . . . [Writing] constitutes resistance. Be-
> cause, in any age, the poet has been a
> protestor of a kind, resisting the thought-
> molds of the day. However, this protest
> might be political, it might be social, or
> it might even be philosophical. At any
> rate, the artist is at odds with the prev-
> alent conduct and thinking of his age;
> this has always been the case.[1]

> Tyranny is the cause of kings' fall
> as it brings the innocent heartache
> Ferdowsi, *Book of Kings*, tenth century A.D.[2]

Poets and writers have always been admired and feared for the
power of their pen by Iran's rulers. This is especially the case today,
three decades after a revolution that toppled the Pahlavi dynasty
and ended two and a half thousand years of monarchy in Iran.
The 1979 revolution, which with the growing influence of political
Islam became known as the Islamic Revolution, was supposed to

---

1 See page 55.
2 My translation. Original verse: "*Setam mayeh-ye azl e Shahan bovad / Cho-
dard–e del-e bigonahan bovad*," in Mostafa Jeihooni, ed., *Shahnameh-ye Ferdowsi, Tashih e enteghadi, Moghadameh-ye tahlili, Nokte-haye no-yafteh* (Isfa-
han: Shahnamehpajouhi, 1379/2000), verse 50.

bring freedom, hope, and prosperity to an oppressed people. Sadly, though, its legacy was nothing less than brutal humiliation, bloody despotism, war, and poverty. The poets and writers interviewed in this book bear witness to this observation. However, in order to understand this point of view, one has to look at the role of the poet in Iran in its historical context. I should stress that this book does not attempt to judge the work of the interviewed poets and writers from a literary point of view. As the aim of the book is to examine the influence of writers and their work in an undemocratic and oppressive historical and social context, the interviewees were chosen not only on the basis of their work and contribution to the canon of Persian literature, but also according to their social presence and significance.[3]

In the ninth century A.D., only two centuries after the fall of the Persian Empire at the hands of Arab Moslems,[4] New Persian (which has been continuously spoken and written for the past twelve hundred years in its present form) was revived as the only formal language that survived the Arab conquest of a multiethnic empire that stretched from the shores of Asia Minor, Egypt, Phoenicia, and Mesopotamia in the west to the Oxus

---

3   It is important to note that the literary voices—however great—of the Iranian Diaspora after the 1979 revolution have not been considered in this project, as the author of the present book was concerned with the role and the influence of the Iranian poets and writers in their post-revolutionary social context within Iran.

4   The Persian Empire fell to the Arab Moslems in 644 A.D. under Caliph Omar. Thus began the eventual extirpation of the Zoroastrian religion and the long process of the Islamization of Iran, which took about two hundred years.

and Indus rivers in the east. Whereas all other major languages of this empire—such as the languages of the Assyrians, Babylonians, Egyptians, or Phoenicians—perished and melted into an Arab linguistic identity, Persian, despite the vast Islamization of Iran, survived. It is in the resurrection and prevalence of the Persian language that Iranians see their glorious victory over all the invaders—Arabs, Turks, and Mongolians—in their country's turbulent history: the language of the conquered invariably became the language of the conquerors. Consequently poets writing in the Persian language are often envisioned as larger-than-life figures that have saved and guarded Iranian identity. Amongst scholars and common readers of Persian literature, the greatest of all these saviors is considered to be Ferdowsi, the tenth-century poet of *Shahnameh* (*The Book of Kings*). Ferdowsi famously wrote about the sacrifices and sufferings that he endured for over thirty years so that he could practice his vocation and thereby raise the Iranians back up from their submission[5] to their past glory by restoring their language.[6] In view of this, it is not surprising that Iran has many large poets' cemeteries, which are regarded as holy places.

---

5 The root of the word "Islam" means not only "peace" but also "submission" in Arabic.

6 The Arab term for Iranians was *Adjam*, meaning "the dumb" or "the tongueless." Ferdowsi claims to have resurrected the Persians by giving them back their language. All Persian speakers know his most famous lines by heart: *Bassi ranj bordam bedin sale-si / Adjam zende kardam bedin Parsi* ("*I suffered during these thirty years / But I have revived the 'Adjams' with the Persian tongue*"; my own translation).

It is important to bear in mind that Ferdowsi, Attar, Rumi, Nizami, Saadi, Hafiz, to name but a few, did much more than merely craft a rich body of literature: aside from being bards who conveyed the beauty of the word, they were subversive exposers of rulers and clergy as well as voices that bore testimony to the injustice suffered by the dispossessed. Their poetry is mystical and spiritual, but at the same time firmly grounded in earthly matters. Their concern is to polish the beauty of the word, as well as sharpen it to unveil injustice and hypocrisy. Many of them paid dearly for their literary and intellectual honesty.

With the dawn of modernity in the nineteenth century, Iran's poets were confronted with new risks and challenges. The legacy that the masters of Persian literature left them was a treasure, but, because the form and diction were increasingly perceived as outdated, also a burden. Nevertheless, Iran was changing quickly. The roots of these changes lie in the sixteenth century. From that time onward, newly formed empires in Europe began to form extensive diplomatic and mercantile relations with Iran. Initially, Iranians did not perceive these new partners—who were also rivals—as a threat to their sovereignty and identity. If anything, they saw them as their enemy's enemies—namely the enemies of the Ottomans—and thus as their friends.

It was not until the late eighteenth and early nineteenth century that Iran's sentiments about European—primarily British and Russian—powers shifted. Since that time, Iranians have had mixed feelings about these powers. They began to regard the influence of Great Britain in particular—and, a century later, that of its young ally, the USA—as invasive and colonialist. The greedy incompetence of the Qajar dynasty,[7] paired with the rising influence of the Shiite clergy,[8] hindered decision-making in favor of the Iranian nation and increasingly turned Iran not into a colony, but into a terrain for proxy wars between imperialist powers that brought misery and famine to the population[9]: an arena for the Anglo-Russian "Great Game"—a game that was to metamorphose into the Cold War a century later.

The star of Iran fell quickly due to these internal and external circumstances. Yet the Iranian intellectuals did not stop believing in an old myth—the rising of the phoenix from its ashes, so to speak. This time, they believed, the savior would come from behind the "enemy" lines: namely, from the West. The fascination of people with the material, intellectual, and artistic achievements of Europe (which only a century later was to be almost wholly overshadowed by the attraction of Iranians to the "American way of life") had as great an influence on public and private life as their mistrust of the Western powers. The intellectuals and educated

---

7   The Qajars reigned from 1796 to 1925.

8   A trend that had been implemented by the Safavid Kings in the sixteenth century as a means to unify the country against the Sunnite Ottoman empire on the one hand, and to exert power over the inhabitants on the other. For an introduction to the relation of the court to the clergy during the reign of the Safavid dynasty, read Colin P. Mitchell, *The Practice of Politics in Safavid Iran: Power, Religion and Rhetoric* (London: Tauris Academic Studies, 2009).

9   Homa Katouzian's *State and Society in Iran: The Eclipse of the Qajars and the Emergence of the Pahlavis* (London: I. B. Tauris, 2009) gives good insight into the fall of the Qajars at the hands of the Cossack officer Reza Khan, who was to found the Pahlavi Dynasty and become its first king in 1926.

Iranians strived to learn from their Western role models how to create a modern, democratic state where freedom, equality, and prosperity thrived. At the same time, the imperialistic and colonialist ambitions of those same "model" states were curbed.

The ascension of the Cossack warrior Reza Khan to the Peacock Throne in April 1926 heralded an era of hope in Iran. Reza Shah Pahlavi, the father of Mohammad Reza Shah Pahlavi (the last king of Iran, whose reign started in 1941 and ended with the revolution in 1979), dramatically intensified the process of "modernization from above," which had already begun in the 1850s despite the corrupt and backward politics of the Qajar dynasty.[10] The Qajars, under the strong influence of both the clergy and the Anglo-Rus-

---

10 Due to the great influence of the clergy both in society and in court on one hand, and the "colonial" politics of the Anglo-Russian powers in Iran on the other, the modernization of Iran under the Qajar kings was not a very successful undertaking. It seemed that for every step forward, two steps were taken backward. The most famous example of this unfortunate process is epitomized in the controversial figure of Amir Kabir, Nasir al-Din Shah's prime minister in the 1830s and '40s. Amir Kabir was a very authoritarian, elitist politician who tried hard to change Iran by sending students to Europe, founding the first Western-style university in Tehran, and modernizing traditional industries, such as the textile industry. He was faced with great resistance in the royal court, amongst the clergy and also on the part of the representatives of the Anglo-Russian imperial powers in Iran. He was found dead in the *Fin Hammam* (Fin Bath) in Kashan in 1852. Up to this day, there is a great debate in Iran about the identity of the "real men" behind the assassins—many accuse the clergy, and many accuse the agents of the British. Others believe that the king, Nasir al-Din Shah, was fearing the increasing power of his prime minister. And yet others see Malek Jahan Khanom, who was both Nasir-al Din Shah's mother and Amir Kabir's mother-in-law, as the mastermind behind Amir Kabir's assassination. Abbas Amanat's *Pivot of the Universe: Nasir-al-Din Shah and the Iranian Monarchy* (London: I. B. Tauris, 1997 and 2005) gives a good picture of Nasir al-Din's and Amir Kabir's era.

sian imperialist powers, were not committed to the "modernity project" that the educated and intellectual elites were undertaking despite all resistance from above. As a result, the large majority of Iran's educated class saw a savior in Reza Shah—at least initially. Reza Shah (like his Turkish contemporary Atatürk) set out to dismantle the largely feudalistic and traditional Iranian society through far-reaching changes. Reza Shah's ambition was nothing short of turning Iranian society both externally and internally into a Western one. The radical measures that he took in order to fulfill his dream of "seeing the phoenix rise from its ashes" included modernizing the army, safeguarding the state's sovereignty, limiting the influence of the clergy drastically, forbidding the chador, and making the population wear European attire. He also introduced extensive literacy programs for men and women, opened state-run schools for girls and boys, confiscated and redistributed Qajar lands, commissioned Western and Western-educated architects and urban planners to rebuild and expand Tehran and other major cities, sent students en masse to the West, and modernized medical and welfare establishments. His son, the Swiss-educated Mohammad Reza Shah Pahlavi, though lacking the charisma and popularity of his father, continued the modernization project even more extensively and hoped to see Iran and Japan as equals in Asia.

However, the dream of father and son did not come true. Iran, despite its riches, the vast modernization programs, and a strong modern army never equaled Japan. Of course, this was partly the result of the superpowers' intrusive interest in Iran's oil fields and partly the result of the country's precarious position in perhaps the most volatile region of the world: the Middle East, the central ground in which the "Great Game" and the ensuing Cold War unfolded. However, the success of an unprecedented revolution in this region and the fall of the strongest power in the Persian Gulf region cannot be seen primarily as the result of the political games of the European empires and its succeeding superpowers.

Many historians see the main reason for the fall of monarchy in Iran in the failure of both father and son to foresee the side effects of their modernization project—or if they did foresee them, their failure to forestall them. Neither leader realized that modernity and a modern civil society can only thrive in a democratic state. They did not accept that critical reflection and self-reflection are inevitable in a democratic society. The majority of the countless students who had been educated in the West, and were supposed to come back and build a modern Iran, wanted not only the material achievements of the West but also Western values. Even those who returned to Iran with a critical view of the West exercised their criticism on the basis of the same principles on which criticism in the modern, democratic world was built. Modernity and democracy seemed to be inseparable and universal.

Oblivious to this insight, both the Shahs and the superpowers—from whose invasive policies the Pahlavi kings actually did try, unsuccessfully, to emancipate themselves[11]—thought modernity and

---

11   Both the left and the Islamic ideologists have long claimed that the Reza Shah's son, Mohammad Reza Shah Pahlavi (reigned from 1941–1979), was a puppet of the Western powers. The CIA-backed coup against the national hero of modern Iran, Dr. Mossadegh—who nationalized Iran's oil industry despite vehement resistance on the part of the British government and the Anglo-Per-

democracy unfit for a "traditional," "eastern" society such as Iran. That none of them were the Iranian people part of the equation—the London-backed and CIA-led coup that deposed Mossadegh,[12] the democratically elected, modern Iranian hero and nationalizer of the oil industry, and restored Mohammad Reza Shah to the throne in 1953—is a telling example of how mistrustful both the superpowers and the Iranian rulers were of the people.

Nevertheless, the modernization project of the Shahs bore fruit rapidly. Despite strong protests from religious conservatives and cautionary skepticism on the part of Western-educated liberals, the people in general, and the urban population in particular, seemed to embrace and profit from the new developments. The changes that had started as a decree from above seemed to be fall-

---

sian Oil Company—and the reinstallation of the Shah to the throne, seems to give evidence for this thesis. However, from the time of his reinstallation to the throne in 1953 to the end of his reign in 1979, the Shah did try to become independent of foreign powers and to reduce their intervention in Iranian affairs. There are those who would even go as far as saying that the revolution in Iran was backed by the West as the Shah was becoming too strong and independent a power in the Persian Gulf region. Today, there are many historians and scholars who see the Shah's complex relation to the West in a more objective and differentiated light. Read G. R. Afkhami, *The Life and Times of the Shah* (2008), and Assadollah Alam, *The Shah and I: The Confidential Diary of Iran's Royal Court 1968–1977* (2008).

12 Dr. Mohammad Mossadegh, a Swiss educated aristocrat and an ardent opponent of foreign intervention in Iranian affairs, was Mohammad Reza Shah's Prime Minister from 1951 to 1953. He nationalized Iran's oil industry despite vehement resistance from the British government and the Anglo-Persian Oil Company in 1951. His passionate speeches at the UN General Assembly and the International Court of Justice in The Hague are legendary amongst Iranians.

ing on fertile ground and were taking root in many minds. The emancipation of women; the increasing literacy amongst peasants, workers, and the lower classes; the growing prosperity amongst middle classes and small-business owners; the improved awareness of medicine and hygiene; and the masses of Western-educated students were now forging a new civil society that wanted all the benefits of a modern state, including democracy, transparency, and freedom.

Tragically, the Shahs reacted to this development by reducing and crippling democratic institutions: political parties were banned (less than two years before the 1979 revolution, there was only one political party allowed in Iran), the powers of the parliament and the judiciary were dramatically curtailed, and censorship of books and the press was made a top priority. Especially under the late Mohammad Reza Shah, anti-democratic measures took an ugly turn in the 1950s with the founding of an intelligence service staffed by CIA-trained officers, whose infamous methods of quelling anti-Shah political activities both in and outside Iran cast a negative light on the Shah.

The new developments brought Iran's intellectuals, poets, and writers up against unprecedented challenges. Modernity and modernization created dissonance amongst the Iranian intelligentsia. Being part of the educated elite, they wanted a modern and prosperous Iran and were aware that it needed to go through painful changes to attain that identity. Some outliers would go as far as to dream of a completely Western, Europeanized Iran both outside and inside, where Eastern, Iranian "race" and "identity" would be completely erased.[13] Most, however, were critical of the bulldozing measures that were transforming Iran at a mind-bending speed. Almost all agreed that there was no way around confronting the contemporary and modernizing developments. The challenge was how to introduce and implement these changes without throwing out the baby with the bathwater.

The Iranian intelligentsia was thus fragmented regarding the ways in which the "modernity project" was supposed to be confronted. Some were more sympathetic toward the royal party's policies, others toward the opposition. There were also those who tried to reconcile the two sides; however, the lack of democratic goodwill on the part of the Shah and his government, and the conspiratorial atmosphere of the Cold War era, made consensus impossible. An atmosphere of mistrust reigned, especially among the liberal and left-wing writers and thinkers, who often sympathized or were thought to sympathize with the Soviet Union. The Shahs, in particular Mohammad Reza Shah, were faced with a vicious circle: the more modernization measures were introduced, the more modernity the people wanted and thus the less control the Shahs held over the people. The Iranians seemed to be biting ungratefully the hand that fed them. The court's reaction to this was to start introducing packages of measures aimed at ever-tighter public control. Political parties, newspapers, books, and

---

13   A popular joke amongst the modern, Westernized Iranian elite regarding the difficult "modernity project" in their country was (and still is) about a nuclear attack on Iran, after which citizens of the modern, Western world would come to Iran and found a new race and new country.

other media were banned. The Ministry of Culture's "guidelines" for art and literature had top priority on the agenda. Writers and artists were not allowed to criticize of the royal family, the state's sovereignty, or the court's official version of Islam.[14]

In this climate, Iranian writers and poets—regardless of their political convictions—became the "mouthpiece" of the oppressed. Inevitably their writing became political and they themselves became spearhead figures in the fight against despotism. Even those who were absolutely apolitical and reclusive were swallowed up by the political atmosphere, and their absence was interpreted in a political context. The televised trial of a young, famous poet, Golsorkhi, who was tried and executed for treason in 1974 (he was barely 30 years old at the time of his execution), added more fuel to the fire. Writers and poets who were skeptical of literature's involvement in politics were seen by their comrades at best as naïve, and at worst as greedy traitors.

The victory of the 1979 revolution and the end of monarchy in Iran provided new spaces for creativity in literature. Amidst bloody upheavals and ruthless power games between revolutionary factions, all of whom claimed the revolution for themselves, writers were experiencing an unprecedented, exciting freedom. Books on Maoism were sold next to booklets on sexual libertinism; pamphlets on feminism were on offer together with guides

---

14   Under Mohammad Reza Shah, many Islamic ideologists, such as the leader of the Islamic Revolution in 1979, Ayatollah Khomeini, were prosecuted and had to go into hiding or exile because their understanding of political Islam went against the court's conception of that religion. For ideologist Mullahs, Islamic law was the one true authority to which all had to submit.

to Sharia law for beginners. Banned Persian and foreign literature was available in the countless bookshops in university quarters throughout the country.

This "Spring of Freedom" was, however, painfully short. Under the leadership of Ayatollah Ruhollah Khomeini (who was the leader of the Islamic revolution until the time of his death in 1989), the reactionary, anti-Western representatives of political Islam prevailed over their left-wing and liberal comrades-in-arms and eventually came to hold great political power through appointments in key positions and by prosecuting their liberal and left-wing former allies in the fight against the Shah. Intellectuals and writers were now faced with a far more precarious situation than they had experienced under the monarchy; namely, an anti-modern regime that was doing everything in its power to undo Iran's struggle for modernity. It seemed that the issue for the new men in power was not how to grapple with modernity while preserving the old values, traditions, and identity, but rather how to eradicate modernity completely from Iranian society. Still, the protests against the Islamic regime, which erupted at regular intervals in the past thirty years, and the bloody efforts to jerk Iran back into a pre-modern age have proved a fatal mistake for the regime and taken a huge toll on the people (the most recent uprising, commonly known as the "Green Wave,"[15] received prominent international coverage). The process

---

15   This wave initially started as a protest against fraud in presidential elections in June 2009. President Mahmoud Ahmadinejad "won" the election thanks to widely practiced irregularities. "Where is my Vote?" has since become an internationally known slogan of the Iranian people. However, the protests did not stop there. They have now become a huge wave, which threatens to topple

of modernization and the project of modernity turned out to be irreversible. The very revolution itself was a modern phenomenon.[16] The introduction of Sharia law into the judiciary, forcing women to wear the chador, segregating boys' and girls' schools, banning dance and music, and "Islamizing" university and school curricula were some of the measures that the new, religious regime took in order to reverse the modernization process that Iran had been going through over the past hundred and fifty years. At the same time, the Islamic regime, ruling over an oil- and gas-exporting country, has shown insatiable interest in promoting trade relations with the Western world (despite its anti-Western rhetoric).

Thus, in order to establish trade ties with the "demonic" West, apologists and lobbyists for the Islamic republic have continually tried to create an image of an up-to-date yet Islamic system, in which illiteracy is at 15 percent maximum, where more than two-thirds of the approximately one-and-a-half million university students are female, and where women have electoral rights (though it is forbidden for them to stand as candidates for higher posts such as Iran's presidency). What these lobbyists hide from Western eyes is the fact that these achievements are all part of the project of Iran's modernization, which had already started in the

---

over the Islamic regime. Thanks to the wide use of the Internet in Iran, the brutalities of the regime against its own people were seen by many (the heart-wrenching death of a young female student, Neda Agha-Soltan, during one of the protests by a bullet shot through her throat from above a building, was seen by millions of people via YouTube). These images have helped the protesters to mobilize a lot of international sympathy for the people.

16   Atashi in particular points this out in the following interviews.

mid-nineteenth century and has deep roots in Iranian civil society (especially in the urban sector). So the number of Iranian students has continued to increase despite the regime's desperate efforts to Islamize the universities[17]; feminist consciousness has grown despite the regime's efforts to segregate men and women in public spaces and despite the Sharia law that considers women's lives and testimonies to be worth half as much as those of men; the importance of pro-Western and liberal education has gained greater weight despite the regime's anti-modern policies; the Iranian civil society has sought to connect and interact with the modern global community via satellite TV and the Internet despite the regime's rigorous politics of isolation. Throughout the past three decades many Iranians have been feeling that the Islamic regime has been trying to force the whole nation back to the early days of Islam. What most hurt their national pride was that the leader of the Islamic Regime, Ayatollah Khomeini, tried to erase the notion of the nation of Iran (*mellat-e Iran*) and replace it with the notion of a nation of Islam (*Ummatolislam*)—an experiment that failed, but whose cost was a heavy loss of lives and minds.[18]

In the eyes of poets and writers, there were indeed parallels between what they perceived as their task and the legacy of the

---

17 It should not be forgotten that after the revolution in 1979 the universities were closed for about three years and "cleansed" as part of the regime's "culture revolution."

18 The eight-year war between Iran and Iraq, mass executions, brutal oppression, and unprecedented corruption caused innumerable deaths (international observers speak of at least half a million deaths on the Iranian side) and led many Iranians to flee the country.

Persian poets after the Islamic invasion.[19] As mentioned earlier, already in the ninth century, only two hundred years after the Islamic invasion of Iran, Iranian poets had started to resist the new, Arab rulers by writing poetry in New Persian and thus resurrecting the Iranian identity. Now the contemporary poets of Iran, who had already grappled with modernization, modernity, and modern values under the monarchy, were also faced with ideological "invaders." Formerly, during the reign of the Qajars (1796–1926) and the Pahlavis (1926–1979), Iranian poets had been faced with a new phenomenon, which had appeared threatening, but at the same time had offered values, such as freedom, individual rights, equality, and the pursuit of happiness and prosperity, that they found desirable. But now, under the anti-Western, anti-modern Islamic regime they were confronted with new challenges and told to bow to an ideology, based on a peculiar understanding of Islam, an ideology that ordered them to discard all modern values. Furthermore, the censorship imposed on them during the monarchy bore little relation to the censorship imposed by the new regime: even under the monarchy, blatant disrespect of religion was not allowed, as the Shahs did not want to fall completely out of favor with the clergy.[20] Now, however, Iran's intelligentsia had to come to grips with a censorship that prohibited the slight-

19   In the following interviews, Mohammad Hoghooghi boldly compares the present time (i.e. post-Islamic revolution) with the times of Arab, Turkic (tribes from central Asia that attacked and invaded parts of the Iranian Plateau and Asia Minor from the ninth century onward), and Mongolian invasions.

20   The critical theologian, Ali Dashti, had to publish his groundbreaking biography of the prophet Mohammad and the early days of Islam, *Bist o Seh Sal* (*Twenty-Three Years*), in Beirut, because Mohammad Reza Shah feared the fury of the Mullahs.

est criticism of religious ideology and invaded the core of their private spheres with unprecedented fury. This new censorship was a mechanism of ideological control that impinged on their most intimate and sexual private lives.[21] Under the monarchy they had to discover and forge a modern, literary identity without losing their old one—and, unfortunately, the result was not always a success. Now they were told to abandon their old—and their new—Iranian identity and let this cultural identity dissolve in the religious (and Shiite)[22] nation of Islam. Indeed, new tools, forms, and strategies were needed to face these new circumstances.

The following interviews testify to how boldly and consistently writers and poets have been facing post-revolutionary circumstances in the past three decades. They talk freely about their untiring hope and endeavor to create "pockets of freedom" in a society where the rulers regularly and brutally stifle any move that questions their legitimacy. They provide insights into their daily struggles to fend off the censorship imposed on every form of artistic expression. Their testimonies show that the regime is en-

---

21   The dissertation of the leader of the Islamic Revolution, Ayatollah Ruhollah Khomeini, conveys this clearly. A large part of his *Toziholmassa-el* (the original copy of which is only found in underground bookshops in Iran) is preoccupied with regulating the behaviour of the Moslem men and women during sexual intercourse (with all dead or living creatures of the Almighty) and after digestion. Atashi and Ravanipour highlight in their own interviews in this book the intrusion of the *Sharia* law into the intimate spheres of personal life after the Islamic revolution.

22   It would not be an exaggeration to accuse the Islamic regime of religious apartheid amongst Iranian Moslems. The fifteen percent Sunnite and other Moslem groups living in Iran do not enjoy the same civil rights as the Shiite majority. A Sunnite could never hold a high managerial, official, or governmental post, let alone run as candidate for a ministerial post.

gaged in a hopeless fight to reverse the clock in Iran and to throw a widely literate, globally networked civil society into darkness. In doing so, they risk broken pens and, more often than not, broken lives. However, they believe that literature is worth the risk, as literature is their means to restore their humanity and dignity. In this sense, contemporary literature is still very political and socially conscious—even (or maybe especially) in its silence.[23] Thus, now more than ever, writers and poets in Iran have become public figures of resistance. In these interviews many of them often point out that writing means resisting.

It is important to note that these interviews were carried out in the last days of Mohammad Khatami's presidency—the reformist politician under whose administration the Ministry of Islamic Guidance loosened its grip on art and literature to some degree. The free manner in which the writers in this book speak about their work in post-revolutionary Iran is to some extent due to the relatively tolerant atmosphere during Khatami's two terms of presidency (1997–2001; 2001–2005). However, Khatami's half-hearted reforms and unrealized "dialogue of civilizations" disappointed the great majority of Iranians, who had elected him as

---

23 Interestingly enough—and sadly in the eyes of Iranian writers, as they state in their interviews—in the worldview of modern, Western scholars and theoreticians, it is the very precarious existence of the writer in oppressive societies that gives literature its meaning and value. As soon as a society like Iran achieves the same status as Western democracies, the poets and writers become unimportant figures that in the postmodern, poststructuralist manner even erase themselves.

the man who would end the reign of terror from within[24] and achieve the peaceful transition of Iran to the modern, free world. His halfhearted reforms also strengthened the reactionary, conservative power structures and paved the way for the power seizure of the regime's reactionary, right-wing politicians and revolutionary guards under the leadership of Ayatollah Khamenei and Mahmoud Ahmadinejad in 2005.[25] During Khatami's presidency many writers, poets, intellectuals, and members of the opposition were assassinated both in and outside Iran at the hands of the reactionary wing before the eyes of a helpless president. The very fact that this book was closely examined by the Ministry of Islamic Guidance for over a year, only to be found unfit for publication,[26] testifies that the changes under Khatami were more or less cosmetic. The poets and writers who are interviewed in this book draw the attention of the reader to the precarious situation in which they live and work. Many of them are bitter about the assassinations and "accidents" that have taken their fellow writers and thinkers away from them, both in and out of Iran, and many of them acknowledge they might be next. In March 2010

---

24   Khatami won the presidential election in 1997 in an unprecedented landslide victory and enjoyed a great backing from the people. However, he disappointed this great majority, who saw in him an Iranian Gorbachev, by bowing to the leaders of the reactionary right-wing of the regime.

25   Mahmoud Ahmadinejad was elected president of Iran in 2005 and 2009. Many observers believe that he won both terms thanks to blatant fraud. The present uprising in Iran initially began as a protest against this fraud in June 2009, but has gradually developed into a movement against the whole Islamic regime.

26   The book could only have been published in Iran if over thirty pages of the interviews were cut.

one of the interviewees in this book, Simin Behbahāni (aged 83) the grande dame of contemporary Persian poetry, was arrested at the airport in Tehran on her way to France to receive a prize for her untiring fight against despotism and oppression. Like Simin, the poets and writers in Iran speak out and unwaveringly maintain that literature's meaning is in opening spaces of awareness in the mind of the reader and pockets of freedom in society.

SHIVA RAHBARAN, 2012

Translator's Note

An old adage advised that "children should be seen, not heard." Similarly, I would suggest that translators should be neither seen nor heard. So it is with great trepidation that I appear here to offer a few explanations.

The exclamation marks and ellipses in the translation, as well as anything in parentheses, are from the published Persian original. The only exception is that English translations of titles are in parentheses; obviously, these are not from the original.

In the few cases where an Iranian book has been published in English, I've italicized the English title as well as the Persian title; e.g. Sādegh Hedāyat's *Buf-e Kur* (*The Blind Owl*). In the cases where, to the best of my knowledge, there is no published English translation, I've only italicized the Persian title; e.g. *Ruzegār Separishodeh-ye Mardom-e Sālkhordeh* (The Bygone Days of Elderly People). Also, where I have been able to find a reliable source, I've used the writers' own preferred English translations of titles.

For the transliteration of names, wherever possible, I've used a person's own preferred English spelling. Otherwise, there is no rigorous transliteration system. I've simply tried to give a sense of how a name or a word is pronounced. Anyone who is familiar with Persian will be aware of the difficulties of transliteration, and anyone who is unfamiliar with Persian hopefully will not notice the inevitable inconsistencies.

The square brackets and footnotes in the text were added by me with the aim of offering clarification where a name, event, or concept might not mean very much to a non-Iranian reader. It goes without saying that I am wholly to blame for any inadequacies in these footnotes. Hopefully, the defects will encourage discerning readers to investigate further.

NILOU MOBASSER, 2012

IRANIAN WRITERS UNCENSORED

SIMIN BEHBAHĀNI

Born in Tehran in 1927, her many poetry books include *She-tār-e Shekasteh* (The Broken Lute), *Jāy-e Pā* (Footprint), *Chelcherāgh* (Candelabrum), *Marmar* (Marble), *Rastākhiz* (Resurrection), *Khatti ze Sor'at va Ātash* (A Line of Speed and Fire), *Dasht-e Arzhan* (Arzhan Plain), *Kāghazin Jāmeh* (Paper Dress), *Kuy va Nāmeh va Eshq* (Alleyway and Letter and Love), *Āsheqtar az Hāmisheh Bekhān* (Read It More Lovelorn than Ever), *Yek Daricheh Āzādi* (A Windowful of Freedom), *Bā Qalb-e Khod cheh Kharidam* (What I Bought with My Heart), and *A Cup of Sin: Selected Poems*.

She received the Carl von Ossietzky Medal in 1999 for her courageous struggles in defense of freedom of expression in Iran.

SIMIN BEHBAHĀNI

Simin Behbahāni is optimistic about where Persian thought and literature are headed, despite Iranian society's many post-revolution disillusionments. She speaks of the ruinous itinerary of the "literature of censorship" and the phenomenon of self-censorship, but she believes that exceptional knowledge has been stored up given Iranian social and cultural resistance to the consequences of the 1979 revolution. This knowledge creates fertile ground for the growth of contemporary Persian literature. From this perspective, the importance of poets and writers for the survival of Iranian civil society is undeniable. Behbahāni points out that this role has been inherited today after a thousand years of attacks on Iran's writers and thinkers.

Behbahāni views her poetry in its historical context. She sees herself as an iconoclast, but has never severed her link with Iran's past literature. On this same basis, far from attaching any importance, as a poet, to "being a woman," she considers any reference to it an insult. In other words, her poetry is part of Persian poetry as a whole, whether produced by men or by women. Behbahāni's poetry is varied and, as she puts it, "multivocal," because her poetry is the poetry of the "moments" of her life—whether the moments of "convoys of war martyrs on their way to the cemeteries" and "lorries carrying the bodies of executed prisoners, dripping with blood" or the moments of happiness. For Behbahāni, a good poem is one in which "today's language, today's events and today's needs" are poured into the mold of rhyme and meter.

SHIVA RAHBARAN: The aim of this study is to discover what impact the 1979 revolution has had on Iranian art and literature, from the point of view of artists and thinkers who are currently living and working in Iran. This study has two parts: in the first part, it tries to come to grips with the post-revolution changes, in terms of the way in which post-revolution contradictions and divides have affected literature. In the second part, we want to look at the role of literature and its effect on society.

The first question is about democracy. What impression do people in Iran have of democracy? Do they think that democracy always produces the desired outcomes? Have Iranian thinkers done anything to inform people about the dangers of democracy or not? Also, many people are of the view that democracy is not suited to Iranians.

SIMIN BEHBAHĀNI: Iranians have more or less the same impression of democracy as do the other nations of the world. Democracy means rule by the people. As long as it doesn't make an about-face and turn into a dictatorship, it's very desirable. Why, really, should democracy be suited to other nations but unsuited to Iranians? Western nations have experienced dictatorships in the past too and no Western nation has had a democratic state at the beginning of its history. Democracy is the product of human thought and reasoning. It's true that philosophers and thinkers have always imagined a utopia in which everything is as it ought to be and the people live in freedom and comfort. But this was not achieved until recent centuries. And it can even be said that, even in the freest and most developed countries, the bounds of democracy are overstepped from time to time. Or, a country that wants democracy for itself sometimes disregards other countries' rights to freedom. So the Iranian nation, too, wants democracy. But I think that it hasn't, in its experience, reached the necessary conclusions in its reasoning for this kind of government. The Constitutional Revolution[1] and the Islamic Revolution[2] were carried out within a short space of time in the hope of gaining freedom. But, from the start, the people's dream of freedom turned into a nightmare of tyranny. But I believe that these kinds of experiences and setbacks are necessary to attaining freedom and real rule by the people.

Today, another Hitler can't come to power and turn Germany into a hellish dictatorship and set the world ablaze. Having had this experience, the German nation will be forever immune to the risk of this kind of government.

Our thinkers, too, are changing in the light of the experiences that they have had under an Islamic state. They will no longer consent to any old kind of tyranny as they would have done twenty years ago. We can see that killing people and imprisoning them no longer has the desired effect! Although proponents of freedom are still sent to prison, the future is bright and we will gradually acquire the knowledge that we need to achieve democracy.

---

1   Popular movement in early twentieth-century Iran aimed at curbing kings' absolute power. As a result of the Constitutionalist Movement/Revolution, Iran's first parliament was established in August 1906.
2   Popular uprising in 1978–1979, which led to the overthrow of the monarchy and the establishment of the Islamic Republic.

S.R. In the West, some analysts call the Iranian revolution "the Iranian experiment." What they mean by this expression is the synthesis of modernity and religion. Do you think this synthesis is feasible?

S.B. I think that the lapse of 1,400 years can never be discounted. Under the Islamic state, punishments are being carried out that are totally inappropriate in this day and age, such as cutting off thieves' hands or stoning adulterous women and men or flogging offenders.

Although Islam always recommends that laws should be in keeping with the times, the religious scholars, jurists, and clerics of our times have not tried to find a way of bringing old laws up to date. It is obvious that the modern world views the cutting-off of hands or feet, stoning, or flogging as a contravention of human rights, and if a solution is not found for bringing these laws into line with the modern world, the success of these kinds of nations will be doubted and require a miracle.

S.R. What is an Iranian writer or artist's assessment of their role in Iranian society today? Bearing in mind that, even including the previous state's policies, artistic activity has been difficult in Iran, how prolific has literature been and what progress has it made?

S.B. Despite my age, I can almost say that I have never put pen to paper without censorship worries. The nightmare of censorship has always cast a shadow over my thoughts. Both under the previous state and under the Islamic state, I have said again and again that, when there is an apparatus for censorship that filters all writings, an apparatus comes into being in every writer's mind that says: "Don't write this, they won't allow it to be published." But the true writer must ignore these murmurings. The true writer must write. In the end, it will be published one day. On the condition that the writer writes the truth and does not dissemble. Of course, whenever the censorship is stringent, most writers resort to metaphors and figurative and symbolic language. And this can help stimulate the imagination. But taking comfort from this fact doesn't lessen writers' dream of attaining freedom.

S.R. So does it become necessary for art to be political?

S.B. Politics is the impact of the prevailing atmosphere on the people and, naturally, on any artist, especially writers. Regardless of how far removed a writer may be from knowledge of politics, it is impossible to rid the mind of the influence of the prevailing atmosphere. Politics becomes a part of a writer's working life. The writer's protagonists are born in the context of the feelings that this atmosphere evokes. How can writers separate themselves from these feelings and create protagonists that come from Mars? Even writers who only write about psychological or internal issues or about love are writing under their prevailing atmosphere, and their writings will take on the hue of the time, place, and mood of their environment.

S.R. Has literature reacted to the anomalies that nations, past and present, have engendered? Has it played a constructive role in changing the mood and creating normalcy?

S.B. Of course. Our literature has always been a reflection of contemporary events. The *Shāhnāmeh*[3] is the greatest epic in history. It is a treasure trove of ideas, wisdom, advice, help, guidance, and rites. With this immense work, Ferdowsi[4] revived the spirit of serenity, magnanimity, and pride for the Iranian nation, which had lost itself under the weight of the Arab conquest of Iran. It empowered divided Iranian peoples to unite. Most of our poets, even those who worked as tyrannical kings' eulogists, have used their poems to remind rulers of the right way to run the state, practice justice, and uphold the welfare of the people. At the time of the Mongol invasion of Iran and the horrific massacres, writers and poets belonging to the mystical school of thought set out to soothe the people's pain and sorrow, and to teach them to be patient and ascetic, because there was no other alternative at the time. In any age, writers have produced works which were in keeping with their society's needs and which helped and guided the nation.

S.R. Writers in the West are envious of third-world countries, and countries that have less freedom. They think that the restriction

---

3   Usually translated as *Book of Kings*. Epic poem by Ferdowsi.
4   Abolqasem Ferdowsi (935–1020) was Iran's equivalent of Homer. He spent 35 years writing the *Shāhnāmeh*, which, along with its epic plot, contains invaluable accounts of Iranian legends and traditions.

of freedom forces writers to be more creative in order to say what they're not allowed to say. According to this viewpoint (based on the American-British novelist Henry James's idea that every story is a window in the house of fiction), the bigger the wall of tyranny, the bigger the opportunity to put in windows. Do you agree?

S.B. I have experienced this as a neoclassical poet and a writer who is committed to literary rules. The more stringent the rules and the more limiting they are, the more the poet and writer is forced to resort to special techniques and intricacies to escape them. And these techniques and intricacies adorn the writing and make it more beautiful. But, in the modern world, linguistic intricacies and embellishments do not attract much attention anymore, and the more sincere and intimate the relationship between a work and its reader, the better. So the countries that don't have walls don't need windows either, because the entire world is their field of vision and they can establish an unmediated relationship with their readers. I, in turn, envy them their free world.

S.R. Do you consider yourself an iconoclastic poet and, consequently, not widely accepted by the public, or the other way around?

S.B. Being iconoclastic is only acceptable and desirable if the public or at least a specific segment of society is open to it. A literature that the public cannot relate to in any form will not endure. I have been iconoclastic, but I've never broken my ties with Iran's past literature. No one can create a noteworthy work without knowing the tenets of their own language and literature. Language is renewed but it never changes its essence, because the contracts that have come about over time for communication cannot be rescinded so easily. It takes a thousand years before a word, among the thousands of words, dies away in a language or changes its meaning.

Literature rests on language. It is a linguistic art. So it cannot sever its relationship with the past. But it can create new methods and styles that differ in structure, form, and content from the past.

S.R. Is the fact that you're a woman important to your art and, if so, does it help you in your artistic work or not?

S.B. The fact that I'm a woman is as important to my work as a poet as the fact that Ahmad Shāmlu was a man was important to his work as a poet. Basically, gender shouldn't be viewed as an advantage in art. If a poem or a piece of writing is good, what difference does it make whether it's by a woman or a man? And, if it's bad, why should its writer's gender make it good? Of course, in the past, we had very few woman poets and writers because the environment didn't allow women to become educated and to learn to read and write. Illiterate women couldn't write anything. So if, occasionally, there was a woman who was a poet or a writer, a particular value was attached to this because it was a skill that was rarely seen among women. And any weakness in her work would be overlooked. But, today, when men and women have equal access to education, why should the fact that I am a woman be seen as a plus? I consider this view an insult and I always want to be compared with men.

S.R. Your new poems that were published in the London edition of *Kayhan* newspaper revealed a new passion that distinguished them from your other poems, which often carry references to blood, war, and injustice. Is this the beginning of a new path for you?

S.B. I have said again and again that my poetry is the poetry of the moments of my life. I've experienced years when the sky over me was blackened with the smoke of missiles and the ground on which I walked turned into ruins under exploding bombs. I've seen convoys of war martyrs on their way to the cemeteries. I've seen lorries carrying the bodies of executed prisoners, dripping with blood, that were being taken for burial in Behesht-e Zahra.[5]

I've stood in long lines, in the rain and under the sun, just to buy a pack of butter or a box of paper napkins. I've seen mothers running after the corpses of their martyred sons, oblivious to whether their headscarves or their chadors or their stockings and shoes were slipping off or not. I won't say any more. In the light of all this, how did you expect my poetry to be joyful or, as in my recent poem, to speak of love? Even so, more than half of my poems are joyful, and they are the product of the moments when I've felt happy. As a matter of fact, my poetry is multivocal. I've spoken about everything. I've written poems that consist of a story

---

5   Tehran's main cemetery.

in minimized form. I've used surreal subjects. I've produced "dia-logic" poems. I've produced descriptive poems. I had one working period which was totally devoted to transforming the foundations of the *ghazal*.[6] I have used about seventy new or disused meters, and this is something that can give the *ghazal* a totally new po-tential and a new mold in which to pour today's language, today's events, and today's needs. You can find any type of poem that you like in my works, and anyone, with any taste, can find something to their liking in them. On the whole, there's a great deal of variety in my works. I can't predict how my poetry will be in the future. It will depend on the state of things and how I'm feeling.

---

6   A poetic form consisting of couplets and a refrain.

MAHMOUD DOWLATĀBĀDI

Born in 1940 in the village of Dowlatābād in the Sabzevar region of northeast Iran, his published works include *Az Kham-e Chambar* (Through the Hoop), *Bā Shobeyru* (With Shobeyru), *Hejrat-e Soleymān* (The Emigration of Solomon), *Āwsaneh Bābā Sobhān* (The Legend of Bābā Sobhān), *Khāneh-ye Ākhar* (The Last House), *Gāvārebān* (Cowherd), *Didār-e Baluch* (Visit to the Baluch), the epic novel *Kelidar*, *Ruzegār Separishodeh-ye Mardom-e Sālkhordeh* (The Bygone Days of Elderly People), *Jâ-ye khâli-ye Ssoluch* (Missing Soluch), and *The Colonel*.

Mahmoud Dowlatābādi

Mahmoud Dowlatābādi believes that any literary work is a kind of "profession of anguish" on the part of the author. It is, in other words, the product of a conflict between the work's creator and his specific internal and external boundaries. Dowlatābādi is aware of the fact that revolution, as a phenomenon, constricts and expands these boundaries, and, hence, that censorship is one of the consequences of revolution the writer inevitably has to grapple with. He hopes that writers and poets in societies that have experienced the upheavals of revolution will understand Iranian writers' apprehensions and appreciate their writings.

Dowlatābādi is of the view that there has always been a deep link between Iranians and their history and literature. Literature, especially in times of foreign domination or social upheaval, has played the role of moderating society and safeguarding both language and social and moral values. In this way, literature establishes a link of such solidity between the people and the creators of literary works as to ensure that the writer does not feel like an outcast in society, especially in times of crisis.

A novelist in a society with a brilliant heritage of literature in verse, Dowlatābādi does not feel like a literary outcast. He is aware of the fact that the novels of "the West" have had and do have a conspicuous influence on Persian novels, but he does not accept the idea that "the novel" is a wholly imported literary phenomenon; he sees the stories, legends, and "romances" of Persian literature in verse as an unquestionable foundation for the Persian-language novelist.

History is of particular importance in Dowlatābādi's novels. He believes that, by reconstructing a historical subject that is fading away, the writer can leave behind a historical foundation stone. Dowlatābādi believes that, between the time of Ferdowsi and Beyhaqi to the present day, there has been a rupture in social historiography and storytelling, and that he took the first step in filling this thousand-year-old vacuum by producing his epic work *Kelidar*.

SHIVA RAHBARAN: In view of the importance of poetry in Persian literature, writing novels in Iran seems to be a difficult thing to do. Iranian society is more accustomed to viewing itself in the mirror of poetry. The Europeans see the novel as unique to their culture as the product of their cultural and historical developments from the Middle Ages to the Renaissance to modernity. How do you see your role in Iran as a novelist? Do you feel like an artistic outcast in a country in which writing novels is a new phenomenon?

MAHMOUD DOWLATĀBĀDI: First of all, when someone is involved in something, they can't really view themselves from the outside—or, at least, I, for my own part, don't tend to look at myself from the outside to try to understand what I am and what I'm not. What we have acquired from our own culture and outlook—or what I have acquired—is the idea of setting aside the self while working. So this whole issue of always having to look at myself and seeing where I am is not important to me. For example, to observe whether, by doing what I do (i.e. writing), I am an outcast in my society or my art or not—that's not how it works. At least that's not how I see it.

As to what you said about Iranians only having viewed themselves in the mirror of poetry, no, this isn't the case. The Iranian people, who are among the nations of the East, have had and do have the oldest tales and stories, and we are still benefiting from them. I'm referring to oral tales that were subsequently written down. One of the most outstanding examples of this genre is the *maqameh*,[7] which is similar to the genre known as the picaresque in the West. Moreover, when our historiographers recorded our history, they paid a great deal of attention to history as stories. So it is true that fiction in the form of novels (in the modern-day sense that you have in mind) first emerged in the West and that we were influenced by it—this is undeniable. We have no wish to deny it, in any case! On the contrary, we have learned so much, humbly, from the West and are still doing so. But our feudal culture, too, contained many "romances," which we were able to read and reread and benefit from our own readings thereof. The fact that a parallel development to these "romances" occurred in the West with *Don Quixote*, which, in effect, offered a new worldview, is a result of the social developments in the West, which had their own logic.

So insisting that we Iranians have only viewed ourselves in the mirror of poetry—no, this is not a hard-and-fast rule. It has to be

---

7   Episodic stories about an ambulant central character, often a beggar.

expressed in a more cautious way, especially so because our classical stories were told in the form of poetry. In fact, I don't feel like an outcast as a novelist, because our modern-day novels have reminded our people of their past as "history-legend." At the same time, over the past fifteen years, one of my novels [Kelidar]—despite the fact that they prevented its publication for four years—has been published fourteen times and the fifteenth edition is just about to be released. My other works have also been republished numerous times. So I have no sense of alienation or of being an outcast in this respect.

S.R. I was comparing you to Sādegh Hedāyat, who felt like an outcast in Iranian society.

M.D. Sādegh Hedāyat had a different personality. He had other sensitivities and a different background and perspective. I don't have that background and perspective and those sensitivities. I have tried to achieve a balance, whereby I avoid succumbing to the strange and outlandish sensitivities that he had, and also avoid becoming like the people who were at the opposite extreme. I have added and divided up all these things and come to an average. In our prose literature and among my country's contemporary writers—if we look at the past hundred years, ranging from Dehkhodā to Sādegh Hedāyat to Nimā and so on—I have wanted to be something of a synthesis; that is to say, to be somewhere in the middle, avoiding either extreme.

S.R. You mentioned Nimā, who was a great poet of our age. I wanted to ask you whether the Iranian novel—bearing in mind that it has been said that poetry, mysticism, and the illuminationist philosophy are very important in Iran—is different from the European novel or not. For example, Mr. Dariush Shāyegān has written, in his book *Henry Corbin: La topographie spirituelle de l'Islam iranien* (Éditions de la différence, 1990), that the novel was born in the divide between the mind and the body, which was the product of European dualism from the thirteenth century onward. In Shāyegān's words, the novel has always been an effort to fill this division. Now, in a place where poetry and mysticism are a mirror for reflecting the "unity of being," is it possible to be a novelist? Or did the advent of modernity in Iran forge a division in this unity, thereby creating fertile ground for the novel?

M.D. Listen, I don't really understand these kinds of theories. In Mr. Shāyegān's words and so on—I have to say that this sort of talk, where we conclude from the existence of a duality that the novel was born out of this division, these kinds of statements are of use in theory but aren't of use in practice. As far as I'm concerned, there is no fundamental difference between the Iranian novel and the Western novel; on the contrary, there is unity between the Iranian novel and the novel anywhere else. And the reason for this is that the subject and focal point of the novel is the human being, and this human being exists and lives everywhere in the world. The chief purpose of the novel is to uncover the human being writ large and, more narrowly, to uncover the human being of a particular moment. Just as, for example, Camus succeeded in discovering the modern, postwar human being. The slight difference in spite of this unity is that, as an Iranian writer, I have my ethos and my past, and a British or a Japanese writer has his ethos and his past. These things create no disparity; they create differences and variety. I have been shaped by the Iranian and Islamic illuminationist philosophy, and it is only by reading mystical and illuminationist works that I can quench my thirst. Naturally, these works will have an impact on me. But this is not to say that this will create a disparity between me and a German novelist, for example. No, not at all.

S.R. I have a question about *Kelidar*. Of course I know that whenever a writer writes a major work of this kind, they resent it in a way because they feel that it casts a shadow over all their other works. *Kelidar*, which can unequivocally be described as a modern epic, has a particular historical grief and longing. It both grieves the past and tries, through this grief, to bring the past back to life. Is this historical grief—as opposed to mystical grief—a modern phenomenon in Iran or has it always existed?

M.D. I don't know. You'll have to ask a researcher. What I can tell you is that history has a particular importance in my novels. And the reason for this is that our history has contained many ruptures. And in this history of ruptures, what I feel our society needs—i.e. continuity and evolution—has not existed in a rational and constant way. So one way or the other, I have homed in on this aspect. But if you have the impression that I devoted fifteen years of my life—from the age of twenty-seven to forty-two—to one work solely out of nostalgia, then, no, your impression is incorrect. I wanted to begin telling the history of my land—the history of a nation—from a particular juncture, which is objectively coming to an end. That is to say, if you examine the backdrop to my works, you will see that it stretches from tribal and rural life, from remote towns and districts and so on, to big cities. And this is like filling the empty squares on the chessboard in a particular way.

In his sociological definition of the novel, Thomas Mann offered an interesting idea, which I read recently, many years after I had finished *Kelidar*. He believed that important literary works only come into being once the relevant historical period has objectively ended or is coming to an end. Minor motives, such as nostalgia, do exist, but only to the extent and limit of nostalgia itself. In creating the work as a whole, the writer is driven by a whole range of motives, of which the writer himself is unaware. Once he embarks on the work, these unrecognized motives come into play and manifest themselves in the artistic work. In fact, *Kelidar* exemplifies Thomas Mann's belief, which I mentioned. That is to say, the society of nomadic tribes and old landowners is fading away, and someone (me), who came out of that village life himself, reconstructs this historical subject, which is fading away, and leaves it behind as a historical foundation stone. It goes without saying that this relationship does contain nostalgia, as well as grief at the loss of moral and spiritual values and the wish to hold together a nation in a situation and in circumstances in which it is fracturing.

Rest assured that if our fathers had created a work like this, or something of its kind, then, there would have been no need for me to do so in their stead. But since, in my view, this was done after a thousand years—i.e. a thousand years after Ferdowsi and Beyhaqi[8]—a kind of unwitting determination came about in me to fill this thousand-year gap, in so far as I was able, and to include the accumulated themes in my work.

It should be said that this system, this order, and these relations (i.e. the relations depicted in *Kelidar*) existed from the start of the Ghaznavid dynasty until the end of the Pahlavis,[9] and it may well have stretched further back (to the Sassanid era and even earlier). So this was a collective need, which was crystallized in me. Some people kindly tell me that I have achieved this and that! I say, Not at all; if I hadn't written these works, logically, someone else would have had to do so. This is a kind of social view of history that I have. In effect, the need was there; that's why it happened.

But within the time frame that I mentioned, we had a series of "romances," which mainly focused on kings and princes, like our tales and legends, such as *Dārābnāmeh*[10] and *Samak Ayyār*[11] and so on. But the idea that someone should revive a realistic outlook

---

8   Iranian historian (995–1077).
9   From 977 to 1979.
10   A twelfth century work by Abu-Taher Tarsusi about the life of a fictional king, Dārāb, and his two sons, Dārā and Eskandar, from two different marriages.
11   A twelfth century work by Farāmarz Ibn Khodādād, it tells the tale of Prince Khorshid-Shah who falls in love with the daughter of the Chinese Emperor. In the prince's efforts to save his beloved from various dangers, Samak Ayyār (Samak, the knave) is his trusty consultant and rescuer.

that existed over a thousand years of history, this is something that I have tried to do in so far as I was able. So I don't accept the notion that I was motivated by a kind of "longing for the past." With this work, I wanted to fill the thousand-year gap, so to speak. Of course, this view and this analysis may be considered to be a product of modernity and its impact on the social and historical aspects of nations, to the degree that they influence each other. You will no doubt understand that what I mean by modernity is different from the kind of superficial perspective that some of our writers are afflicted with nowadays.

S.R. So we can say that you are shouldering the legacy of Ferdowsi, which is reviving a nation by composing an epic. So by retelling that which has been lost, you want to bring a nation back to life, not to bury it alive in its past.

M.D. In fact, my model was Ferdowsi; it was Beyhaqi; it was Nezāmolmolk and Nasser Khosrow. Everyone who wrote prose or poetry actually has been my teacher, and *Kelidar* was written with reliance on them. Of course, I have undoubtedly used Western "forms" a great deal too. As an aspiring artist, I have perused all the literature that was available to me in Persian, ranging from Homer to Tolstoy, to Hermann Hesse, to John Steinbeck, and so on. Also the literature of South America's nations. Yes, I have learned things from all of them, of course. But I by no means make the grave claim that you suggested.

S.R. So your works also reflect a historical-aesthetic union.

M.D. Yes, my aesthetic comes from both the West and the East. I owe part of it to Eastern learning and the Eastern outlook, and part of it to the West's experiences. And, of course, the latter part is very substantial.

S.R. I have another question that relates to comparing you to Western novelists. Henry James considered every novel to be a window in the house of fiction. In this sense, we can see every novel as a window in people's outlook because people have always tried to understand their world and draw near to its truth through storytelling. As you know and as Mr. Muschg said at the Goethe Forum in Munich, many Western writers envy Iranian or Eastern writers. They believe that Iranian artists in Iran have more of an opportunity to open windows because there are more walls. In other words, the Iranian artist is more able and has a greater opportunity to be creative, because there are more walls standing in their way in Iranian society.

M.D. Mr. Muschg's view represents a realistic understanding and an accurate description of the writer's situation in Iran. But these friends who have become sensitive to the position of Iranian writers should recall the following phrase from the great Dostoyevsky: "Sorrow creates art." Romain Rolland, the great French writer, said for his part: "Art is the sacred fruit of suffering." So can these friends, such as Mr. Muschg and Mr. Enzensberger, take note of the suffering that we have endured behind those walls? And is it incumbent on them to do so? Or should we accept that, in the words of Sādegh Hedāyat, each voice only comes out of the relevant person's throat?

We can open windows onto the world and we have tried to do so. But can the world be bothered to hear this voice, and does it have the time to peer through the window and see things that are intermingled with sorrow, torment, and love? It goes without saying that we have come to terms with this situation and we have accepted that we have to live and work in these circumstances, and to keep alight the flame that is known as the culture, literature, and language of Iran—which has been a part of the world's culture, and which we hope will remain so forever.

S.R. Do you not feel that you are more fortunate than a writer in a Western capitalist system?

M.D. I have no idea what the criterion for good fortune is. If I could say what the criterion for good fortune is, then I would be able to tell you whether I am more fortunate than a Western writer or not. The criterion for me is the extent to which someone can be truthful. The more truthful I am in the work that I create and in the life that I lead, the more untainted I feel. The thing that is taken to mean success, fame, or wealth in the West is taken to mean the collective conscience in my thinking. In our society and in my thinking—as a member of this society—fame and celebrity are by no means central. My success and the wealth that I don't have (!) and my fame only take on meaning if I manage to produce a good work. When I manage to write or create a work, I have achieved victory in my own mind, within myself and by my thinking. When I tackle a work, when I create it, I have achieved my quest in my own mind. You can call this good fortune or success if you like.

At the same time, whilst expressing my gratitude to Western writers (e.g. Messrs. Muschg and Enzensberger), I have to say that I'm pleased that, given the realism that is unique to Western culture, they have understood and spoken about the value of my work and the work of people like me. And I believe that their understanding has resulted from that same truthfulness of which I spoke, although, in the seventh decade of my life, when I look well, I can say that I possess no more than a fistful of wind!

S.R. Although you're a very good writer, your works sell very well, whereas, usually, the works of very good writers don't sell well. How do you explain this glaring and unusual success? What effect does it have on your work?

M.D. I believe that this clearly arises from the hidden secret that I mentioned earlier. That is to say, in the moderate synthesis—of past and present—that I have managed to achieve. It is clear that this moderation has led to a logical link between my works and the public. The link between the people's culture and literature and the public shows that, in any age, the people are willing to embrace a work that belongs to them. Just as they safeguarded

Hāfez's *ghazal*s for us, just as they safeguarded Saadi[12] and even [the still more ancient] Ferdowsi. This shows that our people value and safeguard what truly belongs to them and their society, and I esteem this fact. Otherwise, the other aspect of it, in my view, is that these works and these republications bring me some income so that I can provide for my wife and children to a minimal level and not be dependent on anyone in these iniquitous times, so to speak.

S.R. When I speak to Iranian writers in Iran, they say that the Iranian writer feels very close to the Iranian people, as if there is a special pact between them. This is the exact opposite of the feeling that modern writers have in Europe, where they almost see alienation from their society as a precondition for creativity. In your view, has this attachment between the writer and the people always existed in Iran or is it a new phenomenon which has occurred over the past two decades?

M.D. The very fact that the Iranian people have rescued some works from repeated depredations over the course of history and have passed them on to us across the centuries shows that our people, first of all, cannot live without culture. And, secondly, that

12   Saadi (thirteenth century) and Hāfez (fourteenth century) are arguably Iran's two best-loved poets. One of Saadi's verses ("Human beings are members of a whole / In creation, of one essence and soul") adorns the UN building in New York. As for Hāfez, his poetry is inextricably intertwined with the Iranian psyche. If an Iranian house was to contain only two books, they would most likely be a copy of the Koran and something by Hāfez.

they safeguard, with tooth and claw, the culture that belongs to them, that contains their heart and soul. And they try to rescue it from all the depredations. Although there are also many such works that have been lost. Of course, I once said this in Berlin too, this shows that our people are basically devoted to books, story-telling, and language. I cited an example too: After the Arab conquest of Iran and the decline of the Persian language,[13] there were still some places where free-minded people, the old landowners, and Zoroastrian priests, in isolation, wrote about their past so that it would survive. And, in the words of an Arab historian, Ibn-Athir (died in 1233), this treasure trove remained in existence, mainly in Esfahan, until the tenth century, when it was discovered and taken to Baghdad and possibly lost. Of course, this loss did not mean that it was not recreated. It is clear that, in this way, the treasure trove reached the trusted keeper that it was intended to reach and Ferdowsi, the great master, was the true reviver [of Persian culture and language].

In this way, the Iranian people have proved and continue to prove that, if at some junctures they have been far removed from culture, this has been a force that they have always fought against. The people's enthusiasm for and safekeeping of the works of literature that belong to them is not at all surprising in my view.

S.R. So we can say that, for the Iranian people, literature is their bread?

---

13 Persian continued to be spoken in Iran under Arab rule but it was not used for writing/administration.

M.D. No, I wouldn't go as far as that. As it happens, nothing is more important than bread to the Iranian people. I would put it like this: Our people attach a great deal of importance to and esteem serious literature that is related to them.

Mohammad Hoghooghi

Born in Esfahan in 1937, his works include *Zavāyā va Madārāt* (Angles and Orbits), *Faslhā-ye Zemestāni* (Wintry Seasons), *Sharqihā* (Easterners), *Gorizhā-ye Nāgozir* (Inevitable Escapes), *Khorus-e Hezār-Bāl* (Thousand-Winged Rooster), *Dālānhā-ye Boland-e Asr* (Evening's Long Passageways), *Az Bāmdād-e Noqreh va Khākestar* (Of the Morning of Silver and Ash), *She'r-e Zāman-e Mā* (Poetry of Our Times), and a series of books on contemporary Iranian poets, including Ahmad Shāmlu, Mehdi Akhavān-Sāles, Sohrāb Sepehri, and Forough Farrokhzād.

Mohammad Hoghooghi died in 2009.

MOHAMMAD HOGHOOGHI

In Hoghooghi's view, it is undeniable that the 1979 revolution will prove beneficial to Persian literature as a "significant stimulus"—like the Arab conquest of Iran which led to the emergence of Ferdowsi, and the Mongol invasion which led to emergence of Rumi—although it is still too early to make an assessment of this phenomenon. The poet and the writer must wait "until the convulsion and the scattering of forces come to an end, the minds of artists are reformed, and they take up their deep and authentic activity."

Be that as it may, Hoghooghi is not very hopeful that the Islamic Revolution has helped or will help increase the cultural literacy of the common people. As a poet, he believes that his audience over the past decades has been a minority, separate from the common people. And he believes that the Islamic Revolution has compounded this separation.

He believes that censorship is not uniquely a product of the revolution. Over the course of Iran's turbulent history, since the advent of Islam, censorship has always cast its shadow over Persian literature.[14] It can be said that resisting censorship has become second nature to this literature. Even Iranian mysticism, which is considered passive by many, constituted a kind of resistance in its own day. This is why, despite the gap that he sees between the common people and the poet in Iran, Hoghooghi believes that the poet and the writer's creativity has an important

---

14   In the wake of the Arab conquest of Iran in the seventh century.

35

impact on society. Resistance by the creator of literary works to "the thought-molds of the day," whether philosophical, social, or political, is essential to society's progress.

Hoghooghi is of the view that, in Persian literature, "creativity, in the true sense of the word, is exclusive to poets." Persian poetry, with its 1,200-year history, is "blended into Iranians' blood, and Iranian poets believe that poets rank second after prophets, historically speaking." This is why, for the time being, he does not consider the Iranian novel successful internationally. Nevertheless, he is more optimistic about the future of the short story and the novel in contemporary Iran—in view of the course that this genre has taken, starting from Sādegh Hedāyat to Simin Dāneshvar to Mahmoud Dowlatābādi—than about the future of a modern poetry, which has lost itself in a misguided conception of postmodernism.

SHIVA RAHBARAN: The aim of this study is to discover what impact the 1979 revolution has had on Iranian literature and art from the point of view of artists and thinkers who are currently living and working in Iran. This study has two parts: in the first part, it tries to come to grips with the changes and the anomalies that have occurred since the revolution. In the second part, it tries to examine the effect of the revolution on literature and the effect of literature on society.

The first question is a general question about democracy. What impression do people in Iran have of democracy? Do they think that democracy always has the desired results? Are they aware of

the dangers of demagoguery, populism, etc.? Have Iranian thinkers, artists, and writers fulfilled their mission in terms of explaining democracy or not? As you know, many thinkers believe that,
in view of Iranians' experience of modernity and the setbacks they
have suffered, democracy is essentially not suited to Iranians.

MOHAMMAD HOGHOOGHI: I have to say that we have not experienced democracy—i.e. rule by the people or rule of the people by
the people—quite as we should have done. In truth, no country
has achieved it fully; i.e. achieved a totally democratic state. It's
been achieved only relatively. As to whether our intellectuals have
fulfilled their duty to explain democracy and freedom, and acquaint the people with these concepts, I have to say, yes, they have.
As you know, this term was first mentioned in Iran about a century and a half ago, when we were on the threshold of becoming
acquainted with Western civilization. Right from the start, stretching from Fath'ali Akhundzādeh[15] to today's intellectuals, they have
tried to acquaint the people with these concepts more and more,
particularly because, during the Constitutionalist Movement,
the people became aware, in practice, of these concepts' results
and interpretations. Of course, these expressions, democracy and
freedom, were being used in contradistinction to the tyrannical
regime of the time. A state that considered democracy to be contrary to its interests and a people that had to defend its own rights
both became acquainted with the concept of democracy. And, in
fact, with the victory of the Constitutionalist Movement and the

---

15   Writer/intellectual (1812–1878).

establishment of parliamentary government, people were able to vote for their own representatives, at least for several parliamentary terms. But the people whom we are talking about here are not the ordinary people or the *populus*. They are the middle class and above, who can relate to these concepts. And it was the same at other historical junctures, because the dominance of tradition in Iran, and, consequently, the people's backwardness has always led to resistance to modernity. So this may be one of the reasons behind the setbacks that democracy has suffered. But not in the way that you phrased it; not the suggestion made by this or that person that Iranians are essentially unworthy of democracy. But the problem is that they have kept these nations backwards. The underlying factors have to be examined at any rate.

For example, in contemporary Iran, we have had several historical junctures: the Constitutional Revolution; the 1920 coup and the reign of Reza Shah[16]; August 1941 and the sending into exile of the Shah,[17] and the establishment of political parties[18]; the 1953 coup and the fall of Mossadegh; and, finally, the 1979 revolution. Well, we have to examine what this country went through during these years and after each historical juncture. In fact, the people have always been treated as the underlings of the rulers and the powerful. And these power holders have by and large, apart from a few exceptions, been either pro-British or pro-Russian, and, during Reza

---

16   Reza Shah was the founder of the Pahlavi Dynasty (1925–1979) and the father of Iran's last Shah.
17   Iran was invaded by British and Russian forces in August 1941, and Reza Shah, the father of Iran's last Shah, was forced to abdicate and leave Iran.
18   In the 1940s.

Shah's time, favored the Germans and the Nazis. Then, from August 1941 onward, we had almost the only period when there was some activity resulting from the establishment of parties and, first and foremost, the Tudeh Party,[19] which spoke about the working class and the idea of the proletariat in the appropriate conditions,[20] disseminated slogans that workers could understand, and familiarized them with the notion of exploitation and the need for them to defend their interests, thereby bringing the people and especially the working class into the arena of activity and struggle. But, unfortunately, this proper atmosphere did not last very long and, because of the Tudeh Party's excessive support for the Soviet Union, the controversy over Mossadegh and the nationalization of Iranian oil, and the emergence of a new power by the name of the United States, it all led to the August 1953 coup. And a dynamic society was suddenly brought to its knees and stifled. And the return of Mohammad Reza Shah to Iran marked the start of a twenty-five-year reign. And, as the people gradually gained relative economic comfort in a still and lifeless political atmosphere, they drew their heads into their shells. And they slowly became immersed in a pseudo-modernized-Westernized atmosphere, in which social dissipation increased with every passing year, and people became contented with being employed by this or that government department or new state body with a view to buying new household appliances. And this resulted in them becoming less and less self-aware, and the last thing on their minds was democracy and freedom.

---

19   Iran's now defunct communist party.
20   In the growing number of factories and in the oil industry.

All these factors were laid out in such a way that the people were prevented from understanding and grasping true civilization and culture. They not only became content with their modern possessions, they also confused modernity with civilization. This seems to have led some people to suggest that Iranians are fundamentally not worthy of democracy. I have to say that this is untrue because all the people of the world, including our people, are intrinsically worthy of democracy. It was the presence of those factors that condemned them to unworthiness. And this was something that most of our intellectuals were aware of, especially our poets and writers who, by virtue of writing different types of stories and poems, using various modes of expression, have never been oblivious to the events that have taken place in our country. And, throughout all these years and in all the arts, individuals ranging from Jamālzādeh, Hedāyat, Sādeq Chubak, Bozorg-e Alavi, Ebrahim Golestan, Jalāl Āl-e Ahmad, and Mrs. Dāneshvar to Gholāmhossein Sā'edi, Bahrām Sādeqi, Hushang Golshiri, Mahmoud Dowlatābādi, and Ahmad Mahmoud in the field of short stories and novels; Nimā Yushij, Ahmad Shāmlu, Mehdi Akhavān-Sāles, Forough Farrokhzād, and Simin Behbahāni in the field of poetry; Bahrām Beyzā'i, Nasser Taqvā'i, Dariush Mehrju'i, Sohrāb Shahid-Sāles, and Abbās Kiārostami in film; translators such as Mohammad Qāzi, Abolhassan Najafi, and Najaf Daryābandari; and intellectuals such as Fereidoun Adamiat, Dariush Shāyegān, Dariush Ashouri, and a number of other discerning academic figures have all played a role in raising the level of our culture and people's knowledge of social, political, academic, and literary issues. They have all, each within their capacity, played a role in changing the perspectives of various people, but not the perspectives of ordinary people. Now, the question is: why? This is the key question.

What is clear is that we Iranians are very intelligent and have a great deal of potential and talent. Look at how well our children perform at international Olympiads, children who have excelled at a global level in the fields of mathematics, physics, chemistry, and other modern sciences. But it goes without saying that when we talk about the people, we do not mean individuals of this sort. It is the bulk of the population that is called the ordinary people or, lower still, the common people, and there is a great distance between them and our cultural figures, a distance that exists in every country but perhaps not to this extent. Years ago, a British poet who lived in Esfahan for a while asked me: Why is there such a great gap between Iranian intellectuals and cultural figures and the lower class? I have met world-class intellectuals in Iran, but, in contrast to them, I have also met people who have possibly not even spent one second on thinking or reading.

This is quite apart from the people who, I've heard, cannot even read and write, and apparently there are quite a few of them. And, of course, the view that he expressed is an undeniable fact. It shows how difficult it is to establish a link between those intellectuals and these people. And, in fact, it is this absence of a link between the two that brings many people to the conclusion that our intellectuals, and especially our artists, are mostly not with the people and are not committed. And the reason I say "mostly" is because there are some writers and poets who, more or less, do establish this link but only by resorting to sloganeering and by bringing the level of their writing down to the common people's level and ignoring high-level creativity and advanced artistic forms. And this, in turn, keeps their cultural literacy at a low and prevents progress. This is because an artist needs an audience after all, a wide audience consisting of all the segments of the population and not just an elite audience, which may not number more than ten thousand. In the light of all this, I believe that we have no option—aside from creating valuable works, be they short stories and poems, films, plays, paintings, or even music—but to enable the people to connect to these works by working to gradually improve their cultural literacy through universities, cultural centers, newspapers, radio and television, and various media. In this way the people's cultural level will gradually rise and the people themselves will naturally become acquainted with various concepts, including democracy, freedom, civilization, and, more generally, with all the manifestations of culture. And they will slowly reach a stage where they can weigh up cultural works and value them.

S.R. My next question is about "the Iranian experiment." In the West, some analysts call the Iranian revolution "the Iranian experiment." What they mean by this expression is the synthesis of modernity and religion, in the sense that there have always been efforts in Iran to ally modernity and religion in order to prevent society from fracturing. We saw an example of this kind of effort during the Constitutional Revolution, for example, and also at the time of Mossadegh and his national-religious front. And, of course, during the 1979 revolution and under Mehdi Bāzargān.[21] So my question is: do you think this synthesis is feasible? And has it ever succeeded?

M.H. This is something that is rooted in our history. It has been the case from the time when Islam permeated Iran,[22] when we had various early revolts, which were all "national-religious" revolts in a way, and then on to the Zanj revolt[23] and the *Qaramatis*/Carmathians[24]—when Sultan Mahmud, who was a dogmatic Sunni, had thousands of Carmathians burnt in Rey simply because they did not follow the same creed as the "God-empowered" caliphs—as well as subsequent revolts, such as the *Sarbedaran*[25]—who were Shiis and, as it happens, their protest was aimed at establishing a popular state or rule by the people—to the time of the Safavid Dynasty, when Shiism became Iran's official religion, which led to the wars between the Shii Safavids and the Sunni Ottomans, and thereafter, when clerics gradually gained such influence that Shah Tahmasb[26] himself put the government in the hands of Sheikh Karaki. And these were clerics who often hailed from the Jabal

---

21 First prime minister after the 1979 revolution.

22 In the wake of the Arab conquest of Iran in the seventh century.

23 Revolt in the ninth century by slaves and former slaves in Basra (modern-day Iraq).

24 An offshoot of Isma'ili Shiism.

25 Literally, "heads on the gallows." A revolutionary Shiite polity in northeast Iran (1336–1381).

26 One of the Safavid kings (sixteenth century).

Amil region of Lebanon, the most important of which was Sheikh Baha'i. These were clerics who were more inclined toward fiqh[27] and fields based on oral testimonies, so to speak, than Iranian clerics, who were more inclined toward the rational sciences, such as Mirdāmād, Mirfenderski, Lahiji, and Mulla Sadra. It was from this time on, at any rate, that the clergy and the state were either allies or antagonists. Either in accord or at loggerheads. Until the Constitutional Revolution, when we had both types of cleric: clerics who believed that the Shah should derive his legitimacy from the constitution and clerics who believed that the Shah should derive his legitimacy from religion. And, then, during the time of Reza Shah, we had Ayatollah Modarres[28] and Ayatollah Kashani,[29] who were both very political figures and were influential members of the Consultative Assembly. Then, we had the events of 1963 which let to Ayatollah Khomeini being sent into exile until the year when the revolution occurred, 1978–1979. Then, Ayatollah Khomeini returned as the leader of the revolution, the monarchy was toppled, and it was replaced by the Islamic Republic. And this was perhaps the first time that the clergy had become the undisputed power holders in Iran. And now, twenty-four years after the revolution, they are still Iran's rulers.

I've told you all this by way of a detailed preamble in order to answer your question about the relationship between religion and

---

27   Islamic jurisprudence.
28   Ayatollah Modarres favoured a ruling system based on constitutional legitimacy.
29   Ayatollah Kashani favoured a ruling system based on religious legitimacy.

modernity, and to explain how problematic this synthesis of religion and modernity can be in a country with this religious past and this sort of relationship between the people and the clergy—especially so when this synthesis is supposed to take place in the age of the computer and the media, when we live in an interconnected communications universe, and when it is, at the same time, the age of respect for democracy, freedom, and the people's votes, which in fact started with the separation of church and state several centuries ago, during the Renaissance. And, in the subsequent centuries until today, this separation was followed by hundreds of different theories, accompanied by a variety of isms in philosophical, social, political, and artistic fields, such as materialism, idealism, Marxism, socialism, liberalism, secularism, realism, etc., etc., which completely transformed the world and its inhabitants.

The separation of religion from the state is a progressive and pervasive trend, which has been reflected everywhere in the world, sometimes in depth, as in more advanced countries, and sometimes superficially, as in our country. When our young people started going to more advanced countries and studying the modern sciences and modern techniques, and when they returned to Iran equipped with expertise in various fields and with modern ideas, we learned about the manifestations of the West's progress. So our stagnant society was given a slight jolt. In effect, these students were the first ones to consider the close relationship, in Iran, between modernity and religion hard to take. Later, many youngsters from well-to-do families would go abroad and come back to Iran. This process continued until recently, that is to say, the past twenty or thirty years, when we were suddenly faced with a new attitude to Islam in Muslim countries and with the events and revolutions that gradually unfolded; that is to say, we came face to face with a creed or creeds that resorted to a sort of religious revolt under the banner of Islam. In Afghanistan, Algeria, Egypt, the Philippines, and, most importantly and most pervasively, in Palestine, where they are still engaged in that struggle.

In this midst, Iran is the only country where a large majority, opposite a very small minority—which mainly consists of those who are acquainted with Western culture and civilization, in other words, the intellectuals—achieved an Islamic state (which was the aim of all the countries that I mentioned). And this minority is a minority that favors reason and logic, against a majority that favors love and emotion; a majority that is preoccupied with what will help or hinder admission to paradise. And particularly because of their experience of the eight-year war with Iraq, they are in love with martyrdom and meeting their Maker. Of course, this problem also existed in Christianity; a Christianity that carried out Crusades for two hundred and fifty years and fought against Muslims based on this same love. But, then, they had the Renaissance and then the Age of Enlightenment when, with the advent of Copernicus, Galileo, Newton, and others, religion became totally separated from politics and from science.

S.R. But Abu-Reyhan Biruni came to the conclusion that the Earth was spherical and revolved around the sun, not the other way around, three hundred years before Copernicus. Why didn't this jolt us into modernity?

M.H. Because in the Renaissance, the Europeans had the dark times of the Middle Ages behind them. For centuries, they had been cut off from Greek and Roman culture, and it was in fact thanks to the works of Biruni and the translations of Avicenna, Fārābi, and the like that Greek science and philosophy were re-introduced in Europe. And this meant that, after several hundred years of dark and bitter experience, the ground was laid out for them to emerge from the Middle Ages and to be rescued from the ignorance and darkness. But, in Iran, although the age of Biruni and people like him had the legacy of pre-Islamic culture and civilization, as well as the brilliance of the Iranian-Islamic culture of the tenth and eleventh centuries, conditions were not ripe for a total transformation. And because of historical and social factors, sectarian wars, the intolerance of Turkic dynasties, such as the Ghaznavids and the Saljuqs, attacks by various tribes, and the invasion by warmongering Turkic Mongols, the time was not right. Time was moving very slowly and, on occasion, it moved so slowly that it seemed to have come to a halt. These may well have been some of the factors that made Biruni think of going to India, an India that was the fountainhead of ancient culture. It was there that he wrote *Understanding Astrology* and *The Remaining Signs of Past Centuries*. And he stated his view about the Earth being spherical and about it revolving around the sun, along with a question of course: If the Earth is spherical and suspended in space, why does

47

the water in the seas not spill out into space? This was a problem that he shared in writing with Avicenna, without arriving at an answer. Just as Copernicus and Galileo, too, did not uncover gravity. It was only a century or two later, when an apple fell from a tree, so to speak, that Newton discovered the law of gravity.

S.R. Be that as it may, I will repeat my question: Why didn't we leap forward? Why did we go backward instead of advancing?

M.H. I told you why in my previous answer and I'll tell you again: Religious intolerance, sectarian wars, invasions by various tribes and, most importantly, the question of timing. There was a long way to go before the human mind was ready to grasp the modern sciences and the empirical results of science and scientists, in the modern senses of these terms, which are very far removed from ancient scholars and their studies. As well as many other reasons and factors, which, taken together, prevented us from advancing, of course, as I said, in terms of science, not in terms of culture. Anyway, why is your question only about our backwardness and not that of Europe? Have you ever asked yourself why Europe, with the immense cultural record of Greece and Rome, sank into the darkness of the Middle Ages? Why did nothing change after the advent of Christianity? And, basically, why was it that after Socrates, Plato, and Aristotle, on the one hand, and the neo-Platonists, on the other—and with that vast backdrop of epic-writing and drama and the brilliance of people like Homer, Sophocles, Euripides, Virgil, Plautus, Seneca, Ovid, and others—the development of culture slowed down more and more, until it stopped altogether and the Middle Ages plunged Europe into darkness? Why?

S.R. Do all our intellectuals know the answer?!

M.H. Of course. They are all of the same view [as me]. But not the ordinary people, who think about nothing but their daily bread. Because thinking is alien to them. Because they have never been in a position to think. We haven't taught it to them. So the conditions for a Renaissance basically didn't exist here in the way that it did in Europe. Nevertheless, what is clear is that this revolution made us—or, at least, made our intellectuals—think about our authentic selves again and to seek our true face in the mirrors of literature, art, history, and religion, and to recognize our identity.

S.R. You seem to be saying that Iranian scholars have always been outcasts in view of the injustices of various rulers. Do you think that Iranian writers, poets, and artists are outcasts today too? I also want to mention that, in the West, everyone envies poets and writers here and their importance in Iranian society. Shāmlu's funeral procession[30] was one example. But you've just explained to me that there is a very big gap between poets and ordinary people. In the West, they say that, when an Iranian poet holds a poetry reading, thousands upon thousands of people attend. But even the most famous poet in the West wouldn't be able to draw such a crowd. On this basis, Westerners come to the conclusion that,

---

30 The funeral procession drew a very large crowd.

since there is no freedom in countries like Iran, the power of creativity is greater. And, therefore, that freedom is basically inimical to art.

M.H. You seem to think that the fact that poets and writers are outcasts in their country is by virtue of not having freedom. And that the lack of freedom is because of the existence of various regimes that do not allow writers and poets to speak candidly. And, finally, you conclude that freedom is more harmful than beneficial for artists. Let me begin by responding to this last suggestion of yours. You see, an artist who does not have freedom usually adopts a kind of language, form, and method that will allow him to justify the writing of the poem or story if, in sensitive circumstances, he is challenged by a Byzantine regime. He has to arrange the words in each phrase in such a way as to thwart any attempt by the state apparatus to point a finger at it. But when I say "regime," I mean people who are intelligent but who have sold out [to the state]; these are the individuals the artist has to deal with. So he has to resort to a language that is ambiguous, illusive, and figurative. Now, if these kinds of individuals have trouble understanding this or that work or all the works of a poet, then, they hardly expect ordinary people to be able to make heads or tails of it. I am saying this in view of the fact that you referred to the crowd that took part in Shāmlu's funeral procession. What sort of crowd? You can be sure that the crowd didn't include anyone from the bazaar, nor shopkeepers or businessmen, nor anyone from the lower classes, who are only concerned about their daily bread and nothing else. The people who take part in Shāmlu's funeral or who gather at such places [for poetry readings] (and their number isn't small), are mostly university students and teachers, and, at any rate, young, educated people. But Western countries don't realize this and they think that the audience consists of ordinary people. Of course, it has to be said that Iranians have always had an affinity with poetry. They say that every Iranian, without exception, has composed at least one or two verses of poetry. But this is an affinity that is based on the rhythm and music of words—virtually irrespective of the meaning of the poems—and over a thousand-year period at that; not an affinity with the poetry of Shāmlu or Forough [Farrokhzād] or other well-known innovators. No, the listeners and readers of these poems are confined to university students and people from the education sector; no one else.

In any case, has the free Europe [sic] of the twentieth century failed to produce great writers and poets? Writers such as Joyce, Proust, Faulkner, and Kafka, and poets such as Eliot, Pound, Paz, Borges, and others, who rank among the world's greatest writers and poets. Let me emphasize the point again: have these individuals not emerged from that free environment? So the idea that freedom is more harmful than beneficial to humanity's literature cannot be correct; it cannot be a definitive judgment. However, as I said, poetry is infused into Iranians' blood. Even Iranian children use words that rhyme and have an instinctive sense for it. Or, for example, the illiterate, ambulant fruit-seller, too, calls out rhythmic and harmonious phrases to attract customers.

S.R. Yes, I don't dispute that. But one can conclude from what you said about Shāmlu and Forough and the Iranian poet's relationship with the modern-day audience that poets have developed a particular approach to language in view of their resistance to the opponents of this kind of [modern] poetry.

M.H. As you know, poets like Shāmlu and Forough are the shining lights of their times. Their poetry reflects the situation in society, as did Ferdowsi's poetry a thousand years ago. As you know, with the advent of Islam, all the countries of that time not only accepted Islam but also accepted Arabic as their new language—but we didn't. We replaced Pahlavi Persian with Dari Persian in order to resist Arabic. But a language's longevity is never assured until it enters literature and poetry and falls into shape. A book like the *Shāhnāmeh* has to be created so that a language can reveal its beauties and capabilities. Of course, this was one of the important things that Ferdowsi did. The even more important thing that he did was to rediscover the Iranian identity by reconstructing its legends using the art of poetry. The same can be said of Hāfez. Yes, Hāfez, too, can be described as a poet who surveyed the events of his time. Because, while exposing the behind-the-scenes hypocrisies of professed ascetics and Sufis, his poetry also captures the quintessence of ancient Iranian culture in a pristine mirror that shows the guileless wine-sippers of the court of Jamshid.[31] So when the poetry of Ferdowsi and Hāfez reflects the conditions in which they lived, their poetry is just as it ought to be. Now, bear in

31   A legendary Persian king; Iran's equivalent of King Arthur.

mind that our society is a twentieth-century society that remains in the third world. The reason I'm saying this is because there are still hundreds of literary clubs in Iran in which the so-called poets are still happily passing their time with the beloved's gold-spun or ink-spun tresses, the beloved's cypress-like or spruce-like figure, the beloved's crescent-like or arch-like eyebrows, and the beloved's moon-like or rose-like visage.

S.R. Can it be said that it is poets who are perpetually creating the way we think in Iran?

M.H. If I understand you correctly, you mean to say that, as Iranians, the way we think mainly lies in our poetry. To which I have to say, yes. The essence of the way we think lies in our poetry, in the poetry of Ferdowsi, in the poetry of Khayyám, in the poetry of Rumi, and in the poetry of Hāfez. And, of course, in a different way in each of them. But we've had philosophy too. For example, illuminationist philosophy which, we can say, is unique to us. But the thinking of the likes of Fārābi or Avicenna originates in the exposition of Aristotle's ideas. Although they, too, played a significant role in the progression of human thought. The Europeans are well aware of this, even though they try to place Avicenna among the physicians of the ancient world. And bear in mind that his *Canon of Medicine* was, for centuries, the only medical text book and reference book in the world. Of course, it also has to be said that the thinking of almost all our theologians is based on preestablished tenets. But not our poets;

in fact, they are the only ones who are creative, in the true sense of the word.

S.R. Let's go back to the revolution. Even with everything you said earlier, I'd still like to ask you the following question: have the contradictions and divisions that resulted from the Islamic Revolution been fruitful for you or not?

M.H. It's undeniable that they have been beneficial as a significant stimulus. The effect will become clearer in the future; just as the Arab conquest of Iran ultimately set the stage for Ferdowsi, and the Mongol invasion set the stage for Rumi—and just as, more generally, the historical course of events in our land and the different ways of thinking led to a situation in which the essence of Iranian culture was encapsulated in a great man such as Hāfez and was reflected in his poetry. In much the same way, familiarity with European culture and, more generally, their science and literature, brought Iranians into contact with new concepts and with a variety of literary forms, such as novels, short stories, and plays. Well, in the light of all this, inevitably, the 1979 revolution has had and will have its own particular effects.

S.R. Setting aside the effects of the historical and social developments to which you referred, did you also take the question of "censorship" into account?

M.H. Regardless of time and place, you can't say everything candidly anyway. In any given age, the artist develops his own particular language. It takes time before the historical page turns. We can see that, throughout history, the most important factor that has attracted poets to the two key elements of "symbols" and "allusions" is the inability to speak about some particular things.

S.R. So a good poem has to have a kind of dissidence and resistance?

M.H. Well, yes. Poets and writers want to write about the truths of their age from their own perspective, but their times don't allow it. But they do write something anyway. And this writing constitutes resistance. Because, in any age, the poet has been a protestor of a kind, resisting the thought-molds of the day. However, this protest might be political, it might be social, or it might even be philosophical. At any rate, the artist is at odds with the prevalent conduct and thinking of his age; this has always been the case.

S.R. Even for the mystical poet?

M.H. Yes. As I said, our mysticism before the Mongols [i.e. the Mongol invasion of Iran] was different from our mysticism after the Mongols. Our mysticism before the Mongols was born of our social conditions and our way of thinking in the seventh, eighth, and ninth centuries. And our mysticism after the Mongols was born of other conditions. The difference is that the former mysticism was more static and the latter, more dynamic—of course, only until the fifteenth century or so. From then on, it took on a particular shape; the shape of Sufi belief and Sufism. At any rate, mysticism is born and nurtured by love, and love means the core and substance of the human being, because if it didn't exist, the human being wouldn't exist. This is especially the case with ardent mysticism, like Rumi's mysticism, not ascetic mysticism, like Khājeh Abdollah Ansāri's mysticism. I am talking about an ardent mysticism that is more or less in line with the Muhiyeddin Ibn Arabi and Jalaleddin Rumi's notion of "unity of being," in its divine reading. And I'm of the view that you can also have a material reading.

S.R. Now, the question arises: What role can the novel have in such a county's literature? Mr. Dariush Shāyegān—basing himself on Henry Corbin—believes that the novel came into existence in Europe because of the mind-body divide; as a bid to fill this division. But that, in the East and in the land of mysticism, where there is "unity of being," poetry always has the upper hand. It is as if poetry is "divinely revealed," whereas the novel is merely "written." On this basis, how do you see the role of the novel in Iran? How would you compare poetry and the novel? Could we say that the novel is a kind of artistic outcast in Iran?

M.H. As you know, poetry has a 1,200-year history in Iran and, as I said a number of times, poetry is infused into Iranians' blood and Iranian poets believe that poets rank second after prophets, historically speaking. Prophets receive "revelations" and poets receive "inspiration." And "inspiration" is, in fact, the same thing as a "revelation," an occult revelation. Perhaps we can say that revelations originate in "God" and inspiration originates in "nature." Well, relative to this long history and global renown for poetry, we have not been very successful in the field of novel-writing. The Persian language is part of the problem because one of the reasons—and possibly the most important reason—that Latin American novels are valued highly throughout the world is that they are written in Spanish. And Spanish is a direct offspring of Latin and one of the siblings of the modern-day languages of Europe. After English (and possibly after Chinese, because of China's huge population), it may have the biggest number of speakers. Be that as it may, bearing in mind the Iranian novel's short history, we have to acknowledge that we have had some very successful novels, such as Sādegh Hedāyat's *Buf-e Kur* (*The Blind Owl*), Hushang Golshiri's *Shāzdeh Ehtejāb* (*Prince Ehtejab*), Dowlatābādi's *Jā-ye Khāli-ye Soluch* (*Missing Soluch*), Ahmad Mahmoud's *Hamsāyehhā* (Neighbors), and Simin Dāneshvar's *Siāvoshun* (*A Persian Requiem*). And successful short stories from Bozorg-e Alavi, Sādeq Chubak, Ebrahim Golestan, Jalāl Āl-e Ahmad, Bahram Sādeqi, Sā'edi, Golshiri, and some of our younger short-story writers. In any case, I'm very hopeful about the future of short story writing in Iran.

S.R. Am I right in concluding from your remarks that, over the past twenty years, unlike our young writers, our young poets have not been producing very good poetry? You're not very optimistic?

M.H. Some of them are talented, but you can't tell from the poetry of most of them that they are Iranian poets.

S.R. Could you please elaborate?

M.H. What I mean to say is that our modern poetry shouldn't be a direct transposition of European poetry or the modern ideas (often via the original language) of foreign theorists—from Bakhtin to Derrida—without any skill or experience and with total disregard for our own historical background. We have had poets who have used the Persian language and ideas that are unique to Iran to such great effect as to become figures of world renown. But our youngsters are totally unfamiliar with the marvels and strengths of our language. They defend a language that is the quotidian language of communication. They say that this is the language that we should use in our poetry today. They don't realize that they don't even know how to utilize this quotidian language. They take their inspiration from translated poetry. Be that as it may, we can't rule out the possibility that at some point in the future—and perhaps not a very distant future—we may produce another great poet, although the world is going in a direction in which thought and the products of thought and imagination may come to a standstill, a point at which we may witness the defeat of the creative human being by a variety of terrifying artificial media.

S.R. Apart from the fate of art in the world in the future, did you not suggest in your remarks that the 1979 revolution is partly to blame for bad poetry?

M.H. Basically, whenever there's a revolution, it is a historical turning point. For example, August 1941, or the 1953 coup,[32] or June 1963,[33] or February 1979. At such times, the arts, especially the language-based arts, such as poetry or short-story writing, fall into a kind of panic (not to say chaos) and confusion (not to say deviation); that is to say, until daily life and society regain their normalcy. Basically, a kind of superficiality grips people's minds until the convulsion and the scattering of forces come to an end, the minds of artists are reformed, and they take up their deep and authentic activity. This occurs when the artist finds his own line and method. We saw this happen in the 1979 revolution in particular and we saw clearly how some people succumbed to their emotions and produced slogans instead of poetry. And others immediately started writing poems in praise of the revolution. And others still, mainly the well-known, experienced poets, bided their time until they could find their own direction; in other words, until all these events had settled down within their being so they could resume their work.

S.R. My last question is about Western studies on Persian litera-ture. When I've spoken to some literary people, they've told me that when Westerners approach our literature for research pur-poses, we are not very optimistic about them and their work. We often see them as agents rather than as researchers.

---

32   CIA-backed coup that toppled Prime Minister Mossadegh.
33   Uprising led by clerics in Qom, after which Ayatollah Ruhollah Khomeini was sent into exile.

M.H. This, too, is a long-standing debate. And, of course, you may have (accidentally) come across people who, it would seem, are particularly suspicious. It is clear that these views are not well-informed because we have always respected Orientalists. However, it also has to be said that they have not always come to Iran with pure motives and merely with the intention of carrying out research, especially the ones who came to find a particular work with the intention of producing an amended, alternative version, and not for the sake of study and research. At any rate, this has made our intellectuals less than optimistic about these contacts. I mean the intellectuals were asking why the Orientalists don't pay any attention to the contents of our works and their value in comparison with their works. For example, why don't they place Ferdowsi on par with Homer? And, fundamentally, why aren't they the least bit interested in carrying out comparative studies? Of course, this was the "standpoint" of some intellectuals, who looked at everything in political terms and in terms of colonialism. Otherwise, there have been many culture-loving Iranologists who have individually produced very valuable works and shared their love of Iran, its art, and its literature; e.g. A. U. Pope, E. E. Bertels, Minorsky, Jan Rypka, A. Godard, and many others. Also, translators such as Edward Fitzgerald, Marijan Molé, and Arthur J. Arberry. And all the people who introduced Europeans to the poetry of Saadi, Hāfez, Rumi, and Attār to the point where they attracted the attention of the greatest Western thinkers and poets, such as Voltaire, Montesquieu, Hugo, Aragon, Goethe, etc.

S.R. So do you subscribe to the view, which is also often discussed in the West, that when political and economic powers unite, anything that the researcher does (even if it is well-intentioned and leads to good work) will, inevitably, be viewed with suspicion by the person who reads it? That is to say, no matter how much Western universities want to study Persian literature in an "unbiased" way now, the West's power will determine the track that their thinking will follow, whether they like it or not.

M.H. What you said now—if I understood you correctly—is a different issue. This is a purely political issue which may well result from the past record of relations between Iran and Britain. At any rate, I made the points that needed to be made in my answer to your previous question. And I'll emphasize again that, the more we progress over time, the more the ill intentions, especially on cultural issues, fade away. We become better informed and we recognize who has bad intentions toward us and who has good intentions. Because I think that the era of forgeries and treacherous and exploitative intentions has passed; like the case of Ernest Hertzfeld, the German Orientalist, who sold a supposedly very old copy of *Divan-e Manuchehri* (collected poems of Manuchehri of Damghan) to foreign libraries, and many years later it became clear that it was a forgery and had been produced in the last hundred years! (And I have to say that I still don't know whether this story is true or not because Hertzfeld was an Iranologist of some repute and Malekoshoarā Bahār learned Pahlavi from Hertzfeld.) At any rate, this sort of thing has happened. But you can be sure that there are no longer such suspicions on this side and bad intentions on the other side.

S.R. Especially so, since studying and researching Persian literature has become much more commonplace and productive now.

M.H. Yes, definitely.

MANOUCHEHR ĀTASHI

Born in Dashtestān, Bushehr Province, in 1931, his works include *Ahāng-e Digar* (Another Melody), *Āvāz-e Khāk* (Song of Soil), *Didār dar Falq* (Meeting at Dawn), *Vasf-e Gol-e Suri* (Description of a Red Rose), *Gandom va Gilās* (Wheat and Cherry), *Cheh Talkh Ast in Sib* (How Bitter Is this Apple!), and *Zibātar az Shekl-e Qadim-e Jahān* (More Beautiful than the Old Shape of the World). Ātashi has also translated a number of books, including *Fontamara* by Ignazio Silone.

Manouchehr Ātashi died in 2005.

MANOUCHEHR ĀTASHI

Manouchehr Ātashi thinks that the 1979 revolution is a modern, global phenomenon despite its "traditional roots." He views the impact of the Islamic Revolution on contemporary literature and the exceptional growth in the volume of novels and modern poetry produced over the past two decades in its historical context. Ātashi believes that the bulk of Iranian literature is the product of this same historical context, which he dubs "the history of Iran's infelicities." He assesses poets and writers' tussles with the byproducts of the Islamic Revolution—especially censorship—in this same light. The weapon that Iranians have used for survival over the course of a history that has disarmed them has always been literature. And now, too, contemporary Persian literature, which was essentially banned until a while back, has been able to find itself in a far better place than it had been in the period before the Islamic Revolution, and it is now able to aid in the establishment of cultural literacy that Iranian society needs in order to make headway in the global community.

Despite the unprecedented enthusiasm shown by readers for the contemporary Persian novel, Ātashi still does not see this genre as a rival—in terms of quality—for Persian poetry, with its storied past. After mentioning some valuable works in the realm of the novel, he warns writers (and poets) to steer clear of postmodernism and other schools of thought that are not well understood in Iran if they want to offer good works.

He considers himself an iconoclastic poet in the sense that, as soon as he breaks a tradition, he creates a new tradition, which is, in turn, ready to be broken. In writing his poetry, he views not just the wealth of Persian poetry since the advent of Islam as his legacy, but also Zoroastrian Gathas[34] and erotic Sanskrit poetry. His main criticism of the younger generation is that it disregards the freshness of the several-thousand-year-old legacy of poetry and consequently has a poor knowledge of poetry.

SHIVA RAHBARAN: The aim of this study is to discover what impact the 1979 revolution has had on Iranian literature and art, from the point of view of artists and thinkers who are currently living and working in Iran. This study, which is in two parts, will be conducted in the form of interviews. In the first part, it tries to come to grips with the post-revolution changes in Iranian society. In the second part, we want to see what impact these changes and anomalies have had on literature, and, of course, what impact Iranian literature and criticism has had on society, and what direction it will choose to take.

The first question is a general question about democracy and its history in Iran. Many people are of the view that democracy is, basically, of no use to Iranians in view of their traditions and their experience of modernity. Tell me, what impression do people in Iran have of democracy? Do they think that democracy is a good form of government? Are they aware of its latent dangers of dema-

---

34   Hymns in the *Avesta*, the Zoroastrian holy book.

goguery and populism? And have Iranian thinkers acquainted the people with democracy and its dangers? And, finally, what role have Iranian intellectuals played in explaining democracy over the past hundred years, especially since the 1979 revolution?

MANOUCHEHR ĀTASHI: Some time ago, in 1993, I was invited to a SIRA[35] conference in Los Angeles. As it happens, the general topic of all the presentations was the obstacles, in various arenas, to democracy in Iran. They politely told me: Since you're a poet, you can ignore the general topic and speak about poetry. But I believe that when there are discussions of this kind, poetry cannot be separated from other things. Major events and problems that have an impact on poetry cannot be ignored. If you look closely, you will see that the bulk of our literature has been produced over the course of a history that I call "the history of Iran's infelicities," with all its distressing and strange events. In other words, if we have a look, we'll see that our best poets and mystics, such as Abu-Sa'id, Attār, Sanā'i, and Rumi, have all emerged during these periods and these crises; even Saadi and Hāfez, and so on.

And our modern poetry was born in circumstances in which it was hard to know where our country was headed: on the one hand, the Constitutional Revolution had failed to achieve anything and was more or less defeated; and, on the other hand, the Jangal revolt[36] had broken out and been defeated, and the Reza

---

35 Society for Iranian Anthropology.
36 The Jangal revolt (1915–1921) was led by Mirzā Kuchak Khān. It was a revolt in northern Iran against a weak central government that was under the thumb of the British.

Shah dictatorship was back in charge. One way or the other, our society was unable, throughout this time, to experience any calm. You can see that, when Reza Shah's dictatorship came to an end, we had a brief opportunity, in the 1940s, to have a fleeting taste of modernity. And even that fleeting taste did not arrive in our country in an institutionalized way and in the form of thought and philosophy; it arrived in the form of news and journalism.

S.R. Even during the time of Mossadegh?

M.A. Yes, the subject came up precisely during that decade, the 1940s, when there was some measure of freedom. Someone, an individual like Dr. Mossadegh, stands up and talks about a big subject.[37] And, well, naturally, a society, which suddenly has a whiff of fresh air, experiences a jolt. A few parties are established. A few associations and societies are formed. Some newspapers are published. Books are translated. And, to the extent that my age allowed it, this was the sort of thing that we were doing. This is why we see that, in a short space of time, they eliminated Mossadegh and restored the monarchy. Back to repression and the SAVAK[38] and so on and so forth. In this way, these problems, in general, occurring one after the other over the course of history, have prevented our society from taking center stage in history. In other

---

37 The "big subject" that Prime Minister Mohammad Mossadegh is associated with is the nationalization of the Iranian oil industry in 1951. Until then, it was largely controlled by Britain.

38 Persian acronym for the State Security and Intelligence Organization; Mohammad Reza Shah's much-feared security service.

words, I don't see Iranian society as being prominent in history at all. The pinnacle of history was when, after the Renaissance or after the French Revolution, other societies took shape and acquired structures that demanded their own ideas. And the artists and writers created those ideas, wrote books, and produced compilations of ideas. The culture of the French Revolution spread and more advanced societies of Europe arose. The growth of the material sciences, the speed at which these sciences grew, and the associated technological advances all helped things along. And the situation which you see came about whereby Eastern countries were left behind. Well, naturally, some countries had the French Revolution's blessing, as it were. But, over here, people were left without any hope! Over here, it is only individuals who do some things in the field of politics.

It's also evident that we don't have a single historian. I mean that throughout the pre-Islamic period and after it, too, we don't have any record of a single fully-fledged historian. There were people who wrote accounts of daily life at kings' courts, people who wrote reports about wars, incidents at royal hunting parties, and so on. As an exception to the rule, a gifted person like Beyhaqi conveyed something of the deep, bitter truths. But this isn't history, because history cannot exist ex nihilo. History is based on sociology and the ideas and the thinking that took shape in Iran. Iran never got as far as sociology; in other words, sociology did not come into existence in Iran. If you have a look, you can see that Fārābi had read Plato. He'd read Aristotle. He'd read all these people and he explained them well. He became famous as a teacher of other thinkers' writings. But when it came to thinking about society—for example, how all these changes actually come about in society, how a society should be, how it should be governed—because of the longevity of a system of one-man rule, of monarchy, he, too, opted for such a system, but he preferred someone who is knowledgeable and wise and faultless, someone who has never put a foot wrong; he preferred to talk about something like Plato's *Republic*. This is unattainable!

So you can see that there's never been any sign in this country of anything from which democracy—i.e., rule by the people—could be born. Well, things proceeded in this way. Then, as you mentioned, we had Mossadegh. During the time of Mossadegh, we saw the emergence of some kind of basis for the people to act, but they didn't allow it to grow. They crushed it immediately. They crushed it and things reverted to the way they had been before.

S.R. The question is: Why was the Iranian nation unable to safeguard that system against foreign and domestic conspirators?

M.A. The Iranian nation is a nation that doesn't have the knowledge, the cultural underpinning, and the cultural literacy of its day. It has no idea what the word "democracy" means. It has spent its life as a herd of sheep, so to speak. After all, it can't acquire this knowledge out of the blue! Foundations, events, revolutions, or movements have to come about that are based on democracy, whereas most of the movements in our country have either been based on tradition or on monarchy. When we arrived at the February [1979] revolution, again, in the first instance, what we had was something that had not been thought through. That is to say, people were saying: As long as this fellow leaves, it doesn't matter who takes over! Again, there is no sign of democracy or rule by the people and so on. And the [new] state said openly: I want to establish a religious system. It did not say: Let's establish a democratic system. In fact, its claim was that it wanted to establish a traditional, Islamic system. And the population was a population that had, at any rate, never had the chance to act. And it also happened to be a Muslim population. So it just shuffled along, without knowing what it wanted. It said: We'll go down this route and, then, we'll get somewhere and, then, we'll do something! And the years passed and the tumult and turbulence in our society did not die down.

We did not have a backdrop of positive thinking, based on democracy, until we arrived at Mr. Khatami's presidency. It was only then that they started—and only in line with the capabilities of this one man and his associates—to look for elements within the context of the existing tradition, not beyond it (they cannot go beyond it, they operate within the parameters of the existing tradition) that they could align with democracy. In other words, in practical terms, people took part in elections, but taking part in elections, on its own, doesn't amount to democracy. The people will only be able to come into contact with real democracy when they play a part, in full strength, in governing the country. But, as you can see, this is very difficult to achieve and it leads to terrible conflicts. It generates horrific factionalism. The factions cannot get along with each other or, if they do get along, it is with great difficulty and on the basis of mere expediencies.

Our recurring problem is that we don't have anything in our society that might encourage establishing cultural literacy or some alternative basis or element. As a poet and writer, I feel that this is the main thing that our society lacks: a high level of cultural literacy. If our society can increase its cultural literacy and learn about the modern world—that is to say, to learn about and accept today's world—then, it will be possible to tell the nation: "Do this; don't do that." Then, the people will find the basic way forward, one way or the other. But this hasn't happened yet. And this conflict and this tumult will continue until our officials or people who are influential in safeguarding or governing this sphere of life, really undergo a social transformation themselves, to the point where they say: We can't live in today's world but still act as if we live in the past. We have to give in to democracy and accept its consequences and tangible effects.

S.R. You've arrived at the 11 February [1979] revolution. In the West, some analysts describe this revolution as an Iranian experiment. What they mean by this expression is the synthesis of modernity and religion. This paradox or anomaly has always been present in all the modern movements that have occurred in Iran's contemporary history, from the time of the Constitutional Revolution to the time of Mossadegh to today. In order to prevent society from fracturing, pro-democracy politicians and intellectuals have always tried to unite nationalists and religious people and advance together. Has this "Iranian experiment" actually managed to prevent society from fracturing? I mean, has the marriage of modernity and religion proved successful?

M.A. Now we're talking about fellowship between modernity and religion. This is a very broad subject and much of it is beyond my ken. If I say something about democracy, a religious person may come along and cite a religious narrative and say that what I'm talking about is out of the question.

But the thing is that it is the intrinsic nature of humanity and human life that it evolves and moves forward. This isn't a lie. It is a fact that we are witnessing in the world—despite the very contrasting challenges and conflicts that arise in most places. For example, take the question of religion in Europe. Religion hasn't been banished in Europe; it has been made personal. If someone believes in Christ, in the church, he goes to church every week and performs all the rites. In Iran, too, when the character of popular movements becomes such that, while respectfully safeguarding religion, they want to catch up with the advanced countries, to achieve world-level scientific growth, to achieve real democracy and freedom, then, the problem will be solved—without any harm to religion. The insistence on having a religious state—the insistence that religion should rule—is a dogmatic insistence and it causes problems both for religion and for society.

Europe's Middle Ages proved that the church can't rule. During this period, the political power of the church reached its peak. The killing [sic] of people like Galileo by the church reached its peak.

But it gradually receded to the point where, finally, in the twenti-eth century, the same church absolved Galileo and declared that he had not committed any offense. It is thanks to developments such as this that there have been political reforms. This is why, in our society, things must advance to the point where religion can exist as a beautiful thing, not as something violent, domineering, and repressive. Religion should turn into what it is: i.e., faith, in-ner goodness, and the avoidance of the rapacity and repression that really have nothing to do with religion.

We can take Palestine as an example. As they say, the Arabs and the Israelis are brothers. They are all Abraham's children, but they treat each other in the worst possible way. You ask yourself, why? Doesn't the Koran speak of Moses's religion as one of the major, accepted religions, as it does of Christianity? All nations can fall under the banner of that religion: Africans, Chinese, Japanese, etc. But Israel doesn't allow anyone other than its own people to join the circle of its religion. It doesn't allow this religion to become global. This is why it can't get along with any of its neighbors, who follow various religions. And this is the nature of orthodoxy, which infects politics and religion.

S.R. So combining a modern state with religion isn't unique to Iranian culture?

M.A. The Iranian experiment is one manifestation of it. In this sense, it is unique. Russia was the first country to have a revolution and modern reforms; that is to say, it had a Marxist revolution.

But it didn't conceive a plan for banishing the spirit of Orthodoxy. Stalin plainly said that these people—the Orthodox Church— lived with the Tsar and now, too, they expect a Tsar! As a result, the state became Stalinist. And so it continued until the repression reached its peak and it all boiled over.

In Iran, Iranians are Shiis, not Sunnis. The two are very different. In Shiism, there is *ijtihad*.[39] This is why a *mujtahid* can issue a ruling that goes completely against the old rulings. There are many rulings that have been abrogated. Of course, I'm not familiar with the religious terminology, so I can't express it in the way that they do. For example, for many years, eating one or two types of fish was forbidden [*harām*]. Sturgeon and shark, for example. Then, Ayatollah Khomeini said that no, they weren't forbidden; it's impossible for anything to live in the sea and be forbidden.

At any rate, this sort of thing is possible in Shiism. I mean, Iran can't be fundamentalist in the classic sense. Iran always has this asset: its deep and profound culture[, independent of religion,] remains in Iranians' hearts. I mean that Iran's deep culture is intermingled with pure and untainted religious ideas. And this can pave the way for a healthy and constructive development in our country. This is my view.

S.R. Has the 1979 revolution been good for Iran, when we look at the past twenty-three years?

---

39   Formulation of new rulings by senior clerics (*mujtahid*s).

M.A. Well, you could say that our revolution was a real revolution no matter what, because it pushed aside a long-standing monarchical system. It's true that the revolution itself was rooted in tradition and had a traditional, religious credo, but it was influenced by modern-day global developments. Some people within this revolution wanted to try to prevent the people's democratic movement and the people's demand for democracy, but they couldn't. They're the same gentlemen who are trying to impose their social mores. You've no doubt heard that the likes of us didn't dare write or say anything in our universities. Things were such that it was impossible for us to do so. Well, the poets and writers who were most ostracized as "enemies" now chair most of the literary gatherings and debates in universities. The majority of the literary and cultural sessions on the big contemporary poets, on contemporary literary issues, on contemporary cultural issues are chaired by the likes of us. And this is exactly the kind of cultural literacy that we need to encourage; to reach the maturity and a level of development where we will refuse to accept anything that [the rest of] the world will not accept. This is our only way forward and we must act accordingly.

S.R. Along the way, you've always had to tussle with censorship, both under the former regime and now. And, well, this leads to self-censorship. In your view, has all this censorship been good for your literature and your creative force? Has it served as fertile ground? Has it made your poetry more subtle?

M.A. Look, in Iran, censorship after the revolution is not the same as it was at the time of the Shah. The censorship under the Shah

drove our poetry straight into symbolism. Our biggest symbol-
ist poet is Nimā. Except for a few of his poems, everything that
Nimā said was symbolic. In other words, he doesn't deal with
the objective and the real, except in one or two poems, such as
Shabha (Nights) or *Āy Ādamha* (Hey, People!). When you read
Morgh-e Āmin (Prayer Bird), when you read *Qoqnus* (Phoenix),
when you read *Qoquliqu Khorus Mikhānad* (Cock-a-doodle-doo
the Rooster Sings), you find that he is trying to speak through
allusions and signs. Allusions and signs that the majority of the
people cannot relate to, because only well-educated people can
decipher this kind of poetry. In other words, this is the result of
censorship. We don't have political censorship in that sense now.
If someone writes something directly attacking the state, they will
prevent it, but more than having political censorship hanging over
our cultural community, we have a kind of morality censorship or
censorship against sexuality, so to speak. They're mainly sensitive
to this kind of thing; they pick out this kind of thing.

Lots of books are being published in Iran now. I was in Germany just a month ago. One of my friends told me there: "I went
to Iran and I was just amazed! I brought back loads of books.
The books that are being published in Iran—I would never have
dreamed it possible!" And that's really true. I mean, many good
and instructive books are being published in this country. This is
very effective. It will increase people's knowledge. It will educate
people and then there'll be no going back.

S.R. Are the writers of these books indebted to the nascent freedom in Iran or the reverse, the lack of freedom? Because, as you

77

know, in the West, people like Messrs Muschg and Enzensberger say: "We envy you Iranian writers' predicament! Although you don't have the freedom that you should, you can be more important and your voices are heard by many people. You're like messengers who can fill a ten-thousand-seat stadium in your country!" They compare the literary situation in Iran today with, for example, the huge popularity of literature in Russia before the collapse of communism. And, in short, they conclude that freedom is inimical to literature.

M.A. They're just trying to be charitable of course. The more limited interest over there must have other causes, such as anti-intellectualism and the availability of leisure activities.

As for the publication of books and supervision over books, the situation has changed a great deal. In the very recent past, we did have this problem. They very easily prevented the publication of many books. Things have been better for a while now, after Khatami became president. Khatami himself was culture minister once. Many books were published then. But he was finally forced, more or less, to step down. Then he became president and he made Mr. Mohajerani culture minister. Mohajerani not only went so far as to remove the supervision, or almost remove it, but also to make peace with the Writers' Association. I mean, he gave an interview and then he embarked on a kind of conciliation between the Culture Ministry and the Writers' Association. In other words, the state itself was a bit shocked when it saw how badly writers were treated. It recalls how, since the time of Alexander's invasion—not just since the Arab conquest of Iran—this land has always been disarmed. The people were forced to drop their swords, but they didn't drop their pens. This land has preserved itself within its writings. It has preserved itself within the Persian language. And, fortunately, none of them was ever able to crush the Persian language.

I can tell you about an interesting incident. I have a friend who is a doctor. He works in Egypt, for the UN. Of course, he's also a poet. This friend of mine translates poetry, jointly with an Egyptian professor, who has a PhD in Persian literature. He translates Persian poetry into Arabic. One day, the professor asked him: "We Egyptians aren't Arabs; we're Coptic. Everyone knows this. We're from a different race. We're not Arabs. But we became both Muslims and Arabs. How is it that you became Muslims but didn't become Arabs?" The doctor replied: "Go and ask Ferdowsi, ask Attār, ask Rumi, who preserved themselves and preserved us, just as we're doing."

S.R. So our literature has always been the literature of resistance? And has this resistance always created our identity again and again? Is it still doing so?

M.A. When you have books, you exist; when you don't, you don't exist. I remember a film I saw once about the Yugoslav partisans who fought against Hitler. In one scene, there was an old man with a big pile of books in a street. The partisans had ordered people to evacuate the area. The old man was sitting on top of his books and he was saying: "I'm not going anywhere without my books!" They were telling him: "They are bombarding this area! You must go! It's an order!" One of the partisans goes to his commander and says: "Sir, he's saying we have to take his books too." The commander says: "He's right! What we're fighting for is not to preserve our bodies; we're fighting for our culture. It's our culture that must be preserved. Be sure to load up his books in a cart first and, then, leave!" What I mean to say is that this is absolutely true. It's not a joke. We remained alive within this culture. A nation that remains alive within this culture remains alive in its own poetry, its own literature, its own ideas, and its own thinking. It can't be destroyed. It can't be crushed. It can't be told: "Shut up forever!"

S.R. But doesn't this make all its literature political and isn't it harmful to art to be politicized?

M.A. Unfortunately, it is harmful. But, first of all, our younger generations now, after the 1970s, are more inclined toward aesthetics and toward exploring new intellectual frontiers. This is a fact. But, in another way, as you said, becoming politicized along the way can be harmful. As the late Bizhan Jalāli used to say, sometimes it keeps our poetry bad-tempered! Why does this happen? Because it is unavoidable. It occurs in my own poetry too. But, well, this is one of the secrets of our survival too. We don't submit to any old burden that they want to put on our backs. If necessary, we move forward, but we throw the burden off. It would be best if they didn't impose the burden on us; then, we could take the center stage of history and join the convoy of global civilization and head for a good life.

S.R. So in light of the fact that we are on another historical stage, or that we're in a different time and place compared to the rest of the world, how do poetry and the novel compare in our country? Can we say that this "being outside history" makes our poetry very strong? For example, Mr. Dariush Shāyegān has written, in his book *Henry Corbin*, that the novel is a mirror of the West's dualistic thinking; that is to say, it was born in the divide between mind and body that has existed from the Renaissance onward. But in a culture like ours, we have always had mysticism's "unity of being." So we look at ourselves in the mirror of our poetry. Our poet is a kind of messenger to whom poetry is divinely revealed and this doesn't match the role that a novelist plays in a modern society. Don't you think that this is why our novels are weak?

M.A. The novel is young in our country and we have had very few novels. If we were to count them, we'd be able to on just the fingers of our hands. Because we haven't really had novels in Iran. And we haven't had very good translations of novels. But we've had plenty of translated poetry.

Now, the fact that the poetry of the younger generation has not had the same success as the poetry of, for example, the 1960s, or that it has fewer buyers: there are other reasons for this. One reason is that the book market is moving toward money-making and away from poetry and so on. They don't take on young poets' poetry books. When I was young and I'd moved to Tehran from Bushehr, at my first session with some of my old friends, like Reza Seyyed Hosseini, like the late Mohammad Zohri, like Mirsadeqi, and like the late Moshiri, as soon as my poetry was published in newspapers and as soon as I'd read some of my new poems, Mr. Reza Seyyed Hosseini said: "I want to publish your poetry!" And I realized later that he published my book using money that he'd saved up to buy some land. It was 1959. I mean, that's how great his love was for this country and for culture. Now, too, this book has just been republished; it's not new, but people are still buying it.

Unlike other publishers, my current publisher pays me even before he's sent my book to the Culture Ministry for a permit. I mean that this book had sold about 2,700 or 1,800 [sic] copies as of about a month ago. It's unprecedented that a book should sell out before a year is out and be republished the following year.

S.R. But isn't it harmful that publishers aren't accepting young people's works?

M.A. Yes. Our publishing industry and many other things, I mean our cultural institutions, still have their traditional backwardness. Look, a good publisher is a publisher that has a cultural adviser, that has a literary adviser. He has to say, look, this book should be made available. He shouldn't concern himself with fame. I mean, if it's good enough to be made available, a publisher should make it available. Maybe it will take some time before he makes money on it, but it will happen.

This is a problem that the younger generation has nowadays: the publishers don't want to deal with them. The younger generation has to pay out of its own pockets to have its books published. A book that's published in this way inevitably will not sell. They do have this problem. Otherwise, we have some very talented poets in this younger generation. And, as I said, they don't have the political inclinations that people had in the past. They don't want to write political poems. They are all looking for a new kind of thinking in which politics can become part of a poem's essence, rather than being imposed on it.

S.R. But young novelists are more successful than young poets. I mean, even though they don't have that rich literary legacy, they are more successful than poets.

M.A. The novel is successful in a way, to some extent. Iran hasn't had novels. Good novels aren't coming out in the rest of the world anymore either. In the past, when you wanted to read a novel, you would read Dostoyevsky. You would read Balzac, Hemingway, Sartre. Now, their era has nearly come to an end, in a way.

In Iran, for its part, a generation has turned writer and worked at it. For example, Mandanipour, the late Golshiri, Mohammad Ali, Sanāpur, Butorab Khosravi, and so on. It's natural that, when they're publishing poetry, they tell you, the poet: "Go away! This isn't what people are looking for today! Poetry has to be postmodern!" But when it comes to fiction, they say: "Fiction has to have something special." They don't say, it should have a message. They even say that the aesthetics and the language don't really need to be strong either. But when a novel by Mandanipour comes out, they say: "It's full of life. It's full of freshness." It's received well. Whoever he goes to, they'll publish his books. Or someone like the late Golshiri, he had established himself more or less on a par with Sādegh Hedāyat or Chubak. These are things that have made this a good time for the novel. I believe that we will have a good time for poetry too. But what about the generation that was completely wrong for ten years or so and was producing work based on a sham postmodernism? Never mind!

In some of the general discussions that we had with young people, we realized that many of them had taken a wrong turn. They are now coming back home and are connecting to our own culture. We say: First, know and criticize yourself; then, take up modern stuff! You haven't even mastered modernity; what are you doing going for postmodernity?!

So we have these problems and there's a long way to go before we get to new times. Everything has to wait for its time. These processes take time. Here, the reformist newspapers keep coming to us for interviews. They say: "What do you think about the poetry of the 1990s?" Come on! People have been producing poetry for 2,500 years in this country. How do you expect one decade to speak for a century?!

S.R. This brings us to the next question. Are you an iconoclast? We can see that you have a 2,500-year-old legacy, but you break traditions too. Isn't this a paradox?

M.A. I have a collection of selected poems that has a long introduction. It's quite old now. I wrote a long introduction for it. I wrote there that we do break with tradition, but not in order to abandon or banish tradition. A true poet is someone who, as soon as he breaks a tradition, he creates a new tradition; a tradition that is then, in turn, ready to be broken, so that this process can continue. The point is not just to be called an iconoclast. I don't date the history of poetry from Islamic times. I go back to Zoroastrian Gathas.[40] I go back to the *Rig Veda*, which was written in Sanskrit. I go to the Chinese poems of Lao Tse. Poetry has roots and you can plot its journey as a big curve. You can easily take it and reconnect it to the world. This is something that has been done in the past. In the past, Zurvanism, Manichaeism, and the Zoroastrian religion pervaded the whole world. Poems or novels have been translated in which these ideas have been discovered. They've found poems belonging to the Arabs of Andalusia from the ninth to the fourteenth centuries. A friend sent us some translations of these poems and then we realized that Lorca and people like him are heirs to these poems! I mean those roots extend to these modern times. Recently, Abbas Safari translated erotic poems from the Sanskrit period, dating back two thousand years. That is to say, they roughly correspond to the Sassanid era in Iran.

---

40   See Note 34, page 66.

Poems that are fresh and full of life. This is why I'm saying that our younger generation has a problem. It has a poor knowledge of poetry. It thinks that it should start with the Europeans, whereas you won't even find poems like these in Europe itself. So that's not the way to go about it. This is my view.

S.R. Last question. What do you think about academic research into contemporary Persian literature? Some people are of the view that, when a researcher comes from abroad, he is always a tool in the hands of the exploiters (the West), because, without even knowing it or intending it, he assists the superpowers' plans by revealing the Eastern mind or the Iranian mind. And, therefore, that this kind of research only compounds the exploitation. What's your view on this? Are Oriental studies dangerous for the Orient?

M.A. No, that's not what I think. When you read Hermann Hesse, you think that he has read Buddhism well and that that's why he heads for the East. What's wrong with that? As a result, he creates his own masterpiece. Or, on the other side, Carlos Castaneda proposes a kind of Red Indian Sufism. These are not things that you can lock up somewhere. And you can't tar them all with the same brush. The East and the West move along a single horizon, and they run deep. I even want to say that there are traces of the West's footprints in our literature and it will continue to be there.

When I read Eliot's *The Waste Land*, it influences me deeply. I accept it. Why? Because I think: this poet has produced a great work. Immediately after the First World War and the crumbling of Christian values in Europe, he raises his voice. Or I look at what Lorca did in Spain or some other poet somewhere else. This is why I believe that cultures will always be on good terms and be interlinked, especially in art. But not in politics.

MOHAMMAD ALI SEPĀNLU

Born in Tehran in 1941, his books of poetry include *Khāk* (Soil), *Ragbārha* (Deluges), *Piāderowhā* (Sidewalks), *Sandbād-e Ghayeb* (The Absent Sinbad), and *Khānom-e Zāmān* (Mrs. Time, lyrical sketches about Tehran). His research works include *Nevisandegān-e Pishrow-e Irān* (Iran's Vanguard Writers) and *Siāhatnāmeh-ye Ebrāhim-Beyg* (Ebrāhim-Beyg's Travelogue). His translations include works by Albert Camus, Jean-Paul Sartre, and Graham Greene.

Mohammad Ali Sepānlu

In view of the importance of Iranian Islam to Iranians, Mohammad Ali Sepānlu does not reject the Islamic Revolution as a sociopolitical idea, but he believes that the Iranian experience of it has been a failure. He believes this is because, when the idea was put into practice, the clerical class did not become the people's spiritual and religious guides, but rather, this class was put in charge of running all the country's political, economic, and social affairs. Despite this assessment, Sepānlu is optimistic, in a way, about the fact that the revolution took place and about the course it will take. In his view, the revolution helped Iran to advance, because it allowed Iranians to gain a new awareness of their own socioreligious mechanisms.

He believes that the biggest harm that the Islamic Revolution did to contemporary literature was severing the link between poets and their audience (which consists, in the first instance, of university students, high school students, and teachers). This was done not only—as under the previous regime—through official censorship and security controls over schools and universities, but also by robbing the younger generation of hope, a younger generation that should have formed the main core of readers after the revolution. Sepānlu is of the view that the ruinous result of this policy has been artistic exile for poets and writers in their own society.

Despite highlighting the harm that censorship does to literature, he also bears in mind the "positive" aspects of censorship.

Although he believes literature's need for censorship is "like an illness," he believes that the censorship after the revolution has, to some extent, forced poets to use elaborate artistic structures in order to say what they want to say. He is also of the view that the state's attempt to sever completely the link between the creators of literature and their audience has failed. It is true that the link between poets and their audience in classrooms has been broken, but now poets find their audience in the streets and in sports stadiums.

On the subject of the relative positions of the contemporary Persian novel and modern poetry, Sepānlu is of the view that this is a fertile time for the growth of the novel and he knows that the novel is currently more talked about than poetry. Since, contrary to the state's objectives, Iran is moving toward modern urbanization and, ultimately, toward polyphony, the novel, which hinges on this phenomenon, is blossoming rapidly. But, in terms of quality, there is still no comparison between the novel and poetry, a genre which Sepānlu believes is innate to Iran and which has had a long-standing history. Moreover, internationally, it still cannot compete with the novel in the West. This is in circumstances in which, internationally, Persian poetry is "real" poetry and "has something to say."

In his poetry, Shāmlu strives to reconcile and combine classical Persian poetry with "colloquial" poetry. As far as he is concerned, poetry has to be rooted in the "humanism" of Persian poetry and in Saadi's dictum: "Human beings are members of a whole / In creation, of one essence and soul." Poetry's duty is to keep recreating this idea and bringing it up to date; i.e., formulating it as a new historical awareness. To this end, Sepānlu considers himself more in touch with the "elite" of the Iranian public than directly with the masses. The role that intellectuals—such as teachers or university students—can play is to simplify this kind of poetry and pass it on to the masses.

SHIVA RAHBARAN: I would like to discuss the relationship between democracy and the 1979 revolution; about the chance that democracy—which is a system of government that depends on "modernity"—has had and does have in contemporary Iran, especially after the Islamic Revolution.

In the West, especially in France, as you know, some analysts describe the Iranian revolution as the Iranian experiment. What they mean by this expression is the synthesis of modernity and religion. In your view, is this paradox or anomaly, i.e. the marriage of modernity and religion, achievable? And if so, has the Iranian revolution had any success in reconciling religion and modernity?

MOHAMMAD ALI SEPĀNLU: If an experience fails, can the theory be definitively rejected? It may have been possible for things to have turned out differently in Iran. Let's use our imagination. If our leader at the time of the revolution had been someone like Gandhi, would our situation not have turned out differently? For example, a guide who would have supervised things from a distance, someone who would have handed the government over to technocrats. A charismatic leader who could have a calming effect on the chaos after a revolution by exercising supervision from above, in the framework of the law.

I think that all the countries that are like us need a special kind of democracy, because our experience in 1980 in Iran showed that, in a general election, several hundred candidates entered Parliament, each with a small percentage of the votes, none of whom was prepared to compromise in the slightest. In fact, it was like the years after the Constitutional Revolution, when people grew so tired of the insecurity and social disturbances that they were longing for a strong person to take charge of the country. Let's not deceive ourselves; nations like ours still consider themselves in need of a guide who, in effect, has no personal interests. My imagination tells me that if someone like Gandhi or Mandela appears at this stage, we will have had a stroke of historical luck; otherwise, it will just be the same old story.

Well, yes, the answer is that the experience has failed in all instances. The guide made decisions alone, without taking into account any technical experience. You saw an example of this in the delaying of peace with Iraq; in the years when being peace-loving was considered an insult. You see more or less the same mistakes today. In Afghanistan, the defeat of the Taliban was a kind of victory for Iran. How did it happen, then, that we lost out? There wasn't a single Iranian among the members of Al-Qaeda and the September 11 terrorists. So how did Iran end up being called "the axis of evil"? This is solely because of our officials' mistakes. At one point in time, the Al-Qaeda or Taliban regime consisted of dogmatic Sunnis who believed that killing Shiis would help them go to paradise. Then, these same people turned into our officials' clients! I mean our officials turned into their defense lawyers. These mistakes result from the inexperience of people who think that a modern society can be governed with slogans.

We lost nearly a million people in the bloody war between Iran and Iraq. How could we end up in the same category as them; i.e., the axis of evil? It is amazing that some people [some Iranian officials] defend Iraq and Saddam, but, unfortunately, our intellectuals—the ones who know what's what (not all of them know)—don't speak out. Once, I felt compelled, exceptionally, to write a political article, rejecting the argument of those who were saying that we should help Saddam Hussein. I wrote that, if Iraq succeeds at this stage, after gobbling up Kuwait, it will head for Khuzestan.[41] A series of historical mistimings and mismatched theories have led us to where we are. Had it not been for these mistakes, had we had a bit of luck, isn't it conceivable that Iran could have had a democratic religious regime? Read *Humanism in the Renaissance of Islam: Cultural Revival During the Buyid Age* by Joel Kraemer. A thousand years ago, a kind of philosophers' Athens was established in our own town of Rey. It is remarkable.

S.R. This Iranian paradox is related to the conduct of Iranian intellectuals over the past hundred years. For example, Bahman Nirumand is one of the people who says that Iranian intellectuals

---

41   Province in southwest Iran.

have always tried to prevent society from fracturing, using the theory of wedding modernity to Islam. This has been the case from the Constitutional Revolution to the time of Mossadegh to the 1979 revolution.

M.S. Bahman Nirumand is as much to blame as most Iranian thinkers. I mean the research work of most of them is of no use to the unfolding situation in Iran. Before the revolution, instead of critically debating the unrealistic "utopia" of the likes of Dr. Shariati, all their efforts were concentrated on showing off their learning, for example, by exposing the deviations from pure Marxism of the comrades in Moscow. Admit it: in all the thousands of pages of their writings that were being published in Europe and the US before the revolution, you will hardly find anything that hasn't been subsequently disproved. Or, at the very least, anything that has not been proved irrelevant to the Iranian problematic today. Maybe he's realized his mistakes sooner than some of the others.

The problem is that any mistake may lead to another mistake at the opposite end. There was a time when everyone seemed to be writing that the situation in Iran would only improve if the monarchical regime was toppled. Today, they want to prove the same thing about the current ruling system, using the premise that it is impossible for religion and modernity to coexist. Thousands of lines are written in order to eventually arrive at a conclusion that is assumed from the start.

Was it not possible to construct a state without giving special powers to clerics as a privileged group? I mean, was it not possible to allow religion to remain a unifying factor but not have it turn into a ruling machine? (I raised this idea for the first time in April 1979, in Kayhan newspaper.) Because, after all, historical experience has shown that Shiism can be of service as an ideology that safeguards Iran's borders. I am not a religious person, but I maintain that Shiism has played a unifying role in Iran since the time of the Safavids. Do you remember in which regions the insurgencies occurred during the time of Mehdi Bāzargān's provisional government [just after the 1979 revolution], when the law enforcement force had effectively fallen apart? Kurdistan, Turkman Sahra, Baluchestan; areas in which Shiis are not in the majority.

At one point, when the 134-signature letter was published,[42] part of the security apparatus was putting pressure on us to make some of us withdraw our signatures and, then, possibly, to suppress the others. And the scenario went like this: They would ask each of the writers who had signed the letter, "Did you realize that foreigners would exploit your signature? If you didn't, now that you know, are you willing to withdraw your signature?" Some of our renowned intellectuals withdrew their signatures with great fanfare, as if in protest at foreign interference. In a long interview with *Ettela'at* newspaper, I tried to analyze this issue, from every aspect. First of all, yes, I knew that the foreign governments that are opposed to the regime would milk the letter for all its worth. But does this mean that we shouldn't point out the failings of our own system? Aren't all the things that our own government says

---

42   Reference to a letter against censorship signed by 134 Iranian writers and sent to the Islamic Guidance and Culture Ministry in October 1994.

against the U.S. Administration obtained from American news sources? So there is nothing wrong with the critical things that we write and it is completely in keeping with democracy. And, secondly, I pointed out that opposition to the regime doesn't make us traitors to our country. We're not willing to abandon our country and, for example, become mercenaries for Iraq. It was there that I spoke about this historical role of Shiism, to which our thinkers today—with their affection for abstractions—seem totally oblivious. When the Ba'thist Iraqi regime attacked Iran, did we have to defend ourselves or not? With what ideology did Iranian soldiers and volunteers walk over minefields at the battlefronts and resist Iraq? How should we equip the nation for defense? The *Shāhnāmeh* alone is not enough. We have to appeal to Imam Ali and Imam Hussein too. I'm aware that, in the thick of all the super-modern debates, my remarks seem a bit old-fashioned. But they have historical roots.

S.R. So you believe that creating the national-religious front during Mossadegh's time wasn't a mistake?

M.S. Dr. Mossadegh's theory was right. He used to say: "My actions are based on two values: Iran and Islam." And we saw how, with this compound ideology and without any repression, the hot-headed Islamists were sidelined. Today, too, we must proceed on the basis of the existing realities. We don't have a privileged class by the name of the clergy. Islam doesn't recognize such a thing. But, despite all the pressure that I've endured or witnessed—all the censorship, all the deprivation, all the imprisonments, all the repression, etc.—I have enough self-control to say: We should have a state that uses religion to good effect for the sake of national unity and progress. Was the constitutionalist state—despite the article about a council of *ulema* and about Shiism being the official religion—not a secular regime? A state that considered its powers to be derived from the nation. A state that said that the nation was the font of power and believed that all the members of the Iranian nation were equal before the law; i.e., regardless of their creed or ethnic group. If Iranians love both Imam Hussein and Rostam,[43] why are there efforts on both sides to try to eliminate one of the two?

S.R. So you're saying that this Iranian experiment and this Iranian paradox can succeed?

M.S. It could have been successful; I mean it was possible. But recent bitter experiences and historical reversals have raised a generation in Iran that has no hope. If our generation suffered from a surfeit of ideals, this generation has been disheartened by a dearth of ideals. When the experience of Marxism, a national state, and, finally, a religious state lead nowhere, if, one day, the country is in a difficult spot, our intelligent kids will say: "We don't want

---

43   Imam Hussein was the Prophet's grandson and is revered by Shiites as the third Imam (after Imam Ali and Imam Hassan). Rostam is the hero/strongman in Ferdowsi's epic poem, *Shāhnāmeh*. Sepānlu is highlighting Iranians' attachment to both Islam/Shiism and Iran/Iranian culture.

to know. We don't want to repeat our fathers' bitter tale." What's happening in Iran today doesn't bode well. I mean people are losing their hope in the future and surrendering to any event or any change, without calculating the consequences. The symptoms of this illness are more clearly reflected in today's literary products than anywhere else, especially in the popular and best-selling part of it. Sartre said that, when a society loses its hope in the future, it will have a consumerist literature. We see a profusion of consumerist literature and art in Iran today.

S.R. Do you think that the 1979 revolution was a historical necessity?

M.S. It's hard to say. I think that the Shah's system, too, demeaned the people in a way and, finally, the system imploded.

S.R. How do you view the role of foreign powers in all this?

M.S. The foreigners were only able to speed up the process. How could they possibly have sparked a revolution in Iran if the objective conditions for it hadn't existed? They met in Guadeloupe and said: "The Shah is on his way out, so let him go more quickly." I suppose you've heard of the report of the George Ball committee and the Massachusetts analysts? They'd reported that Iran was on the threshold of an explosion. Of course, they were mainly worried about the communists and the Soviet Union, that they might create a situation like the one they created in Afghanistan. The George Ball committee wrote: Before the communists exploit the contradictions in Iran, it would be better if we changed the Shah's regime ourselves, in a less harmful way, by opting for the religious and national forces. Carter has been quoted as saying, "We believe in God and so do they!" But maybe they hadn't reckoned with the psychology of Eastern people and its shadings. Many Eastern leaders don't know the meaning of national interests. Look at the way Saddam Hussein is treating Iraq. No sane person would subject his own people to chemical bombardment or throw them into mass graves. It isn't even a question of interests; it's a question of the psychological effects of power. I always quarrel with my friends when they say: This or that president is an agent of this or that foreign government. I tell them: If he were, then at least he would act logically.

I knew what a disaster the invasion of Kuwait would be for Iraq. But my intellectual friends were suggesting that there had been some kind of behind-the-scenes deal. These places are lunatic asylums. If Saddam had a nuclear bomb, I'm sure he would have used it. The leaders of these countries, whom any doctor would diagnose as psychologically unhinged, are largely responsible for events. When they talk about executing people, their faces fill with glee. If these people were in democratic countries, they would be kept in mental hospitals.

S.R. I have a question about Persian studies and, more generally, Oriental studies. This is an issue that is discussed not just in Iran, but in Europe, too, by philosophers such as Michel Foucault and Edward Said. For example, my Palestinian friends at Oxford—

well-educated Palestinians—always say: "As we're studying here, they're exploiting us. They're studying our thought processes so that they can rule us again . . ." And this idea of theirs is accepted by many of the Europeans or Americans who are teaching post-colonial studies. What's your view on this? On this basis, is it ever possible to carry out productive studies into the contemporary literature of "the third world"?

M.S. We are like the losers of the third world. I remember how once, Dowlatābādi and I were sitting at one of the sessions at the Berlin conference,[44] and we were observing a discussion between Iranian journalists and the Germans. One of our compatriots was saying with great emphasis: "We haven't come here to fall for any-one's words and to be duped. We don't want to dupe you, so, don't dupe us." The person next to me was a clever man. He scribbled down a note for me. It was a bit rude. He wrote: "It's like telling someone, you can't . . . me." What nonsense! Saying this sort of thing shows that there is a trace of a slave mentality, a bit of an in-feriority complex in the speaker. This is how we end up in the po-sition of the loser. If they're going to dupe you, they're not going to tell you about it. So what's the point of this sort of twaddle about, "You can't make me say anything I don't want to?" This is just the kind of indignation that someone from the third world displays when he wants to make himself look important. He wants to say,

---

44   A cultural conference attended by a group of Iranian writers, intellectuals, and journalists in April 2000. Some of the participants were subsequently put on trial and jailed in Iran for attending the conference.

"I have things to say that you'd want to hear, but I'm not going to say it." And he has nothing to say that you'd want to hear.

I'd say that over the past thirty or forty years, most of our friends, who are good artists or who are very knowledgeable, haven't even noticed the calamity that is unfolding, never mind about analyzing it. This is why you constantly come across pieces of writing in which someone says: "We made a mistake then." No one notices that they're also making a mistake now.

S.R. So the 1979 revolution, with these kinds of intellectuals and artists—

M.S. It couldn't have turned out any better.

S.R. Did it take us one step forward or one step toward the Middle Ages?

M.S. In my view, it took us one step forward. Because the masses experienced a religious state. As a result, the Iranian people's mindset is now ahead of that of all the other Islamic countries. The day when, in Turkey, in Egypt, in Pakistan, in Indonesia, etc., a pseudo-Islamic revolution begins to unfold, only the Iranians will be able to understand the difference between the pledges of justice and the reality of the state.

When, at the time of the Shah, people used to ask them [the clerics], do you want to stone women? do you want to cut off people's hands and feet? and so on, they would reply, hah! You make it sound so simple. There are very detailed provisos. For example, you have to have four fair-minded witnesses. And so on. Now, in the stonings that have taken place in Iran, did they really abide by all the provisos? But I know that radical extremists are making the same arguments in Egypt today and people are falling for it. Whereas, here, since the people have experienced it, they know how it turns out in practice.

Of course, when I talk about an Islamic state, I mean rule by clerics. Otherwise, the people cannot be parted from their religion; not after 1,400 years or so.

S.R. I'd like to go back to what you said about the Safavids. Mr. Dariush Shāyegān has written, in his book *Henry Corbin*, that Shiism's downfall was when the Safavids used it to make the Iranian nation homogeneous, because Shiism is the religion of rebellion, so it cannot rule. In other words, it goes against the grain of Shiism to be made part of "the establishment."

M.S. Mr. Dariush Shāyegān's argument is only interesting in the realm of theory. But, as Dr. Safā wrote in his history of literature, by making Shiism the official ideology of Iran, the Safavids managed to reestablish all the borders of the Sassanid period. Because, on the basis of the initial teachings of Islam, any Muslim, however foreign, can rule over a Muslim country, such as Iran. Like Bin Laden in Afghanistan. I believe that it's not a joke when we say that it was only the Shiite reading of Islam that prevented Iranians from being dissolved in the Arabs. It is not for nothing that our greatest national poet, Ferdowsi, was a Shiite; the national poet in a society where the Sunnis were in the majority. Of course, as long as you're in the opposition, you're very meek. You're viewed as a very compassionate human being. But when you take control of the state, you, like everyone before you, make mistakes and are repressive.

Now, what if someone were to come along and say: In this big world and, especially, in this age of modernity, national borders don't mean anything. Unfortunately, Iran cannot be partitioned peacefully like Czechoslovakia. If we want to avoid Yugoslavia's fate, if we believe that our children shouldn't kill each other in a war, if we want to avoid repeating the ethnic and territorial clashes that we saw in Bosnia and Kosovo, we better pay attention to the consequences of our slippery-slope arguments, especially if we happen to be sitting in the safe haven of a European library, having just had a full meal, accompanied by a sip or two of a little something. Let me put it plainly: I most humbly ask our analyst friends to try to modify their one-dimensional analyses, which see the cause of Iran's misfortune or the way to its salvation in a single factor only. I'm worried that, in the future, they will again say, "We made a mistake."

S.R. Please say more about your role as a responsible poet in Iran today—bearing in mind the policies of the former regime.

M.S. I've tried to do my bit in two areas. First, in my profession, i.e., poetry and literature, which is my main, essential work. Secondly, in the field of social action. I have done my best to avoid being beguiled by ideologies. There was a time when most of our intellectuals were indebted to or in awe of the left-wing movement. And they used to call us "liberal" as an insult, and the religious regime, too, repeated this. I wrote my book *Chahar Sha'er-e Azādi* (Four Poets of Freedom) about our popular experience as reflected in the literature of the constitutionalist period, and in the two elements of love for our homeland and democracy, which produced the historical experience of the National Consultative Assembly and the rule of law. At the time, I had the sense that my reaction to these things isolated me from many people. But those were my natural sentiments.

S.R. What period was this, before or after the revolution?

M.S. The year before it and, of course, the year after it. What I mean to say is that I tried my humble best to avoid the fashionable political trends of the day. I say, with utmost humility, that I have no expertise in social affairs. But I am an innovator, at any rate. I have written a kind of poetry that is an experiment in combining literary Persian and Persian as it is spoken by people in the streets. Within this same method, I have tried to lend dramatic resonance to the poetry's diverse cadences. Perhaps my contemporaries have not understood me well. But I have expanded my work slowly and in depth. Now, we find that a group of our intellectuals and artists is striving to present a culture to the nation that may be rooted in the "humanism" of Persian literature; that is to say, they are bringing it up to date, formulating it as a new historical awareness. It goes without saying that we are not masters of all knowledge. We each do our small bit. As to what my bit has amounted to, others must be the judge. During one's lifetime, there are hundreds of non-cultural considerations, including personal enmities, so I'll leave it for the future to decide.

S.R. Don't you feel as if you're an outcast in your own society? As you know, during the period of modernism and with the advent of individualism and the growing importance of the individual over the whole in Europe, the poet has felt increasingly distanced from the people. For example, Virginia Woolf viewed with envy the English poets of the Middle Ages who were like megaphones, whose voices conveyed the combined voices of all the people. And, after, no one even remembered the names of the poets; it was as if they'd dissolved in the collective. But, from the Renaissance onward, poets became increasingly separated from the people and being outcasts from the people became a necessity for them. Are Iranian poets immune to this affliction in the light of the strong tradition of "unity of being"? And if they do have any sense of being "outcasts," is it not mainly related to the political conditions and the state?

M.S. Of course, Virginia Woolf could not speak to the masses in view of her reserved, intellectual manner. But, at the other end, there was Stephen Spender, whose poems were read very widely. You can have someone like Neruda, whose works were read by the masses throughout the world, or someone like Eliot, who addressed the elites. (Of course, I prefer Eliot.) The work that some of us produce is not addressed directly to the masses. The master of modern Iranian poetry, Nimā, usually wrote for a select group of educated people. The educated people simplified it and entrusted it to the masses. Each person works in one of these directions. For example, Simin Behbahāni's poetry is more simple and has a broader reach, and my poetry mostly deals with elites, except for a few oratorical works, which were addressed to the majority of the people and were well received.

As for the sense of being an outcast that you mentioned, as a matter of fact one of my poetry collections is called *Tab'id dar Vatan* (An Outcast in My Land). The historical irony of it is that it includes poems from both before the revolution and after the revolution. Anyhow, there are two ways in which you can feel like an outcast. One of them is when what you write is too complicated for the average understanding of your day. In other words, as I phrased it in one of my poems: "In a horde of Mongols, you speak of civilization." This way of feeling like an outcast is like belonging to another age and time. The second way is when censorship prevents the publication of your works. Between 1973 and 1978, that is to say, until a year before the revolution, no one was allowed to publish anything by me. All my works were banned. As against that sense of being an outcast in time, here, I felt like I was an outcast in my land. And, two years after the revolution, when all the universities were closed down, I experienced another way of being an outcast and it lasted several years.

I remember how, in 1973, wherever I went, after a trial period in a job, they would tell me: "SAVAK hasn't approved you." And then I'd be unemployed. Through the mediation of the head of a government department, I met an official from the security agency. He said: "We have a culture and you oppose it. So we won't allow you to be in contact with young people or to teach in universities or to have things published in newspapers." And from 1981 onward, there was, again, no place for me—based on a similar argument—in the new university setup. I mean, having imagined that my sense of being an outcast would end after the revolution, I felt it return. Maybe I feel slightly less of an outcast since Khatami became president.

S.R. What about self-censorship? Self-censorship is related to the taboos of Iran's traditional society, not with government censorship. Don't you think?

M.S. Self-censorship is when you think about having your work published. Very slowly, you get into the habit of not saying some things. At a time when the word "breast" is considered obscene in this country, you have to use the word "chest" everywhere. Under the Shah's regime too, there were things you couldn't say. I wrote in an article once: Then, we couldn't translate Ionesco's play *Exit the King*, and now we can't translate Apollinaire's play *The Breasts of Tiresias*. Of course, you should write whatever you want to write in private.

S.R. But this absence of freedom and this self-censorship makes many writers in the West envy writers and poets in Iran. Based on Henry James's idea that every story is a window in the house of fiction, can we say that, since you have more walls, you can put more windows in it? And, of course, your work in this society is more meaningful than the work of writers in the West. They feel as if not just their words, but they themselves are of less importance to their people, although their works sell in much larger numbers than the works of Iranian writers. As an example, the head of the Goethe-Institut cited the fact that, in Iran or in other Eastern countries, when a famous poet gives a poetry reading, it can attract thousands of people, whereas this isn't possible in the West.

M.S. This is another one of the contradictions of life under censorship. We could have brought together thirty thousand people in Amjadieh Stadium for a commemoration of Ahmad Shāmlu, something that would be impossible anywhere else in the world. But they didn't authorize it. I remember how, once, Yevtushenko, the Russian poet, had gone to the United States to give poetry readings. More than ten thousand people were turning up at each session. An American poet wrote him a letter, saying: "How lucky you are! If you write one poem against the situation in the Soviet Union, they might execute you, but in the US, no one pays any attention to us!"

Censorship makes the imagination construct elaborate forms and reverberate words differently. Be that as it may, being in need of censorship is like an illness. But the position of Persian poetry may reveal a special phenomenon. In Iran, hearing poets recite their own poems still has a wide appeal, especially so because people like the "didactic" aspects of poetry. They look for a message in it. Even when literature conveys hopelessness and despair, they seek a reflection of their own lives in it. But I don't like to see Persian poetry today attracting interest only because of its political messages.

A few years ago, when I was visiting New York at the invitation of American PEN, at a meeting with publishers, one of the publishers told our group of writers: "Remember how, ten years ago, when the Soviet Union had not yet collapsed, Americans were very keen to read contemporary Russian literature; now that communism has been toppled, they no longer look for translations of Russian books." I replied jokingly: "It seems that we should be grateful to our government." But one likes to attract interest for one's own sake, not for the sake of the country's political situation. Nowadays, apart from our classics, headed by Rumi and Khayyám, it is only Sādegh Hedāyat's *Buf-e Kur* (*The Blind Owl*), among the contemporary works, that is consistently republished abroad. I long for this situation to change. I mean, I hope that, like Iranian cinema, our contemporary literature, too, will start attracting interest because of its own intrinsic value, which isn't slight.

S.R. In a book entitled *Hāfez-e Andisheh* (Hāfez, Keeper of Thought) [Hāfez is both the pen name of a poet, and a word that means "keeper" or "protector"], Mostafā Rahimi has said that reconciling irreconcilables (by "irreconcilables," he means paradoxes) has been the eternal duty of good Iranian poets, especially Hāfez. Do you think that you've inherited this duty too?

M.S. Each poet looks at the problem from a particular angle. A poet like Hāfez was combating the prejudices of his own day—the duplicities of self-professed ascetics and Sufis, and local officials—and defending the sanctity of love. All lives and all countries are full of contradictions. Sometimes art expresses the contradictions, sometimes it tries to heal them, sometimes it fights them, and sometimes it surrenders to them. In Iran today, for example, are we all trying to heal the contradictions or are we—as the politicos put it—"antagonizing" them? In Iran, for at least four generations, many artists have struggled for human rights. But since they have had conflicting interpretations of human rights (some people think that *human rights* means the rights of the working class), they have produced differing works.

I believe that literature becomes lasting because of the values it generates. As Faulkner put it, love, brotherhood, peace, freedom, honesty, and so on.

S.R. Don't you think that art becomes politicized in such a politicized environment?

M.S. It inevitably takes on a political shade. But, I repeat, deep within itself, literature evokes values, evokes the true meaning of words, works for peace and beauty. Nowadays, when they tarnish a beautiful visage, the work becomes political.

S.R. The next question is about the comparative positions of the novel and poetry. What's your view on the position of the novel in Iran? We're a country that has always viewed itself in the mirror of poetry. Dariush Shāyegān says that the novel is a modern, European phenomenon born of the divide between mind and body, which has existed since the Renaissance. The novel has always been an effort to fill this divide and, in a way, to achieve "unity of being." But, since we've preserved this unity and have had our mysticism and illuminationist philosophy, we always view ourselves in the mirror of poetry. It is as if poems are divinely revealed; but not novels. It's true that we're seeing a quick growth in novel writing in Iran today, but, still, our very important literary movements have occurred in poetry. In view of Nimā and Parvin E'tesāmi and so on, our twentieth-century literary revolution took place in poetry, unlike the West.

M.S. I'm not badly informed about Persian fiction. I've written a kind of history of literature myself, entitled *Nevisandegan-e Pish-row-e Iran* (Iran's Vanguard Writers). I may have been the first to articulate many of Iran's literary developments. I've written the first article about many subsequently famous writers. But I can say that Iran's fiction writing, despite its quantitative growth, has qualitative flaws. For example, in comparison with the European novel, we rarely witness the required critical intelligence. I mean the writer usually places preconceived, ideological answers before the reader's eyes.

They say that the novel is a modern phenomenon and they usually refer to *Don Quixote* as the starting point. But the question is: Do we not have models, in old Iranian literary story writing, that remind us of *Don Quixote*? We don't have to look very far; in the early days of the Safavid era, in other words, roughly contemporaneous with Cervantes, the author of *Don Quixote*, we have a work like *Badayi'-al-Waqayah* (Marvelous Events), which views with the same satirical eye the exciting events that it narrates. And, at some points, it seems cleverer than Cervantes's work. So I can't totally agree with everything that Mr. Shāyegān is saying. Be that as it may, it's true that Iranians have tried to say the key things that they have wanted to say through poetry. As a result, a rich legacy has been amassed in Persian poetry which is highly valued by the world to this day. In Europe, it is perhaps comparable to Britain's legacy of poetry or that of Greece. As a part of my literary travels, in 1997, I attended the international poetry biennial in France. We had five poetry readings, along with poets from other countries. One of the most interesting comments that I received from the audience was: "In your work, we came to true poetry, because the word games played by these people—meaning, some of the postmodern poets—don't give us anything." Well, this is an aspect of contemporary Persian poetry which—if it is correctly publicized—has many eager takers.

It may be that the point that some thoughtful experts make, i.e., the "polyphonic" diversity of the novel, has not become generalized in the Persian novel yet. Is this because it is a society that has a single god? Gibbon noted, in *The Decline and Fall of the Roman Empire*, that the fact that Christianity has one god destroyed the methodological and cultural democracy of Greece, and led to a thousand years of the Middle Ages. I'm not an expert on philosophy, but I think I know which avenues can offer us polyphony. Most of our novelists give the reader an ideology, a specific message, a definite solution. Usually, our novelists are on the side of one of their protagonists. In the modern novel, such as the works of Kundera and Saramago, we're not so likely to see this support for particular fictional characters. In order for the Persian novel to become polyphonic, it has to come out of its ideological phase.

S.R. So can we conclude that if democracy is established in Iran, Persian poetry, which is monophonic, will be worse off?

M.S. I don't accept that all of Persian poetry is monophonic. At any rate, poetry has a hidden magic, that is to say, it has an innate aspect, with which the reader connects. This magic will pertain in a democracy too, because one of poetry's intrinsic characteristics is that it doesn't surrender to ruling systems.

S.R. Do you see yourself as an iconoclast or do you think you're following a course that's traditional too?

M.S. I don't consider myself a professional iconoclast; I lean on traditions, but I don't remain fettered by them. In any event, our poetry is connected to our history with strong, mysterious roots.

S.R. One problem with democracy is that meanings become equal and, consequently, meaning is destroyed. Many people believe that, in a country like Iran, there is meaning because of the absence of democracy. But you are of the view that, if we continue like this and if democracy does not come about, our younger generation, too, can arrive at a kind of meaninglessness. So what's to be done?

M.S. I think that, first, we have to try to give meaning to ourselves. Inevitably, others would then be encouraged to find a meaning for their own lives. Nihilism and the denigration of all values seem to combat creations that have an eye on the future, unless nihilism is presented as a symptom, as in the works of Dostoyevsky. Surrendering to nihilism is surrendering to despair and acquiescing to the gradual destruction of everything. The idea that meanings come into existence in the absence of democracy is very strange, because literary meanings are several thousand years old; in that time, history returns human beings to democracy, which is their home, and values become entrenched and, naturally, meanings are tied to expanding values. Unless, instead of creativity in democracy, a kind of reaction comes about, an obstinacy that leads to meaninglessness or silence. For the time being, it's better if we seek ourselves. For now, if we can't find what we've lost, we should try not to lose ourselves.

S.R. To this end, will Iranian mysticism be helpful or should it be thrown away?

M.S. Mysticism, too, like our entire cultural legacy, should be examined with a critical eye. Going it alone and turning inward has given the Iranian individual a sense of resistance in difficult times. Like a kind of meditation. But can you support society in modern life with meditation? I don't know! But, obviously, mysticism has been the weapon of a vanquished society—in order to preserve human values or, at least, to avoid dying of grief.

S.R. You mean it's for the hereafter, not for the earth?

M.S. It's for the individual, not for society. More or less like religion. You can use it to keep away from sin and injustice. But can you run a complex society with it?

S.R. But isn't it the case that in modernism, too, the individual wants to find himself and not be dissolved in the collective?

M.S. There's one difference. I repeat, mysticism gives us an inward sense of resistance in times when moral or social values have been negated. In modernism and democracy, rationalism grows in life. It inevitably moves from anti-idealism toward sociability; that is to say, it accepts cooperation with others. As a mystic, you establish a direct relationship with Truth. Others don't matter to you, except as rays of the overarching Truth. So we see that, if mysticism is a medicine, it's for treating depression, loneliness, the temptation to commit suicide, and so on. But it can't be recommended for society, unless we intend to establish a one-member mysticism party and be laughed at by dervishes.

ALI ASHRAF DARVISHIĀN

Born in Kermanshah in 1941, his published works include *Az in Velāyat* (From Hereabouts), *Ābshurān* (Ābshurān, short stories), *Fasl-e Nān* (The Bread Season), *Selul-e 18* (Cell 18), and *Sālhā-ye Abri* (Cloudy Years, a novel in four volumes). In the field of children's fiction, he has published *Abr-e Siāh-e Hezār Cheshm* (The Black Cloud with a Thousand Eyes), *Gol-e Talā va Kelāsh-e Qermez* (Gol-e Talā and the Red Slippers), and *Ātash dar Ketābkhāneh-ye Bachehhā* (Fire in the Children's Library). He has also edited the memoirs of Safar-Khān, a selection of stories by Samad Behrangi, and contemporary Kurdish short stories.

ALI ASHRAF DARVISHIĀN

In view of the literary advances that were made in the first few years after the revolution, Darvishiān believes that the 1979 revolution was a major bid to express the demands for freedom and independence. But in view of the rapid moves toward the monopolization of power and the imposition of restrictions on everyone outside the circle of power, the censorship of books and progressive publications became a daily affair, and only literature that propagated the official line was left unrestricted. In this way, literature was prevented from flourishing for a long time. In Darvishiān's view, the most important regrettable consequence of this monopolization and repression from above was that writers were separated from their audience—the Iranian people—and poets and writers became outcasts either within the country's borders or beyond them. On this basis, Darvishiān sees the 1979 revolution as a cultural regression that will be difficult to undo.

Darvishiān believes that the relationship between writers and poets and their audience, on the one hand, and their determination to resist the state's efforts to separate them, on the other, have been an ongoing issue in Iran, especially since the Arab conquest. Hence, literary resistance has always been crucial to the survival of Iranian society. From this perspective, the efforts made by writers and poets to withstand the consequences of the 1979 revolution have—despite the many occasions for despair—been a positive force for the country's progress. Consequently, a return to the earlier climate of repression and censorship seems difficult to imagine. All the same, Darvishiān cannot speak of a literary explosion, since not only does censorship continue to be exercised from above—albeit less forcefully than in the early years after the revolution—but it has also insidiously pervaded writers' minds, preventing them from producing world-class work.

As a novelist, Darvishiān believes that novel-writing is difficult in Iran. He doesn't see the youthfulness of this genre as the main reason for its backwardness. Censorship, Iranian society's antediluvian feudal core, and the pervasiveness of European languages, especially English, are more important reasons for the backwardness of the Persian novel. For Darvishiān, the novel in particular is an arena for finding the divisions among human beings and, at the same time, filling them. He tries to achieve this important aim by retelling historical events in the form of novels, because understanding the past is the lamp that lights the way to the future. To this end, Darvishiān favors a bold language and realism.

SHIVA RAHBARAN: The first part of this project tries to come to grips with the post-revolution changes. Many Iranian and foreign analysts are of the view that the past two decades have wrought dramatic changes in Iranian society, leading to many paradoxes and anomalies. We want to examine and understand these changes, and then to discover what impact they have had on literature. In the second part, we want to look at the role of literature and its effect on society.

The first question is about democracy and about the anomaly or paradox of democracy: What general impression do people in

Iran have of democracy? Do they think that a democratic government is a good government? Are they aware of the dangers of a democratic system? (For example, Nazism came to power through a democratic system.) And is democracy, essentially, good for the Iranian people? As you know, both under the previous regime and now, many people are of the view that democracy is basically not suited to our particular traditions and customs. And, finally, have our intellectuals, artists, and writers fulfilled their mission in terms of explaining democracy and its highs and lows to the people?

ALI ASHRAF DARVISHIĀN: Let's start at the beginning, i.e., the change that has come about in our society since 1979. I believe that the most important change in our society occurred in those first few years, in 1980–1981. Because, during those days, everyone, from all the different segments of the population, was involved in the revolution. People with different views. And there was no apparent distinction between them. It wasn't a question of this one ruling and that one being ruled. Everyone rose up together for a common goal and achieved victory. For freedom, for independence. But, unfortunately, after a year or two, a particular line of thinking gained the upper hand by exploiting people's emotions. And the newspapers, journals, and books that were being published suddenly disappeared with the emergence of barriers and impediments, such as the Islamic Guidance and Culture Ministry and censorship. All of a sudden, a particular climate descended over a society that had just freed itself from its fetters. A particular group of people became the rulers and they took all the country's affairs under their own control. And the monopolization of power and the imposition of restrictions on everyone outside the circle of power began.

I think that it was all over within that first year or two despite some scattered resistance. For at least a twenty-year period, our society remained in the grip of repression and authoritarianism. Books and the press began to be censored, and progressive newspapers were banned. Only those journalists, writers, and poets who were completely affiliated with the state and who sang its praises were allowed to work. So when the war broke out, all writing had to be in support of and propaganda for the war, and hardly anyone dared object to this state of affairs.

People whom the state deemed "outsiders" were being prevented from going to the battle fronts. Marxist forces were so ruthlessly repressed and crushed that, if the United States had spent billions of dollars to achieve this end, it wouldn't have succeeded this well. And any kind of objection to this repression was seen as a sign of collusion or complicity, incurring prosecution and punishment. Over these nineteen to twenty years, especially in those first few years, they separated dissident intellectuals from the people. Some were jailed and destroyed; some fled the country. Writers and intellectuals were treated in such a way that none of the newspapers and no media dared to mention the name of any progressive writer, any dissident writer, or anyone who objected to the situation. So a deep rupture emerged between the younger generation and the preceding generation. This rupture revealed its harmful effects and results later, as we can see today.

S.R. Were these intellectuals, who were outcasts in their own country in a way, unable to put the people in the picture?

A.D. The link was completely severed. Many of our friends went abroad. They emigrated and were, unavoidably, separated from [Iranian] society. They were unaware of the changes in society and only received news of developments with delays. And the ones who remained in Iran had no access to newspapers or journals to communicate their views and thoughts. Everything was being censored. The Writers' Association—which also suffered a hiatus for several years—tried to assert its existence by various means. For example, by trying to organize story-reading evenings, or trying to produce a newspaper or journal, or trying to help the victims of natural disasters, such as earthquakes and floods. But it was prevented from asserting its existence in any way whatsoever. The works and books of the Writers' Association's members remained under the censor's blade, and there weren't any journals that would publish their works. Even when its members met now and then, they did not do so under the banner of the Writers' Association; instead, they met as "a consultative group," because it was dangerous to mention the name of the Writers' Association.

But, slowly, the consultative group began to thrive and the members of the Writers' Association registered their first protest—since the hiatus—against the detention of Sa'idi-Sirjāni.[45] Then, there was the 134-signature letter in protest at the repression and censorship. It was published at the height of the repression and the

45   A writer. Died in detention on 27 November 1994, aged 50.

members of the Association were able, in this way, to declare to the whole world their protest at censorship and all the difficulties in the cultural sector.

S.R. But you also suffered many fatalities.

A.D. That's true. Of course, Sa'idi-Sirjāni was not a member of the Writers' Association. In fact, his thinking and his beliefs were opposed to those of many of our members. But since the Writers' Association believes it has a duty to defend freedom of opinion and freedom of expression without exception, it protested his detention and issued a statement. And some of the signatories were summoned to court and interrogated because of the statement. As a result of the pressure, several people, about five people, had to withdraw their signatures. But most members, that is to say, about 130 people, stood by what they'd said and went on to new battles. And, of course, they suffered some consequences too. At least four of them were killed, including Ahmad Miralā'i, Ghaffar Hosseini, Mohammad Mokhtāri, and Mohammad Ja'far Puyandeh,[46] who were brutally murdered.

---

46 Mohammad Mokhtāri and Mohammad Ja'far Puyandeh were two of the victims of what became known as "the serial killings" in the autumn of 1998, when a number of political activists and writers were killed in Tehran by "rogue" agents from the Intelligence Ministry. Although the killings in 1998 were particularly striking, many writers and journalists maintain that they were not the only victims of the Islamic Republic's security forces; hence, the other names that Ali Ashraf Darvishiān mentions.

S.R. So do you see any future for democracy in this country, or will the democratic movement suffer the same dangers and nightmares again?

A.D. Of course, as long as a nation is kept in a state of ignorance and illiteracy, tragedies of this kind can recur. But I believe that the era of those nightmares is over. Of course, in a society such as ours, it is difficult to predict the future. But we must not forget that, in the light of the current global situation and today's extensive international communications—the Internet, satellite channels, and equipment that is constantly making international communications easier—it would be difficult to go back to that climate of repression and censorship. At the moment, the spirit of opposition to dictatorship and the monopolization of power is growing among various segments of the population. Protests in various cities, workers and teachers' strikes—after years of being under the thumb of state-controlled trade associations—protests by young people on various occasions, such as on firework night before the Iranian New Year and at football matches, are all signs of this growing consciousness among the people.

The House of Workers and the House of Teachers, which are state-controlled associations, have lost their credibility. Everyone realizes now that they've been cheated and they're starting to protest. While they're standing in line for bread, standing in line for chicken and eggs, standing in line for a bus, people complain openly. As for democracy, it is the natural demand of people these days; they want to live in freedom.

I have often said that Mr. Khatami's election in 1997 was not a command from above; it was pressure from below, from the people. Of course, when there's just three candidates and you have to pick one of them, you pick the one who says better things. The people noticed the candidate who was saying, "Iran is for all Iranians," and was not preaching to them like the other two candidates. That candidate showed a kind of respect for the views of the people. Never mind that he proved ineffective in practice. It was in his nature; he couldn't have acted in any other way. Basically, in view of his class background, he couldn't really fall into step with the lower classes. And he was unable to fulfill his pledges because, as he said himself, his aim was to strengthen the ruling system. So inevitably, he lost his credibility. But the people sometimes act cleverly and astutely. They try to opt for a way that will produce the fewest casualties. After all, you can't expect the people to sacrifice their young adults once every twenty or thirty years! So they decided to put this candidate at loggerheads with the other two candidates, so that they would quarrel among themselves and contradict each other for a while, which is what happened. They chose the candidate who spoke about Iran, about freedom, about respect for human beings, and about civil society. (Of course, he later changed "civil society" to "the Prophet's Medina"!)

These were the problems that arose in our society. The so-called religious intellectuals came into existence as a result of these conflicts. The killings, the inefficiencies, the corruption, the repression and censorship set this group of intellectuals thinking, because some of them were intelligent and farsighted. They could see that young people were increasingly turning away from the system. Since these religious intellectuals had worked in the intelligence services in the past, they were aware of society's problems. Bear in mind that, in the Soviet Union, Gorbachev, who was the head of the KGB, later spoke about the country's problems and shortcomings. It was because he'd witnessed all of his society's problems and protests, and he could see where the weakness was. In Iran, the people who had been in the intelligence services knew what the problems were. And, in view of these problems, they began delivering talks and writing pieces about the situation. Because these religious intellectuals (I am, on the whole, opposed to this expression) could speak freely at their gatherings and in their journals. But dissidents and "outsiders" continued to be hamstrung and censored.

The managing directors of newspapers could see that, by publishing news about protests and strikes in this or that corner of the country, their circulation figures would keep going up and they could sell as many as two or three hundred thousand copies. The state realized what was happening and it started to ban newspapers. Suddenly more than thirty newspapers and journals were banned in one week. So people no longer crowded around newspaper kiosks, and newspapers' circulation figures have suddenly dropped, to the point where some of them have stopped publishing. Along with newspapers being banned, some people were also detained or they were summoned to various places. All the newspapers are now publishing similar, repetitive things. I mean that I can see that the eight newspapers that

I buy and read contain nothing interesting and they aren't even capable of demagoguery!

S.R. How do you mean?

A.D. Demagoguery means making people believe something that isn't true. For example, saying that all the Iranian people are totally opposed to establishing relations with this or that country. It means deciding for others and foisting the decision on people. For example, saying that we have freedom, all the people are leading peaceful lives, and our economy is in very good shape. Our education sector is very good. All young people support us. In my view, these are attempts to dupe people. When people compare these statements to the realities of their daily lives, they don't add up. When they switch on the radio or sit in front of the TV, they notice the discrepancies. They are being told things that, basically, don't match their lives. This is the point at which people raise their voices in protest and reality imposes itself. Reality makes its presence felt. An individual compares these things and sees that he is being duped. But the things that a writer or a poet says are things that emanate from these people's hearts. They reflect the people's lives. The writer or poet takes these things and recreates them, makes them artistic, and gives them back to the people. And the people compare these things with the realities of their lives and are moved by them.

S.R. This brings me precisely to the following question: Is the Iranian writer or artist an outcast or a part of society?

A.D. Either way, if his heart is with the people, he will say what he has to say.

S.R. But you're saying that the writer or artist derives what he says from the people's hearts.

A.D. That's right. He was forced into isolation for sixteen, seventeen years, and wasn't able to publish his writings. But he could stand in line for various things and hear the people speak about their concerns and establish a link with them. Because, in this situation, he is part of the people.

S.R. So the writer or artist hasn't detached himself from the people? For example, like modern and postmodern European intellectuals, who always feel like outcasts, as if they are removed from their society.

A.D. Not at all. I believe that, even when he was an outcast, he was working actively and intelligently, and striving to observe and learn about the shortcomings and injustices. He's been by the people's side, sharing their concerns.

S.R. I'm thinking of Sādegh Hedāyat who, like modern French writers, felt as if he was detached from the people, detached from the Iranian people.

A.D. I think that Sādegh Hedāyat felt like this toward the end of his life. I mean it was because of the defeats that the people had suffered; many of his hopes had turned to despair. It was impossible for a thoughtful and very sensitive writer like Hedāyat to remain detached from the pervading atmosphere of his society. When we read *Alavieh Khānum* or *Hāji Āqā*, we see the extent to which Hedāyat viewed the lives of the people with sensitivity, love, and interest.

Those idioms, those vivid and totally new images could only have been produced by a writer who was close to the people, who was intimate with the people. Real and realist images. But when defeat arrives and an atmosphere of dictatorship is imposed on society, the artist, unavoidably, is unable to lie to the people or to himself.

S.R. Most of the writers to whom I've spoken within this project have no sense of contempt for the people who are the subjects of their works. This is very interesting to me. Because, for many of the big writers in the West, contempt for the common people or, at least, a sense of alienation from them is the first prerequisite of writing.

A.D. This is the first time I'm hearing this strange idea. Of course, any writer or intellectual is pained by ignorance or backwardness in others. But if you examine the causes and motives behind the ignorance, you'll see that the people alone are not to blame. I don't see this sentiment, I mean hatred of and contempt for the people, among Iranian writers. Maybe this is another postmodern phenomenon! I don't sense this contempt at all, despite all the ploys that the regime has used to create a rift between the people and writers and to set them at each other's throats. For example, by dismissing writers as "coffee-shop Vietcong" or by accusing them of all manner of offenses or by publishing propaganda against them in state-owned newspapers, without granting them any right of reply. And independent and progressive writers have nowhere else to publish their replies. Yet, all of this has had the opposite effect for the writers, poets, and intellectuals whom the state has tried with all its might to erase from people's minds. The best-educated, most well-known, most independent, and most respected poets and writers have gathered together in the Writers' Association of Iran and have resisted this censorship and repression. And, fortunately, we can see that the young people who, as a result of the state's pressures and plans, were supposed to have been raised without ideals, are very quickly turning toward popular and independent writers, and are reading their works. I am not at all despondent in the way that some people are when they see the rest of the world moving toward democracy. Because there is no going back to the nightmares, and the killings and the detentions of free-minded people that we had in the past. It would be impossible.

S.R. In the West, analysts see the synthesis of a modern state and religion as "the Iranian experiment." Is such an anomaly, i.e. wedding modernity to religion, achievable? And if so, has the Iranian nation had any success in reconciling religion and modernism?

A.D. Modernism cannot be squared with these people's interpretation of religion. Modernity is forward-looking and this is incompatible with these people's view, which is backward-looking and focused on reviving past traditions, which, in many instances, are best left unrevived. Not all traditions are good. There are traditions that we should now set aside, because they are of no use to today's society. At the same time, there are traditions that are vital to keeping the Iranian people alive and resisting tyranny. For example, they've been trying for years to do away with the celebrations on the occasion of Nowruz[47]; whereas our people have a sense of oneness and solidarity with Nowruz. As soon as people feel that spring is on the way, they begin preparing for the celebrations. Or, for example, the firework night that precedes Nowruz. Or the celebration of Mehregān,[48] which has ancient roots in our culture. These traditions can't be destroyed.

At the same time, from the point of view of a modern human being, marriage between an eighty-year-old man and a ten-year-old girl is a kind of crime. To do this is to commit a crime, which carries a prison sentence. But we see that this crime can easily take place in a religious society. Or, for example, preventing people from using the Internet or banning satellite dishes. Some religious people, like Mehdi Bāzargān, tried to reconcile religion and science in a way, but they failed.

---

47   Iranian New Year, corresponding to the first day of spring.
48   Autumn festival, which, like the Iranian New Year, dates back to pre-Islamic, Zoroastrian Iran.

S.R. So was the Iranian revolution a move forward or a move back?

A.D. A move back. Over these past twenty-two years, we've slipped back five hundred years by today's standards. And it's very very unlikely that we'll be able to undo this backwardness and catch up with the industrial countries. Japan has now reached the post-industrial stage and is pursuing other issues. We're still at the stage of assembling manufactured products. We've failed in industry. We've failed overall in the education sector. According to government figures, 114,000 of this country's best teachers have emigrated. These are big losses. Our youngsters who have won medals at Olympiads have all gone abroad as a part of the brain drain. We don't know whether we can undo these losses or not.

S.R. But I think that the synthesis of modernity and religion has always been a part of the revolutionary movements of the past one hundred years; I mean in Iranian contemporary and modern history, since the constitutionalist period until even the time of Dr. Mossadegh. Many national-religious groups have been viewed as the engines of Iran's modern movements. Do you mean to say that our progression toward a modern state and democracy has failed?

A.D. The popular movement of Mossadegh's time lasted two years and four months. And traditionalists, such as Ayatollah Kashani, were definitely influential in its defeat. I believe that never in Iran's history have we had a more popular, more sympathetic, and more independent government than that of Dr. Mohammad Mossadegh. I remember what the press was like then. I was ten, eleven years old. I was very interested in newspapers and I used to read most of them. I used to spend all my pocket money on newspapers. All the papers freely wrote what they wanted to write. They used to say whatever they wanted to say about Mossadegh. Mossadegh himself had said that all newspapers were free to write whatever they wanted about him, but that they should be careful what they wrote about others. There were so many cartoons of Mossadegh. They used to write things, very critical; but they were free. That was real democracy. I've said many things in this regard in my four-volume novel, *Sālhā-ye Abri* (Cloudy Years). Mossadegh's government and his fate were both very similar to those of Salvador Allende's in Chile. Some groups and parties made a mistake about Dr. Mossadegh, and, by the time they realized their mistake, it was too late.

The 1979 revolution started with the people. The people deep within society. Impoverished people. Intellectuals, too, had been pained for years by the Pahlavi regime's financial corruption, the repression, the arrests, and the brutal acts perpetrated by the Shah's SAVAK. We had political prisoners. Progressive individuals, intellectuals, poets, such as Golsorkhi and Dāneshiān, were executed. The deaths of Forough Farrokhzād, world champion wrestler Gholamreza Takhti, and Samad Behrangi were suspicious. Bizhan Jazani and a number of Mojahedin-e Khalq members were savagely put to death by firing squad after spending years in prison.

The resentment over these events gradually accumulated over the years. There was popular discontent. Were the people not Muslims then? Were they prevented from performing the ritual prayers? Were they not free to go to mosques? I don't think the people rose up in a revolution for the sake of religion and a religious state. The people rose up for freedom, prosperity, justice, and equality, and for bread. And, then, a bunch of people came on the scene and exploited the justice-seeking people's emotions. Everyone, with every kind of view, took part in the revolution. A revolution that was unprecedented in the world. But a bunch of people took the revolution away from the masses and prevented it from becoming deeper and more thoroughgoing. A particular bunch of people with traditional views. They didn't allow anyone else to defend their own rights, and if anyone did defend their own rights, they'd end up in jail or be executed.

Ruthless purges and horrifying executions emptied the nation of intellectuals, of thinkers, and of free-minded people; emptied it of thought. And a bunch of opportunists and dogmatists took up the reins of power. And, now, we can see how they've turned out, what crimes and abuses they've been prepared to commit, and how vicious their infighting has been over the spoils. They're pillaging the country's wealth, which is the product of the direct or indirect taxes paid by poor old men and women. They pillage and then they leave. They take millions of dollars and flee the country.

S.R. Do you feel that this heap of smoldering ashes or this quagmire is fertile ground for the creation of literary works? It's been a long time since I last visited Iran, but I have the feeling that there's been a literary explosion.

A.D. I wouldn't say an explosion, but there have been some changes. You can't speak of a literary explosion in a society that is beset by censorship. Bear in mind that we're a country with a population of nearly seventy million and a typical print run of 2,000 for books. Don't forget this point. I've said in various articles and interviews—in so far as I've been allowed to publish or say anything at home or abroad—that censorship has dealt a horrific blow to books and book reading. There are various reasons why people don't read. But the measures taken by the state have been very, very influential in separating people from books.

But, in the last few years, the tight strictures of the past have been set aside, because people want uncensored books. Their pressures and struggles have pushed censorship back a bit (I say a bit, it's not ideal), and good literary works have been produced which do a good job of portraying society's highs and lows, the terrible nightmares, the despair, the isolation, and, even, the people's struggles. Women, in particular, have excelled in recent years, in all the arts, in film, in short story writing, in painting, in novel writing, and they have aired their own concerns and problems, and those of their society. Women who work both at home and in the workplace have always shouldered the concerns of their husband, family, and children in this disordered society. Anyone who is responsible for children in this society is always anxious about the problems that they may run into every time they leave the house. Will these children be arrested because of what they're wearing? Or because a few locks of hair that may have been left uncovered by a headscarf? The burden of this anxiety usually falls on women.

At any rate, women have shown what they're capable of in all the artistic and even political fields. And distinguished women writers have emerged and I'm very hopeful about the future. I have to say that, even in the darkest years, 1981–1988, when the arrests and mass executions began, I never lost my hope that things would change in the future, because I could see that the groups that were gaining the upper hand were acting against people's wishes and against human nature. If they really allowed a referendum under the supervision of international organizations, about ninety-five percent of the people would undoubtedly vote against this establishment. The people have realized that they were swindled and they understand their predicament. One example of this was when they voted for Khatami in 1997 against the establishment's expectations, and they repeated this four years later. This time [2005 presidential election], they'll either vote intelligently or they won't vote at all. Because they're realized that independence is pointless without freedom; it isn't possible.

People want freedom. In many areas, we're dependent on other countries. In industry, we're dependent. But only democracy, freedom of opinion and expression, and the lifting of pre-publication censorship on books are now matters of concern for our society.

S.R. So we can say that expressing these afflictions has fueled literature and art to some extent?

A.D. Yes, absolutely.

S.R. To what extent has Persian literature always been fuelled by these divisions, so to speak? For example, in a book entitled *Hāfez-e Andisheh* (Hāfez, Keeper of Thought), Mostafā Rahimi writes that reconciling irreconcilables (by "irreconcilables," he means paradoxes) has always been pivotal in Iranian literature, especially so in the work of Hāfez. So have you inherited this duty too? Is it something historical and cultural?

A.D. I think that an intellectual is always a protestor, someone who protests against the inhuman aspects of society. Against the disorders. Against the injustice and the trampling of rights. An intellectual always looks at things with a critical eye; this will always be necessary. I believe in the philosophy of Marxism. I love its philosophy. But if, one day, we happen to be living in a Marxist state and we see that it has turned into a dictatorship and is mistreating people, I'll oppose it. I'd struggle against that state too. So you have to recognize that this protest will always remain with a writer who looks at society with awareness.

S.R. So the politicization of literature is an unavoidable necessity?

A.D. I don't think that the term "politicization of literature" is being used correctly nowadays. A literature that is aimed at gaining power is totally political. We have to distinguish between a literature that is struggling for freedom of opinion and freedom of expression, and a literature that is affiliated to the state and is aimed at gaining power. Writing with the aim of establishing freedom of opinion and expression inevitably involves words. And when they try to impede words, it unavoidably has to struggle against the impediments. This is when it becomes political. This is when it turns into a protestor against a state that is opposed to freedom. If you see this as political, then, yes, such a literature is political. But a writer who puts all his works at the disposal of a state and the consolidation of the state and who will himself one day join the higher echelons of the state—such a writer and his literature are totally political. But I call a literature that resists a repressive state "committed and responsible literature." This is a literature that is forward-looking. It is a literature that grumbles against the status quo. It is a literature that is alive. It is a literature that is produced by someone who protests, who views society with commitment and vigilance, and who does not in any way expect to become a minister or a member of parliament one day. Far from expecting it, he risks imprisonment, torture, and even strangulation by one of the reactionaries.

S.R. So do you think that the literature of Hāfez, Rumi, and Rudaki is committed literature too?

A.D. Yes, I do. Committed in relation to human beings and to human suffering. Ferdowsi stood up to Sultan Mahmud of Ghazna. The poetry that Hāfez wrote was in protest at the hypocrisy and severity of state officials and constabularies. And it's been said about Rudaki that they hit him on his head so many times with his book of poetry that he went blind. For these people, political literature is a literature that performs its duty in a committed way, and non-political literature is the literature that is formalist and tries to be pretty formally and technically, but has no content. For me, a literature that doesn't speak of people's pains, struggles, and joys is not a committed literature; although I'm not opposed to it, because I respect freedom of expression. For example, if they tell me one day to separate these different types of writings, I won't do it; every kind of voice and view should exist and should be heard. Civil society is a society in which you can hear every kind of voice. In Nicaragua, Daniel Ortega's government was a government that I liked; it contained different voices, because the cabinet included Marxists, capitalists, and priests. He really created an interesting and democratic blend. It should be the same in literature. There should be something for every taste. Things should be written freely, but, ultimately, it is the people who choose the writings and the poetry that they like. When it comes to this, no one can bully them. No one can tell them, buy this book; don't buy that book.

S.R. Do you not draw on Iranian mysticism?

A.D. Absolutely not. I don't like mysticism and things like that.

S.R. Why?

A.D. I'm a writer who lives on this earth and writes about the people on this earth. Because my life has shown me in practice that what matters are these earthly things. I'm not concerned about the sky. If I look up at the sky, it's because I want to know whether it's going to rain or not.

S.R. In the West, many writers envy the success and the situation of Iranian writers. They say that, although people buy more books in the West, what Iranian writers do is much more meaningful. They say that this is because Iranian writers don't have freedom. On the basis of Henry James's notion that every novel is a window in the house of fiction, we can say that every novel is a window in people's mind. Western writers say that since there are more walls in Iran, there is a greater opportunity for putting in windows. So freedom is detrimental to artistic work.

A.D. I'm really amazed by these statements. Being detached from reality is so detrimental! There's no relation between their remarks and our experience. In Europe, literature and art is of a really high standard because there are fewer impediments and restraints on writing there. No literature or art can flourish under censorship and repression. From the time when we're children, we're always censored. The education system destroys all the creativity and imagination in us.

S.R. Can't the beauty of Rumi and Hāfez's works be attributed to censorship?

A.D. In those days, censorship wasn't as it is nowadays. A poet would recite his poetry. Then, it would circulate by word of mouth, until it was heard by the state. I mean, in the past, when someone created a work of art, it wasn't as if a censorship office would intervene before it could be published.

S.R. But they had to make sure that what they said couldn't be understood by everyone, for fear of the king.

A.D. First of all, if it's going to be something that not everyone can understand, then, of what use is it? Secondly, where Hāfez was concerned, he didn't tend to write his poetry; he'd recite it to his friends and students. Years later, one of his students, by the name of Mohammad Gol-Andām, who had memorized the poems, wrote them down. So censorship couldn't have played a part. Hāfez couldn't have been afraid of censorship. Of course, it's true that they were constrained by something known as religion and they used to use figurative language. And the use of symbols and figurative language continues to exist in our literature today. But the important point is that we start being censored from when we're children. "Say this. Don't say that. If you write this in your school composition, we'll get into trouble. Don't ever say that when you're at school." From here onward, everyone's creativity is quashed. And we grow up with this kind of self-censorship. There are always impediments that prevent us from saying what we ought to say, from writing what we ought to write, and from criticizing. And what lies behind all of this is tyrannical and dictatorial rulers. We always see some barriers in front of our minds and we can't express every aspect of our lives, whereas the European or American writer can speak about many things. For example, Jean Genet could say everything about his life, but this is impossible to do in Iran. This has meant that, even in translations, we can't read the texts of foreign works, because these works are severely censored.

S.R. But, on the other hand, you have to be far more skilled and this makes your language far richer.

A.D. No, not at all. I think that their language is richer, because they've cultivated it in freedom. They're experienced. They've worked far more with that language. And they've, in effect, helped it grow richer. In truth, what's our standing now in terms of poetry at the international level? What's our ranking in terms of literary fiction and novel writing?

S.R. Don't you think that this is a political issue? Just as peripheral societies were exploited, so to speak, over the past four hundred years, economically and militarily, now, they're being exploited culturally. That is to say, we read the works of Europeans, but they don't read our works.

A.D. Absolutely. This is one of the impediments that I was talking about. One of the dozen or so impediments to the growth of our literature is that a third-world writer has to do the work of newspapers and journals too, because newspapers in these countries are encumbered by censorship and they can't tell it like it is. Here, a writer has to use his works to make revelations, in a way, and to report the news, and this unavoidably lowers the standard of his work and damages it. But when you look at, for example, Saramago, the Portuguese writer and Nobel laureate, his works are political and he is political. Of course, not political for the sake of gaining power, but for the sake of being committed. Or even Gabriel García Márquez, the Colombian writer, is political in *One Hundred Years of Solitude*. A train sets off from somewhere with two thousand banana pickers. They don't arrive at their destination. And no one knows what's become of them. It is a political novel.

S.R. Don't you think that writing novels is difficult in Iran? In a country that has mainly viewed itself in the mirror of poetry. For example, Europeans see the novel as a phenomenon that's unique to them, the cultural fruit that has come down to them from the Middle Ages and the Renaissance down to modernism and postmodernism. Dariush Shāyegān has written, in his book *Henry Corbin*, that since we, in the East, didn't have the dualism of Western thinking, we never experienced the split between mind and body. Our "unity of being" remained as it was. So our poetry was "divinely revealed" or "inspired" in a way; whereas in the West, the novel has always been an effort to solder or fill that division. So doesn't the fact that you're a novelist in Persian literature make you an outcast? I mean artistically, not politically.

A.D. We're outcasts because Persian doesn't have a global reach. It's not like English. But the fact that the novel form is overshadowed by poetry here is because we're a late arrival to modern times. We've been under the yoke of feudal rulers for many years; even as recently as fifty to thirty years ago. The novel form is related to modern society, a society in which industry has grown, in which there are printing presses. A society that produces paper. There is a difference between this and a society that has not become civilized yet, that has no publishing industry. Novel writing in Europe has a three-hundred-year head start on us. Our novel writing is only one hundred years old, and, for the first forty years of it, there were only some resemblances to the novel form. The effects of feudalism are still ingrained in our minds. The short story belongs to modern society, a society that is forward-looking. I mean a fully industrialized society that has conditions that call for short story writing. When Jamālzādeh wrote his first short story collection, *Yeki Bud Yeki Nabud* (Once Upon a Time), it had already been years since James Joyce and Marcel Proust had written and published their most technically advanced novels. This is not at all to say that, since poetry has prospered, the novel form could not emerge.

S.R. So you still don't see grounds for progress for the Persian novel?

A.D. I said it before and I'll say it again that, as long as the evil shadow of censorship hangs over our literature and other aspects of our lives, there's not much hope of progress. But I hope that, as a result of the struggles of the people and intellectuals, these impediments and fetters will be removed, so that we can say what we want to say in a free society, and write freely. And so that poetry, too, can rescue itself from this obsession with theories and this turmoil, and put this period of crisis behind it.

S.R. I have a question about your four-volume novel, *Sālhā-ye Abri* (Cloudy Years). It is a historical novel. I would liken it to Dowlatābādi's *Kelidar*, which is also a historical novel that starts in the distant past. I asked Mr. Dowlatābādi if he thought that writing this kind of novel was like worshipping the past.

A.D. You'll rarely come across a novel that deals with current affairs. Many writers are unable to write about something until it is at some distance in the past. There's a difference between novels and articles. In *Kelidar*, Mr. Dowlatābādi has portrayed village life, with all the mishaps and misfortunes that it has had to endure, a kind of life that is disintegrating. And in *Sālhā-ye Abri*, I portrayed events spanning from 1941 to 1979 for the benefit of a generation that has had its link with the past severed. I think that one of our problems is the absence of a link between new generations and the past. I said this in the novel too; there are points at which there are ruptures between the generations. And we don't know where to find the missing links. We have to find them. We mustn't lose them. History is the perpetuation of a nation's life and culture, and it is a writer's duty to show this link to the other generations, so that they can find their way to the future.

S.R. You mean the path to the future is opened up by keeping an eye on the past?

A.D. We don't keep an eye on it, we need it, because the past is the lamp that lights the way to the future. Unless we're acquainted with the past, our future will be problematic. The problems that exist in the United States are caused by the absence of a history that they can lean on.

S.R. You don't try to disguise reality in any way in your novel. This kind of novel is a kind of autobiography. I mean, you're basically telling it like it is. You don't flinch from using bold language.

A.D. Because I believe that one of our problems in novel writing is that the writer really keeps himself hidden. But European and American writers don't write like this. Their presence is candid and unaffected. They can write about Christ, about government officials, about sacred things, even about the police and its conduct, and this is because of the free-spiritedness and frankness that they've learned since they were kids. But we always live under a cover, under a mask. That's what I wanted to achieve in *Sālhā-ye Abri*. I didn't flinch from saying things, although not to the ideal extent.

S.R. Your realism has a very violent feel; it jolts the reader. We very rarely see these kinds of realistic scenes in Persian novels.

A.D. It's very important to me that a novel should jolt people. A novel that makes you toss and turn in bed. Why do we read? To become informed, to learn about what's happening around us. A novel should stay in your mind for a long time. You should live with it and you should think to yourself, why do people live like this? why should a family live in poverty and destitution, while the Shah or a state official pillages the people's wealth? I think that you have to jolt the reader by portraying people's real lives. The pain, the suffering, the hopes, and the nightmares of a nation. You have to jolt readers, in order to force them to think. Otherwise, of what use is art and literature? Even if it's entertaining, it has to carry a message too. Today, we see that it's not even entertaining. I mean, the presence of the human being is fading away in novels and literary fiction. The human being is absent. We can use time and place, but we mustn't forget about the human being, in all his dimensions, in all his complexity. Why do we write novels and stories? Do we write them for ourselves? If we only write them for ourselves, why do we publish them?

S.R. That's precisely what I was going to ask you next. Who does a writer write for?

A.D. I definitely attach importance to the reader. Some say: We write for our own sake. If you write for your own sake, then, sit at home and read it, day and night, for your own sake! Why do you publish it then? You publish it because you want the reader to come and buy it and read it. And to feel some affinity with your work at any rate. So there has to be human relationships in your works with which the reader can connect. These human relationships are exactly what takes place in a society: universal human emotions, to which you draw attention. This is the key to Shakespeare, Hāfez, and Khayyám's success. Drawing attention to humanity's common pains; a deep understanding of human life. This is why, even today, people still consult Hāfez's poetry when they want to make a decision. This is why Khayyám's poems pierce you to the core of your being and make you tremble. This is why Shakespeare's *Hamlet* still glues you to your seat.

S.R. What happens to love in your novel? In it, you find love for a mother, but love for a woman—erotic love—is like a light or a window that's ajar. It shines, but it goes dark again.

A.D. Yes, it's because I was raised in a society in which you have to lower your head when you see a woman. They didn't teach me to look into a woman's eyes, to look at women's lives. They didn't teach me how to fall in love, and I was always faced with the issue of what religion allows and what it doesn't allow. It doesn't allow looking at a woman. Don't look at her life, don't look into her eyes; just steal a few glances at her flesh! This is how I was raised. This training has had bad effects on us; it hasn't been able to bring itself up-to-date with your society. In the past, it may have been possible to fall in love with one glance and to internalize it. But what about someone who externalizes? I believe in realism, meaning, everything should be "in the open," but our society and our upbringing has robbed me of this. Now, our young people, especially teenage girls, suffer from depression and they have to spend most of their time in their rooms. This is why they're so successful in the national university entrance exam. Success in the exam means memorization. The more you read, the better you succeed.

I said, I want to write everything "openly," but our tradition has forbidden this. Dilapidated traditions are the biggest dictators. So I can't write what goes on in my heart. If I could write about matters of love, I could have said a lot more about the love between Sharif and Shahrnāz. Censorship doesn't allow it, a censorship that's based on bad traditions. Even the love for the grandmother was censored in the book.

Censorship says that a grandmother mustn't dance at her son's wedding. There must be no dancing. Write, feet-stamping! And most important of all, a grandmother mustn't snap her fingers to the beat of the music! Whereas many readers wrote to me and praised the beauty of the dance scene. Mrs. Simin Behbahāni loves this scene. The scene depicts how a religious woman dances at her son's wedding; how, as she's dancing, she tries to make sure that her chador doesn't slip back from her brow. Then, she ties the loose ends of her chador around her hips and jiggles around in front of the bride and groom, and dances and snaps her fingers to the rhythm of the music. This is why I say that everything in our lives is one-dimensional. Joy is forbidden. But all manner of offenses are committed on the sly. You have to maintain appearances. You can do whatever the hell you want out of view.

This dance scene caused a big problem for me. After the first edition, *Sālhā-ye Abri* was refused a publication permit for two years. It was stuck at the censors, because of the grandmother's dancing. They were saying: You have to modify 700 pages of the book's total of 2,400 pages! I didn't agree. It was published later, after Khatami was elected. And, of course, I changed the word "dancing" to "feet-stamping"!

S.R. By this token, is writing in Iran worth the hardship?

A.D. All our struggles, all the time spent in jail, all the torture we have endured and are enduring is so that we can have a good world, in which we can write and speak freely without being afraid of being thrown in jail, without being afraid of being strangled, without being afraid of being tortured. A world in which there are no prisons, no wars, no censorship, and no bloodshed. A world in which my dear friends Mohammad Mokhtāri and Mohammad Ja'far Puyandeh wouldn't have been strangled by reactionary and mentally backward people.

Javād Mojābi

Born in Qazvin in 1939, his poetry books include *Fasli barā-ye To* (A Season for You) and *Bar Bām-e Bam* (On Bam's Rooftop). His short story collections and novels include *Az Del beh Kagaz* (From the Heart to Paper), *Qesseh-ye Rowshan* (A Clear Story), *Borjha-ye Khāmush* (Silent Towers), *Obur az Bāq-e Qermez* (Passing through the Red Garden), and *Mumia'i* (The Mummy). His works for children include *Pesar-e Cheshm Ābi* (The Blue-Eyed Boy) and *Sibu Sār-e Kuchulu* (Sibu, the Little Starling). He has also written a number of plays, including: *Shabah-e Sodom* (Sodom's Ghost), *Ruzegār-e Aql-e Sorkh* (Age of Red Reason), and *Tābut-Sāzān* (Coffin-Makers).

JAVĀD MOJĀBI

Javād Mojābi sees the Islamic Revolution as the product of the conflicts of a hundred years of contemporary history, relating to Iranians' bid to find their identity in a world that is changing at an unprecedented rate. But, less than three decades later, he does not think that the time is right yet for assessing this phenomenon and how it has affected the trajectory of contemporary Iranian society and literature. Mojābi is aware that contemporary Persian literature is beset by official censorship and unofficial taboos, but he does not see this as necessarily unique to contemporary Iranian writers. He believes that censorship has been poets and writers' perpetual prison throughout history, and he knows that it is only thanks to a Hāfez-like spirit and "joyful sorrow" that they are still struggling against these limitations.

The Islamic Revolution and its calamitous outcome for contemporary Persian literature—the banishment of Iranian writers and their works from the global community of writers—has forced Mojābi to grapple with the question of poets and writers' identity in a world that is becoming ever smaller. He is opposed to Stalin's "universal homeland," on the one hand, and to capitalism's "globalization," on the other. While calling for the "stripping of identities," he dreads "identity-lessness." The ideal, to his mind, is a kind of "global village," based on the values and ideas of the humanism of the Age of Enlightenment, and a love of humanity "à la Saadi."

Mojābi sees a possible connection between the unprecedented growth of the novel in the two decades since the Islamic Revolution and a decline in the appeal of mysticism and illuminationism in a society that is moving rapidly from monophonic feudalism to polyphonic urbanism. He believes that this multivocal backdrop will be fertile ground for the growth of the "multi-identity" art he has in mind. Drawing on an analogy by Einstein, Mojābi sees himself—in his capacity as a poet, writer, painter, and intellectual—as a "mouse-butterfly" that can find room for maneuver even under the tightest constraints and forge enough space for creativity.

SHIVA RAHBARAN: What impression do Iranians have of democracy and what's their assessment of it? Are they aware of the dangers of populism? Is democracy, ultimately, of any use to Iranians? Because some contemporary Iranians have always said that democracy is incompatible with Iran's traditions.

JAVĀD MOJĀBI: I'm not a politician to spin lies in the name of the people; I can only tell you what my own opinion of democracy is and what I think would be beneficial for the nation to which I belong. I don't think that there's any nation in the world to which democracy is of no use. Of course, a democracy is weighed up against a situation in which there is tyranny; it is relative. It's been said that democracy is the lesser evil. We mustn't imagine that democracy is an absolute good. In the process of moving toward a democratic space, we should also criticize it in an informed way and correct our country's particular relations in the context of global democracy. It is via this rational evaluation of democracy that we close the way to a return to tyranny and pave the way for the attainment of more freedom by the people.

The thing is to figure out what understanding nations and thinkers in any society have of democracy at any given stage, and to what extent their impressions coincide with that understanding. I think that democracy's most important challenge is to harness power to the people's advantage. If overt and covert power are not controlled by an array of people-powered forces and institutions, we will, ultimately, have overt or covert tyranny under an official veneer of democracy. If primitive tyranny, as in Saudi Arabia, for example, under the all-encompassing rule of the almighty king is reprehensible, in the United States, the mafia-like power of transnational firms or the influence of warmongering militarists is just as dangerous to democracy. Just as the Stalinist cult of personality and the horrifying mass killings in his labor camps were dangerous to the Soviet people and to world peace. And just as, now, the chaos favored by the Russian mafia that controls prostitution and drug networks can lead to political repression. I even think that forcing people to choose between two parties, considering how people are brainwashed from every side, is far from democracy; although, of course, the fact that the people are steered by the media seems unavoidable.

S.R. Like Sharon's Israel or Berlusconi's Italy?

J.M. The existing powers in society are engaged in a kind of war because of the conflict of interests. Ultimately, the legal mechanisms of democracy must operate in a way that ensures that the main controlling power rests with the people, whether via media, associations, parties, or any other legal institution. But there are times when an institution that is representing the people decides to use its power to protect the interests of its own managers. The clash between the other forces in society and the offending side brings in the mass media and the law. If the law and its implementer are unbiased, if people's rights have been taken into account in the laws, and if the people are constantly kept informed about corruption and the overt and covert pressures that exist in society, then the likelihood of mistakes diminishes. We have to recognize that democracy is a historical experience, from ancient Greece down to today. And it is still correcting its systemic flaws, assuming that the interests of cartels and trusts, and military forces, and conspiratorial politicians do not impede its gradual evolution and progress.

S.R. For example, we see that, because of September 11, there is talk, on the pretext of public security, of doing away with all the organs of democracy in the United States.

J.M. A society's rulers will only have legal credibility and their conduct will only be acceptable if they safeguard the people's individual and group rights. And this isn't something that's vague and general; the details have been specified in human rights declarations and in the many laws relating to citizens' rights. I believe that in the constant battle between old tyranny and new democracy, which is rooted in individual and class interests, tyranny has not disappeared; it has retreated and waits in the shadows only to reappear through various cracks and in various disguises in order to protect domineering capitalists, warmongers, and totalitarians. In effect, the tyrannical representatives of capital and power will always lie in wait for any opportunity.

S.R. In an article published in Iran, you said: "I am a tyrannical person who has democratic inclinations." How do you mean?

J.M. I explained in the article that just claiming, "I'm a democrat," doesn't solve the problem. First you have to see what kind of atmosphere you're living and breathing in, in terms of tyranny or democracy. What are the historical and social conditions of your society, and what are the implications of its political reality? Then, you have to be honest with yourself and come clean about the extent to which you avoid tyranny. I mean, how hard have you tried, in your individual and collective life, to respect freedom and democracy? And, if, in a society that's beset by tyranny, you want to establish a democracy regardless of the conditions and their implications, is your atypical conduct not as inappropriate and baseless as the bellowing of a tyrant in the context of a free and democratic society? Reviewing your own conduct and, then, reviewing the conditions of your society will bring you closer to reality, on the condition that you rid yourself of your delusions and you're not intimidated by the prevailing trend.

S.R. As an intellectual, what's your duty in society?

J.M. Where the mechanisms of civil society, such as parties, trade unions, NGOs, media, and various checks and balances, exist, the task of an intellectual, strictly speaking, is to produce ideas and theories, and to criticize the status quo with a view to improving it. Where these conditions don't exist, part of the duties of the missing parties and institutions falls on intellectuals, and this may well prevent them from performing their intrinsic duties. But they cannot disregard these social duties because society expects it of them and they, too, are favorably inclined because they want to see themselves and the people move on from the existing historical conditions. It makes no difference to the situation whether this inclination is heartfelt or an unavoidable necessity. The circumstances of most writers in Africa, Asia, and Latin America are such as to implicate writers and artists, shoulder-to-shoulder with the rest of the nation, in the long struggle to attain democracy, freedom, and peace, despite the fact that these unavoidable commitments sometimes bring them up against death or exile. This is the price that the holders of a sincere vocation have to pay for their modern thinking, because they don't have politicians' conspiratorial minds but they've been unavoidably driven into the same arena. In advanced societies, too, a writer and artist like Günter Grass performs the duties of a political intellectual, in addition to his literary work, and he expresses his views and is in the thick of things, from the Rome Conference to the quarrel over the Berlin Wall, shoulder-to-shoulder with Willy Brandt. Party activities may generate some opponents for him, but they don't send him to the Gulag, like Solzhenitsyn, so that he can later fall victim to the manipulations of Western politicians.

As an intellectual, I see myself as belonging to a global tribe and I try to familiarize myself with the customs of this scattered, cultural family, and to see the norms of the tribe—which has considered itself committed to humanity and beauty over the course of history—as my own moral principles.

S.R. Is the global tribe of intellectuals close to the idea of globalization or the universal homeland?

J.M. No, not at all. Look, concepts like peace, freedom, and democracy are part of the global heritage. Human beings, in different societies, have tried for centuries to elevate and advance these concepts, and they have tested their practicability. Now, too, the world is striving to achieve them. But expressions like "the universal homeland," which was exploited by Russian communism in its quest for power, and "globalization," which has become an instrument for political domination by the West, especially the United States, are unrelated to general human experiences, such as democracy and civil society. Every now and then, the world's dominant powers brandish a theory, which is deceptive in appearance and deadly in its consequences. Like globalization. Or even an expression like "postcolonialism," which is intended to assess the status of cultures that are emerging from the grip of colonialism; but the fear is that the West's sense of political superiority and the cultural discrimination in the minds of many of its theoreticians will further perpetuate the growth of cultural colonialism. And the tools to achieve this, such as the Internet and cultural propaganda power, are also available. Will these powerful networks for the propagation of Western civilization and culture not make African and Asian nations ever more accustomed to purchasing consumer goods from the West and make them ever more subservient to Western culture? Although it may well be that, this time, the West's domination won't be imposed on the basis of cultural discrimination and colonialist ideas. Instead, it might be imposed on the basis of a theory for establishing a global homogeneity that will turn the whole world into a market for their economic products, just as it's already an arena for the new masters' cultural products. Of course, in this unavoidable satellite and Internet interchange, I don't want to put all the blame for the weak performance of vulnerable and underdeveloped governments and nations on a domination-seeking North. But outside this modern, technology-ridden sphere, we, in the economic South, have been nations with our own spiritually rich cultures and lives. Will we not lose our authentic identity in the future in this process of cultural homogenization?

S.R. In your capacity as a member of "the scattered tribe of intellectuals," how close are you to the people? It's been said that most of the intellectuals in the countries of the South are ivory-tower dwellers for various reasons.

J.M. In the decades that we're putting behind us, intellectuals in our country were of the view that culture is a one-way street and that they had to stake their claim to leading the people while remaining in the great heights of their ivory towers, as you put it. But this belief is gradually taking a more practical shape: although we are the select members of a nation, our human voices will only carry if they're woven into the silent voice of our nation. We're individual voices. We may, at some historical junctures, also be able to represent the voices in society that usually go unheard; representatives, not leaders. Being an intellectual is a kind of duty, not a claim.

S.R. Some analysts in the West, describe the revolution in Iran as "the Iranian experiment." Do you think this is an apt description? Is the paradox of wedding modernity to religion achievable?

J.M. Sociologically speaking, religion is part of a nation's culture and a nation without rites is inconceivable to me. Even the modern world has shown, in practice, that it needs spiritual beliefs; in fact, the inclination toward religion has taken on a kind of exotic form. But "the Iranian experience," i.e. a religious state, is a different matter and its success depends on the sincerity of its rulers and the correspondence of this goal to the people's social demands.

S.R. What I meant was that, in contemporary history, Iranian revolutionaries and intellectuals have always tried to join up religion and the state in some way, as a way of averting Iran's problems;

from the Constitutional Revolution, to the national-religious movement of the time of Mossadegh, to the Islamic Revolution.

J.M. In the intellectual community, over the past hundred years, the conflict between modernity and tradition has always kept this problem fresh. For example, Āl-e Ahmad and Shariati believed that most Iranians are Shiites; that Shiism has always been a religion of protest; and that this is part of the people's culture, which people-minded intellectuals must take into account. Of course, there have also been some Iranians, over these hundred years, who have tried to reject religion with the aim of integration into global modernity, but historical experience has proved them unsuccessful. Nowadays, religious intellectuals—having taken into account our national experience as a whole, and the need for global growth and development—have arrived at a middle ground in terms of synthesis of religion and politics. Of course, non-religious intellectuals have also given a great deal of thought to this historical and present-day concern.

S.R. Can we say that the Iranian revolution was, in Marx's words, a historical inevitability? And, by the same token and in view of the history of modernity in Iran, was the revolution—far from being a leap back—not a totally modern development?

J.M. We have to consider the foundation of our people's collective beliefs. There has yet to be a comprehensive study on this culture's mental and practical inclinations. And conditions over the past hundred

years—in terms of freedom of expression and freedom of opinion—
have not been such as to allow people to reveal their identity in an
uninhibited way, apart from a few instances over the past twenty-five
years when the masses have shown reactions to the revolution and
the war and acted in a telling way in elections. Every group—with its
own knowledge and its own mental system—has arrived at its own
particular interpretation of these national actions or reactions and
generalized it. Those who have studied history will know that, for
historical reasons, the Iranian people are more complex than they
make themselves out to be. Hence, in the absence of precise information about people's changing inclinations, national inclinations are
discussed in a kind of generalized and subjective way. But there can
be no doubt that we are facing forward, toward modernity. This is a
society which, in the age of the information explosion and in view of
its economic and political conditions, is rapidly moving away from
its rites-oriented shape. And, on the basis of its imperative social
demands, it is entering a new world. But although it is acquainted
with the shape and aims of the new world, it is, for whatever reason,
deprived of the conditions in which it can bring about the society it
wants. In these conditions, our nation wants exactly what all civilized nations want: political and economic development, prosperity,
freedom, democracy, human dignity, and cultural fulfillment. But,
in the light of our geopolitical position, will the domineering world
leave us be? And will officials and power holders be able to respond
to the people's real demands? Solving this problem on this or that
person's instructions—even Marx—isn't simple.

S.R. Do you feel happier than Western writers and thinkers? They envy you your situation and your lack of freedom. On the basis of Henry James's comment about art and the fact that he likened fiction to opening windows in people's minds, do you have more opportunities for putting in windows than Western writers do—bearing in mind that you have more walls?

J.M. With the utmost respect for everyone who envies our situation and who wants to put windows in walls, I would like to invite them to swap places with us as soon as possible; although, deep in my heart, I don't want to see a large number of the kind of romantic people Henry James had in mind die of frustration and grief. Joking aside, the feeling of happiness is related to individuals' character and temperament; to the state of their nerves and their lives; and, ultimately, to the way they look at the world and at human beings. For me, external conditions, such as the state of society, freedom, security, a decent standard of living, and development—whether on an individual scale or in terms of collective possibilities—are very important. How can an inactive cultural atmosphere and a rupture in the cultural link with the people be cause for joy for the person who has to put windows in walls? But our skill is to work in the realm of possibilities and in the existing conditions. We belong to this people and this culture. And we have done our work patiently and with the joyful sorrow that is our heritage.

What makes a writer work persistently is an explosion of internal energy that seeks an outlet through which to manifest itself—even if the world and human beings oppose it. No mighty wall—whether of steel or of paper—prevented Hedāyat, Shāmlu, Brodsky, or Havel from saying what they wanted to say. Maybe we move in the radiance of an everlasting outlook; an outlook in which "business" is unimportant.

S.R. I have a question that's related to the talk you gave last night (at the Goethe-Institut in Munich) about the duties of writers and artists in peripheral societies. Can we say that artists in these societies have a bigger obligation to the people? In a country like Iran, is this a literary and cultural heritage? I'm also thinking about Mostafā Rahimi's idea that, in Hāfez, you see a poet who reconciles irreconcilables (paradoxes), and resolves them into a kind of unity. Is it within the capabilities or the hopes of contemporary Iranian poets to find a solution to people's mental and social divisions, in the way that Hāfez might have done?

J.M. Solving problems is within intellectuals' expertise, but I don't think that it is within artists' expertise. In my talk, I spoke about three kinds of intellectuals who work in the relatively independent spheres of politics, philosophy, and culture. In the political and philosophical spheres, intellectuals keep an eye on power. In the cultural sphere, artists and writers keep an eye on what's happening within human beings and on the blossoming of human minds. For historical reasons, these functions have become confused in Iran and artists have unavoidably had to perform the grave duties of philosophers and political thinkers.

This confusion in our destinies has had positive aspects, but it has also had drawbacks. Of course, now, because of the rapid developments in society, the divisions between intellectuals' duties are becoming more precisely demarcated. So while preserving our organic link to neighboring spheres, we strive to deepen culture and art, and this releases us from the delusion of being society's sole guides.

The role that Hāfez played belonged to a closed feudal society, in which people's hopes were pinned on literary prophets' utterances. In fact, let me set your mind at rest. Nowadays, there's no such thing as authentic Iranian, American, Chinese, or African culture. What we're seeing is a composite culture, which inevitably takes on a native shade in each country and whose measurements tend to change constantly. In effect, there is a relatively unchanging native base, over which pass a variety of global experiences. When book lovers in Iran read as much Camus, Dostoyevsky, and Márquez as they do Rumi; when people in France and Germany can see as many films by Kiarostami and Angelopoulos as they do in Asia; and when African culture has had far more influence on modern music, painting, and sculpture in Europe and the United States than Africans' clothes and food have been influenced by Westerners, then it is no longer very realistic to talk about peripheral societies as opposed to central societies in terms of civilization and culture. After all, this is a term that was invented by Westerners, who are trying to practice cultural discrimination as a replacement for the practice of racism. We are navigating the boundaries of cultures and we are steered by border culture. This is not to denigrate our own national culture, but to mitigate chauvinism and closed borders.

S.R. But you can't deny that your mission is different from that of other thinkers and writers, in view of the environment in which you live.

J.M. If a culture and a nation take the messages of its elite offspring seriously, this lends self-confidence to the creators of art and literature. Of course, this relationship has to turn into a constant dialogue between the people and the artist, so that we can achieve the kind of cultural democracy that I mentioned earlier. In the absence of vocal speakers who can convey the collective's voice, our individual and, at times, weak voices sincerely reflect the absent voices until we can arrive at a time when the people can have their own voices, through a variety of associations, and writers can focus on deepening their intrinsic duties.

S.R. Mr. Mojābi, you're a writer, a poet, a painter, and a thinker, all at the same time. Don't these multiple identities make you feel like an outcast?

J.M. I believe that there's something miraculous about the creative mind. If a creative mind is unable, for whatever reason, to pursue its work in one artistic field, such as painting, for example, it will not come to a halt; it will redirect its energy into another field, such as poetry or the cinema. The movement of artists from one field to another, whether by choice or by compulsion, is a well-known phenomenon in the history of art. There have been many instances of it. And I'm no exception to this rule of movement between various media or, as you put it, being cast out from one field into another. There's nothing strange about this. Bear in mind that, sometimes, an individual may be prevented from pursuing an activity; in which case, he has to opt for another medium through which to express his ideas. It seems Einstein once said that some people are like mice, digging holes and going down into the depths, and others are like butterflies, flying around in broad and varied expanses; the ideal for me is to be a mouse-butterfly.

S.R. I was thinking of Sartre when you were speaking about the "mouse-butterfly."

J.M. Maybe our generation began its new model of intellectual activity with Sartre and Camus. It's not a question of comparing one person to another; it's a question of the norms and conventions. Of course, contrary to the prevalent idea that Iran's first intellectuals emerged at the time of the Constitutional Revolution and our acquaintance with Western modernity, I'm of the view that intellectual activity in Iran dates back to when the first moral tracts were produced and a sense of an intellectual-social mission emerged in our midst. And, later, the burden of this work fell on literature and especially poetry. But I won't go into that now.

I've written monographs about two of our progressive, combatant literary figures: Shāmlu and Sāedi. In order to express their ideas and to perform the duty that they felt they had toward the native human being and the universal human being, they did a bit of everything: writing, translation, research, giving talks, traveling, and going to jail. Multidimensional individuals have sacrificed themselves for their societies. Of course, I don't mean to suggest that artists should sacrifice themselves for their aims; I don't believe in having a Sufi-like death wish. On the contrary, I think that it's an artist's right to enjoy the blessings of a respectable life, like any other citizen. But what can you do when you're born in the Middle East? You acquire a strange destiny, which I've dubbed the Middle Eastern destiny. You have a term written in the column indicating your birthplace that situates you deep within a several-thousand-year-old history, with several-thousand-year-old traditions, and several-thousand-year-old do's and don'ts. And you put your childhood and carefree times behind you, and, in your youth, you imagine that this old world is as young as yourself and you try ever so hard to change it. Maybe you don't realize that thousands like you, over the course of this long history, have tried to achieve this same simple goal—to change the world—and so they became Ferdowsi, Ayn al-Qozāt, Sohrevardi, Amir-Kabir, Mossadegh, Dehkhodā, and Hedāyat, with all their battle scars. In your reflective years, you find yourself among these beloved departed ones, who try to warn you, with signs and gestures, against being hasty and naïve. But sometimes the language of the dead is incomprehensible to us, and their ambiguous signals convey the reverse of the intended message.

This isn't a paradox. It's a kind of grotesque, a mixture of tragedy and comedy, which, in the modern here and now, fits us out with a historical destiny. You see that you're someone living in the heart of a ritualistic society and that you don't resemble the other members of the society very much. For a time, rightly or illusorily, you consider yourself attached to the mental conduct of progressive human beings living in other societies, but you know that, even if you lived in those societies, you wouldn't belong to that culture and to those people, and that they see you as a transplanted organ; you feel a pervasive sense of foreignness, in your homeland and in any other land. If this Middle Eastern destiny doesn't make you burst, it may eventually lead you to a happy end.

So you're left with a homeland and a culture that, in your mind, you take with you everywhere. You grapple with the question: Where, then, are you from? One answer is: Uncommon-land. One answer is: I'm from the Middle East. I'm not from an African culture. I'm not a Spanish-speaking person. We speak to a global audience which is sometimes right in front of our eyes and tongue, and sometimes continents and centuries apart. So "the scattered global tribe" or "border culture" or "the audience in the global village" all become comprehensible terms. Or maybe these are just the hollow musings of a disgruntled intellectual and a dissolute mimic. You've echoed things to yourself and some people have overheard you or there wasn't even any time left for overhearing anything. But, anyway, it was clear that you were speaking and this is enough for someone who felt compelled to speak and to write.

S.R. How do you feel within the Persian language?

J.M. Language is the main work tool of us poets. At the same time, language is the flag of our identity and our nationality. It's what's made us different, preserved us, lent us meaning, and will perpetuate us.

By plunging into the depths of language, the poet uncovers the depths of himself and his tribe, and he shares it with those people who want their daily lives to be more profound. Everyone translates themselves into the language with which they are familiar and, in Iran, we usually translate ourselves into poetry and emotion. The Persian language is my resting place and it will be my cradle, always in motion.

S.R. But you paint too.

J.M. The first thing that I learned to do was painting and I still tend to paint in the recesses between my classes on joy and sorrow. Painting is what I do naturally and with ease, like breathing and sleeping, without any need for preparation. Painting taught me the subject of composition in poetry. For the past few years, I've been producing poetry ceaselessly and I've come to the conclusion that I was a poet who spent his effervescent energy as a poet on writing novels, short stories, and articles.

In writing poetry, the composition that is my mind reveals its varied faces. These new and innovative faces, which I was not aware of before, astonish and please me. As I write poetry, I become conscious of the hidden corners of my mind and this amazing game acquaints me with my hidden self. Maybe poetry is the most intimate art and the most abstract, with a function similar to the mind itself. Or at least that's the kind of ease and revelation that I reach in poetry.

I don't believe in external innovativeness, which is a deliberate effort. I believe that when you renovate your mind with reflection, experience, and awareness, whatever you say will pass through the new thoughts in your mind and will take on a new form.

S.R. In relation to freedom, what do you think about illumina-tionism and mysticism? Has mysticism pushed us into backward-ness and captivity, or to freedom?

J.M. I believe that, in mysticism, you, as an individual, are freed from all the attachments of this world, and this is a kind of bound-less freedom. But, ultimately, this freedom is bounded by submis-sion to God, which reveals the constraints again, the constraints that are associated with this submission. In mysticism, mavericks have turned this relationship of submission into a relationship of love, thus also releasing themselves from the constraints of reli-gion. Maybe mysticism liberates the individual from himself and unites him with the beloved, and this is beautiful. But this school of thought, which can provide felicity and freedom for the reclusive individual, offers no prescription for collective happiness. It views the collective as a mass of individuals, which isn't correct. Maybe art, too, like mysticism, is more concerned with individual—rather than collective—pleasure and release. And its pleasurable and magical secrets are perceived in private. The question is: can we inject mysticism's spirituality, as a social ethics, into society's dynamics? I think it's possible, because mysticism's concepts are sufficiently formless and varied. With its ideas of unity of being, love, liberation from attachments, and freedom, it may be able to adjust itself to any unexpected situation. Mysticism's suggestion that you should love others as thyself and that you should forget yourself is a kind of narcotic against the torment of the self by others.

S.R. What's worth noting in relation to spirituality and the meaning of life is that, in the West, after Wittgenstein, the question of language became so important that the idea of language as a game gained currency. Writers, such as Barthes and Robbe-Grillet, wrote in a language that was empty of meaning. After September 11, some philosophers, most notably Richard Rorty in the United States (who was always of the view there is no reality other than the non-reality of language), suddenly seemed to descend from the high clouds of their games and make a complete about-face on the realities on earth. Now, not only have they discovered reality, but they also speak anxiously about the need to save the world by exporting Western ideas and values—in Rorty's words—by military force if necessary.

J.M. Yes, this is also what His Royal Highness [the Shah] used to say. His Royal Highness, too, liked to say: We have to civilize this nation at any cost; if necessary, by force. This isn't a kingly idea; it's a stupid idea. Sometimes it's His Royal Highness who makes decisions for heaven and earth, and for language and culture, and sometimes it's a writer, a philosopher, an intellectual or this or that mighty, power-holding institution or party. Language is a way of conveying understanding. A human being thinks, speaks, and acts with language, and connects on the basis of the meaningfulness of language. Now, what would you hope to achieve by stripping language of meaning, other than to strip connections and the comprehension that you've achieved thanks to your nonsensical, mediocre civilization? Perhaps we might say that the meaning of language is being stripped. In totalitarian regimes or in the deluded relationships of capitalism—modern-day slavery—this may be a fact. But your insistence—in your capacity as a poet or a philosopher—on deliberately stripping meaning makes you an ally of regimes that want to hush the people's silence even further. The people want to speak and to hear others speak, and for some meaning to be achieved therein which might be of use to them in improving their lives. Is it your duty, as a novelist and a philosopher, to strip language of meaning in order to help strip individuals of their identity and, ultimately, to produce a nonsensical collective space? I'm prepared to strip intellectuals of their leadership identity, but I'm not prepared to try to strip the collective of its identity; unless I have a bee in my bonnet à la His Royal Highness or Rorty-style.

Unfortunately, the move toward the non-reality of a language that's stripped of meaning has gained supporters among young people these days. This may be an overreaction to the meaning-centeredness of poetry over the past few decades. But we must be vigilant, because a kind of political-cultural fascism can grow in the context of meaninglessness and identitylessness, especially for us, as we stand on the threshold of discovering the meaning of civil society and have yet to acquire enough meaning to want to try to get rid of it with these kinds of games. As it happens, the plurality and variety of novels in the decades after the revolution—and, especially, the active presence of women in this kind of writing—shows that, first, language is seeking and reflecting multiple meanings and plural voices. The novel, as the tool of urban dwellers, has been used more than single-voiced poetry to this end. Secondly, the people's enthusiasm for reading novels underlines the fact that people seek a meaningful connection in which they can better find themselves.

Amir Hassan Cheheltan

Born in Tehran in 1956, his published works include *Sigheh* (Temporary Marriage), *Dakhil bar Panjareh-ye Fulād* (The Steel Window), *Digar Kesi Sedāyam Nazad* (Nobody Called Me Anymore), *Chizi beh Fardā Namāndeh Ast* (Not Much Time Left to Tomorrow), *Rowzeh-ye Qāssem* (Qassem's Story), *Tālār-e Āyneh* (Hall of Mirrors), *Mehr-Giāh* (The Mandrake), *Tehrān, Shahr-e Bi-Asmān* (Tehran, the City Without a Sky), *Eshq va Bānu-ye Nātamām* (Love and the Unfinished Lady), and *Sāʾat-e Panj barā-ye Mordan dir Ast* (Five O'Clock is Too Late for Dying). Cheheltan is also editing an anthology of contemporary Persian fiction (translated by Gustav Carlson) for the book fair in Gothenburg, Sweden.

[Cheheltan's latest novel, *Tehran Revolutionsstrasse*, has been published recently in a German translation by Susanne Baghestani. —Trans.]

Amir Hassan Cheheltan

Amir Hassan Cheheltan does not, on the whole, have an optimistic view of social developments in Iran over the past century and he describes modern Iranian thought and literature as "congenitally deformed." Be that as it may, he acknowledges the importance of the Islamic Revolution as "a full-length mirror that showed us to ourselves," although he believes that the cost of this self-knowledge was the loss of almost all the capabilities of the Iranian nation.

All the same, he considers the "mirror" of the revolution to have been beneficial for the growth of contemporary Iranian literature—especially the novel. Over the past two decades, Cheheltan has witnessed unprecedented enthusiasm for novels in parallel with a notable decline in the reading of poetry. He interprets this phenomenon as a shift in society from emotion and mysticism to rationality and levelheadedness. He welcomes this development and is of the view that, in this way, contemporary literature can clothe Iran's revolution-stricken society in the garb of a new, global identity and rid it of old sediments and superstitions.

Although there is always a distance between society and writers, in their capacity as society's observers, Cheheltan does not feel alienated in his traditionalist society, which is beset by censorship. As far as he is concerned, even Hedāyat, who can easily be said to have been the epitome of an alienated artist in a traditionalist and backward society, would not have been able to produce valuable works without some "commerce" between himself and his society. Cheheltan's novels are fueled by the contrast between Iran's urban society—especially in Tehran—and Iran's legend-based history. So in his novels, he tries to depict this "modern, legend-based" history in everyday life.

SHIVA RAHBARAN: The first question is a general question about democracy in Iran. What impression do Iranians have of democracy? Do they think that this form of government is a good government? And, finally, a related, general question: Many people are of the view that democracy is, basically, of no use to Iranians in view of their rites, traditions, and history, and that it will never succeed here.

AMIR HASSAN CHEHELTAN: Let me begin by telling you about the things that distinguish Iran from all other comparable societies, i.e., all the other Islamic or even Asian countries. This may, to some extent, make us conscious of the particular complexities of this society and its approach to modernity and democracy. Iran was the first country, outside the American and European region, to acquire a parliament, in 1906. The movement for the rule of law and election-based democracy bore fruit in Iran even earlier than in Russia, where its social movement suffered a setback in 1905. So you can see how many years ago the need for democracy was first felt in Iran. But the question is: why isn't it possible to achieve democracy in Iran? Why is it that, despite feeling the need for the rule of law and the opposition to arbitrary power, our people do not make shrewd efforts to achieve democracy?

Incidentally, I should add that I'm of the view that human societies only have the potential for gradual change; revolution is an impossibility.

Our important problem is our strategic position over the past century as an oil terminal, added to which was the problem of having the Soviet Union as a neighbor. Of course, this difficult position has helped Iran at some historical junctures. In the modern era, Iran never became a colonized country, in the way that India was, for example. In other words, it was never ruled by foreign powers, although there were times when it had very little control over its own affairs. So I can't totally discount the role of foreign forces in impeding the attainment of democracy. Without a doubt, the eight-year war with Iraq was one of the events that halted the growth of democracy in Iran.

S.R. But do you think that intellectuals have also been to blame or not? Iranian intellectuals—starting from the Constitutional Revolution, which you mentioned, to the time of Mossadegh, to the 1979 revolution—have tried to arrive at modernity and democracy via a paradox, i.e., synthesizing religion and the state. Don't you think that this paradox or anomaly is to blame for the failure of democracy in Iran?

A.C. I don't agree with your assessment. Yes, democracy has suffered a reverse in Iran. If intellectuals showed fellowship with what happened in 1979, it was because they had no choice. The events that unfolded around that time displayed more clearly than before the strong presence of religion in the inner layers of Iranians' minds. Religion doesn't only manifest itself at religious events in Iran; religion is a spirit that also reveals itself in people's conduct and in legal and social forms. The people reacted against the modernity that Reza Shah wanted to establish in Iran. The criticisms and analyses that are made of his rule have persuaded me that, if he had enjoyed a minimum of popularity among the people, he would have been able to display some resistance to the pressure that the Allied forces put on him to leave the country.[49] My father told me that, when Reza Shah left, the people started killing neighborhood policemen because they didn't represent security; they were the instruments of domination and coercion.

I think that that the level of success of any new program in a society directly depends on the people's capacity to absorb and accept it. The solutions that intellectuals or politicians devise will not lead anywhere unless this important factor is taken into account.

S.R. So where has the mission of intellectuals and artists got to in Iran today?

A.C. You have to bear in mind a couple of points. Artists are not necessarily intellectuals. Intellectuals produce ideas. Artists produce beauty. The ideas that are produced in our age rapidly become

---

49   Iran was invaded by British and Russian forces in August 1941, and Reza Shah, the father of the last Shah of Iran, was forced to abdicate and leave Iran.

politicized, and they may be of use for only a passing moment. But the artist has a broad horizon; the world is his audience.

Moreover, over the past fifty years, our intellectuals have always been anxious to perform the mission of rescuing the people; this anxiety has made them hasty and sometimes they've been drawn toward extremes. At one point, they were drawn into the Tudeh Party.[50] Then, they were drawn to the idea of guerrilla warfare. And then there was the "return to self" movement, of which Jalāl Āl-e Ahmad was one of the standard-bearers. I have no idea who "the self" is in the twentieth century or where he is to be found. *Gharbzadegi* (Westoxiation) is a masterpiece of illiteracy. Just taking a short course in sociology would suffice for anyone to see what demagogic nonsense this book is. What's interesting is that some of our intellectuals are absolutely devoted to Jalāl Āl-e Ahmad. We suffer from a poverty of thought. No one produces thought. And the bigger tragedy is that Iranian artists and writers imagine that they are committed, so that they can fill this void. Yes, of course, Nazim Hikmet, Pablo Neruda, Yiannis Ritsos, and others have produced political poetry, but their love poems far outnumber their political poems. We've always missed the depths of developments and have, consequently, remained dwarves. This is why what we know as political literature in Iran doesn't have one iota of aesthetic value. A political declaration intended to generate excitement: that's all! Iran's artistic community has suffered so many casualties because of this misunderstanding. These casualties have suddenly and tragically hurled the contemporary

---

50   Iran's now defunct communist party.

Persian language—which has been deprived of good poetry and good short stories—into the world, where it can see that is lacks many things, including revolutionary poets, revolutionary writers, and revolutionary parties.

S.R. The impression I got from what you were saying is that, if anything, it has too many of this kind of poets and writers!

A.C. Of course. But why? Because it immediately wants to compensate for what it lacks. This haste removes things from their natural reality and everything becomes mere fantasy. We suffer from a kind of congenital deformity and dwarfism in all things and in all spheres. It's the same with democracy. It wants to be born somewhere where it's impossible for it to grow. The infant's delivery has proved unsuccessful so far.

S.R. Do you think we can say that the revolution in Iran was a historical necessity?

A.C. I think so. Moreover, this revolution displayed this society's essence to Iranian intellectuals for the first time. This society was like a small pool with a thin layer of translucent water on the surface which made us unaware of the depths of the old sediments, because we're such emotional, perfunctory, and hasty people. This revolution was like a full-length mirror that showed us to ourselves. But did we have to pay such a high price for this achievement? Now, that is to say, in these few years since 2

Khordad,[51] everyone is asking themselves how to go through this transitional period [to democracy] at the lowest possible cost. The belief has finally come about that we must reexamine our historical past in order to extricate ourselves from the impasse. The Iranian nation lost almost all its capabilities in order to arrive at this awareness. In fact, one of the amazing things about this nation, historically, is that it has always gone to the very edge of an incontrovertible abyss, but has somehow been able to find the strength to rebuild something again.

S.R. Like a phoenix rising from the ashes?

A.C. Maybe this is our last refuge. When the mind's powers can't uncover the hidden logic behind events, we inescapably seek refuge in fairy tales and legends. Sometimes I think the fact that Iran was the only country—among all the countries that were conquered by the Arabs—that was able to preserve its language is more like a miracle. In fact, the Persian language is itself a miracle. Among the European countries, Italian—I mean the language that people speak in Italy today—is possibly older than the rest. The oldest books available in this language are Dante's *Divine Comedy* and Boccaccio's *Decameron*, which were written less than seven centuries ago. It would seem that there are no older books than these two in the languages that are currently spoken in Europe.

---

51   Date on the Iranian calendar corresponding to 23 May; election date on which Mohammad Khatami unexpectedly beat the establishment candidate to become president in 1997.

But Ferdowsi's *Shāhnāmeh* was written eleven centuries ago and even schoolchildren can understand it today.

S.R. Your answer brings me to the following question about Iranian thinkers and artists and their heritage: Mr. Dariush Shāyegān has suggested that, because mysticism and illuminationism have formed an important part of the Iranian heritage, the novel has never flourished here, because the novel is the offspring of European reason from the Renaissance onward.

A.C. I agree with him. As it happens, over the past two decades people have started showing some enthusiasm for novels and novel writing has grown in Iran. It would appear that our society is gradually turning toward reason and thought. In fact, while Iranian literature revolved around poetry in the past, short stories and especially novels have taken pride of place over the past two or three decades. Poetry is generally considered to be the realm of the imagination and emotion—something that is, of course, still very much needed by human beings today—but novels are the realm of thought. Among all the literary occupations, none is as linked to contemporary life as novel writing. It was necessary for us to push superstition and emotionalism slightly to one side at last.

S.R. Is Iranian mysticism or Iranian poetry part of your heritage or not? Or is it only important to you as something that you have to go beyond?

A.C. Well, I go for useful things. For example, I'd only put old objects on a shelf in my room if they formed a pleasing ensemble with the present-day objects; otherwise, I'd send them off to the storeroom. We don't have to accept unconditionally everything that relates to our past or, even worse, be fanatical about them. I view the treasure chest of classical Iranian literature from a historical perspective and I see it as a philosophical, moral, and literary aggregate. Moreover, I look for the aesthetic aspects of this literature; I don't accept the definition of being that it contains. Our current problems are not related to the conditions that produced this literature. Its meaning-component is only of historical value as far as I'm concerned. The attraction of this literature for me is discovering the Persian language. Because every time I turn to it, it shimmers with changing colors, reveals its hidden potential, and sets the strings of my soul vibrating endlessly.

As for the things that Dariush Shāyegān says, they are very good in as much as he is someone who has the courage to explain ideas, which aren't even that abstract and which directly concern the world of us Iranians. He's the only one who tries to give an account of our situation in a rational way. We're an oral nation. When we see each other, we can talk for hours about any subject, but we never set down even a couple of sentences of it on paper. But sometimes I think that he's trying to rationalize and excuse our situation.

S.R. He talks about the failure of modernism and, in my view, looks onward to postmodernity. In other words, Shāyegān talks about postmodernity "turning away from" reason and moving toward mysticism and illuminationism.

A.C. Yes, that's right. For example, he believes that the growth of technology, prosperity, and progress in Japan is tenuous and fragile. Perhaps he's right. But I can't turn a blind eye to Japanese people's happiness. I envy them. What is happiness after all? Happiness is the fact that, when a Japanese writer leaves his house, he's sure that he won't be stabbed by someone who is lying in wait to kill him. When the Japanese fall ill, they don't have to worry about how they're going to pay for the doctor and the medicines. Yes, this is happiness. Of course, these same Japanese people may become depressed or they may feel sad at night, before they fall asleep, about the fact that they've become disconnected from their ancestral roots.

I can't see Japan as an example of failure. And I wouldn't make the following recommendation to any nation: If you come from an Eastern, mysterious, and mystical background, you better appreciate your ancestral heritage!

S.R. But hasn't Iran always risen from the ashes thanks to its legacy of myths? Hasn't Iran always been the land of miracles?

A.C. If we believe this, we'll never do anything. We can't just sit and wait for miracles. In order to come out of this impasse, I need tools that will help me find solutions.

S.R. So do you see novel writing, which goes hand in hand with realism, as a difficult thing to do in this miracle-prone nation?

A.C. Of course. Look, our contemporary poetry has thousand-year-old parents. But our contemporary novels have a lineage of only sixty or seventy years. I can't view the samples of classical Persian writing as the predecessors of modern novel writing. So Persian isn't very proficient in the realm of novel writing. Persian and poetry have been wrestling together for a thousand years, but the Persian novel is a newborn infant.

S.R. So don't you see yourself as an artistic outcast in this land? I mean, isn't your art, novel writing, sidelined by poetry?

A.C. No. But I suffer from a dearth of readers in general, of course.

S.R. You mean the writer and the poet are outcasts here, in their homeland?

A.C. Maybe. Iranian writers write in a vacuum. A print run of a few thousand is very small.

S.R. What role do literary studies play in improving this situation? Many people abroad, in the departments of literature in Western universities, are of the view that literary studies can, at the same time, be a kind of display of power by the West vis-à-vis the East and a new method of colonizing the Eastern spirit and soul.

A.C. Paying attention to these things and striving to unravel them has turned into a way of life for the Western human being. Even if I think that the airplane was invented for dropping bombs, I still can't hide my joy and satisfaction about the fact that it can take me from Tehran to London in just four or five hours' time.

We haven't made any effort to unravel ourselves. Western curiosity about everything, including things that relate to me, is not a conspiracy in my view. But I confess that I find it unpleasant if people look at me, at my life, at my history, and at my past as they would look at things in a laboratory. Knowledge must be gained in proportion to understanding. Maybe one day a more equitable relationship will be established at last and we, in turn, will be able to unravel unknown aspects of the Western human being.

S.R. But since there is an imbalance of power, there's little chance that Iranian research will catch up with Western research.

A.C. Perhaps. But this conundrum is a product of our own stupidities. Sādegh Hedāyat's works are banned now. Even Saadi is censored; they're not authorizing the publication of Saadi's *Ghazaliyat*.[52] There's no mention of contemporary Iranian literature in schoolbooks. Schoolchildren and university students aren't taught to be interested in contemporary literature. I don't accept the idea

---

52   Known in English as Saadi's *Lyrics*.

that research work by Westerners is an imperialist conspiracy. It may be that intelligence organizations use the information too. I'm not in a position to say. But I find it appealing that some people are interested in finding out, for example, who I am, what I write, and why I write. This is pleasing to me.

S.R. It's not good for art to become politicized. But this has always happened in Iran, for social reasons and because of the reverses that we've suffered in our experiences of modernity. The phenomenon of modernity has taken strange forms in Iran, and it has always been combined with suppression and repression. But, in the West, many people envy this situation. They believe that the severe anomalies and divides that have emerged in contemporary Iran have produced good grounds for Persian literature. Moreover, the creators of literary works enjoy a level of respect here that is rare in contemporary Western societies. Although the print run of books is low and books don't sell as well as they do in the West, you and your colleagues can, as writers and poets, fill a sports stadium with enthusiasts! So they've come to the conclusion, in the West, that freedom is, all in all, bad for producing good poetry and novels. Basing themselves on what Henry James said about novels—that every novel is a window in the house of fiction—they say that since you, Iranians (or third-worlders), have more walls, you can put in more windows, so your work is more important and more meaningful.

A.C. I don't know. But if I was the owner of the literature that's now being produced in Iran, I would be prepared to give it up and to have a free and happy society instead. The enthusiasm for writers here is because we're a legend-minded nation. Iranians think that words have magical powers. Writers produce words. Nowadays, when soccer players or TV actors are the new legends, the presence of a writer somewhere produces a sudden hush and an atmosphere of sanctity. There's another reason too: in Iran over the past hundred years, where the dominant aspect has been suppression and repression, there's been a porthole that they've never been able to close. The name of this porthole is literature. In the most difficult political times and at the height of censorship, Iranian poets and writers have never stopped working. In such circumstances, the simplest words—against the backdrop of the existing conditions—take on a figurative aspect and fulfill people's needs. This turns writers into charismatic figures.

S.R. So is the absence of freedom good for literature?

A.C. It depends on whether the writer is clever enough to turn the restrictions into a springboard. We've been able to turn the restrictions into a literary form. For example, in a modern short story, I may just speak to you about a corner of a table and then the arm of a chair, and, on this basis, you're supposed to picture the rest of the room in your mind. I mean, limitations on what you can say has an aesthetic aspect too. The censors always want us to write a story in which we don't say anything. This helps me raise the aesthetic level of my work, if I approach things consciously of course.

S.R. Hasn't this censorship turned into self-censorship in our midst? Hasn't it created a situation in which we avoid saying many of the things that we want to say?

A.C. In Iranian-Islamic culture, this is known as *taqiyeh*.[53] It means that you should be silent for now, you should not protest, you shouldn't say anything so that you can live to speak some other day, when the situation has improved. Moreover, not saying exactly what you mean is ingrained in Iranians because of some historical experiences. It is difficult to know who to trust: not your neighbor; not your colleague; not your fellow student; not even your spouse. We talk a lot, of course, but only in order to hide a substantial part of the facts, and this has turned into a social characteristic.

S.R. You've turned into a very strong realist. In this respect, your *Rowzeh-ye Qāssem* (Qassem's Story), for example, seems "more modern" than the more epic-like and poetical *Kelidar*.[54] Do you see yourself as a writer who is more "contemporary"?

A.C. I can't answer that. Our writings are different. Moreover, *Rowzeh-ye Qāssem* is the first novel that I wrote—of course I wasn't allowed to publish it for a full eighteen years. I'd like to be judged by my subsequent novels. For example, by *Tehrān, Shahr-e Bi-Asmān*

---

53   "Dissimulation"; a practice generally associated with Shiites. The idea behind it is that Shiites, who were often in the minority in their societies, were allowed to or even duty-bound to practice "dissimulation" and to say that they were not Shiites if saying otherwise would have placed them in danger.
54   Novel by Mahmoud Dowlatābādi.

(Tehran, the City without a Sky). This short novel, with a very succinct language, is the social history of our past five, six decades.

S.R. Are you an iconoclast or not? Many Iranian novelists, such as Dowlatābādi and Mandanipour, say that an important part of their heritage and their bedrock consists of the classics, such as *Samak Ayyār*,[55] *Kelileh va Demneh*,[56] and *The Thousand and One Nights*. Are you an iconoclast to the extent that you turn your back on your Iranian heritage and only view Western novels as your bedrock?

A.C. Iranian storytelling is part of my heritage. But I'm also a citizen of the world. It goes without saying that part of the past hangs in the air that I breathe today. But I don't surrender to it. I may have more in common with Kafka, Joyce, and Proust than the works that you named. I can't sit at my computer, tremble in fear at the undoubted supremacy of the lunatics that rule in this or that corner of the world, and feel fellowship with antiquated literature. I have reached a peaceable agreement with the past, which belonged to my ancestors; a restful nostalgia that is a source of spiritual calm for me.

S.R. Iranian society is more modern now than at the time when Hedāyat was writing. He was totally alone. Do you suffer from less isolation?

---

55   See Note 11 under Mahmoud Dowlatābādi, page 24.
56   Persian translation of the *Panchatantra*.

A.C. I am constantly engaged in commerce with the society in which I live. Without this society, Hedāyat and I couldn't have existed. But there's always a distance. There's always a distance between the individual and society. But how does it happen that this distance sometimes becomes calamitous?[57]

Three, four generations ago, it became possible for some Iranians to become acquainted with other ways of life. But it wasn't possible for all Iranians. Our society's current crisis in fact results from this: a wrangle between the supporters of two different ways of life. Hedāyat was in an absolute minority.

S.R. It was interesting to me, in *Rowzeh-ye Qāssem*, to see how you exploit our superstitions and turn them into everyday life. That is to say, you create a realist structure out of the delusions in our minds, as if they have an external, real existence. But now, if I understand you correctly, you're saying that you don't want these sentiments to exist in Iran, although you use their aesthetic aspects.

A.C. I look at myths with a surrealist eye. At the same time, in *Rowzeh-ye Qāssem*, I make a point of recreating these myths in everyday life. Myths are a part of our everyday lives. I take advantage of these elements to lend color to the fictional atmosphere, in an aesthetic sense.

S.R. Aren't you creating new myths in this way?

---

57   Sādegh Hedāyat committed suicide.

A.C. Maybe people who wear suits and use computers have taken on the role of those myths now. We change, but much more slowly than we imagine.

S.R. Do we need myths as mirrors in which we can look at ourselves?

A.C. No! They're a nuisance. They rob us of the capacity for pure thought. We must consciously distance ourselves from them.

HĀFEZ MUSAVI

Born in Bushehr in 1954, his works include *Dasti beh Shishehhā-ye Meh-Gerefteh-ye Donyā* (A Hand on the World's Mist-Covered Panes), *Satrhā-ye Penhāni* (Hidden Lines), and *She'rhā-ye Jomhuri* (Republic's Poems).

Hāfez Musavi

Hāfez Musavi has an optimistic view of the Islamic Revolution and its effects. He believes that, over the past hundred years, after every revolution or movement that has marked a historical juncture in Iran, there were efforts to consummate modern thinking—a thinking that revolves around "I" or "the individual." But he argues that these efforts were redoubled after the Islamic Revolution—a revolution that, in Musavi's view, did not have any effect on spiritual and religious values, but only on the availability of the products of modernism and modernity. These efforts take the form of intellectual and literary grappling with contradictions that were brought "right under the spotlight" with the advent of the Islamic Revolution. Musavi traces the roots of these contradictions to a particular historical juncture, the Reza Shah era, but he believes that the era of the Islamic Revolution is the time when the contradictions reached their full-fledged form. The intellectual and literary grappling with these contradictions constantly pushes Iran's society toward a kind of reevaluation and self-knowledge, which is imperative if the society is to enter a real modernity of some kind. On this basis, Musavi sees Iran's revolution-stricken society as fertile ground for contemporary literature, and he hopes that this process of literary and philosophical battle will lead to a kind of thinking that's free of the old slogans and ideologies. Only in this way will contemporary literature have a positive impact on Iranian society.

As for the poetry-novel distinction, Musavi believes that the Iranian novelist's task is more difficult, because the novel is a genre that was born of Western modernity and is a product of its multivocal society. But he is also of the view that Iranian society is on the threshold of entering a multivocal and modern society, which will not only create suitable grounds for the growth of the novel, but will also call for deep changes in the field of contemporary poetry.

SHIVA RAHBARAN: The first question is a general question about democracy. What impression do Iranians have of democracy? Do they think that it's a good form of government? Are they aware of the dangers of populism and ways of preventing it? Have Iranian thinkers fulfilled their mission in terms of acquainting people with democracy? And, finally, many people, whether under this regime or the previous regime, have been and are of the view that democracy is not in keeping with our disposition, our way of thinking, our particular characteristics, and our traditions. What do you think?

HĀFEZ MUSAVI: There's been a great deal of debate in this connection in Iran in recent years. I mean, the question of democracy has been discussed a great deal over the past ten years. Maybe what I'm going to say now is a summation of the things we've read or heard over the past few years, and it has been a serious debate. The most clichéd verdict is that Iranians have no experience of democracy. Of course, this cliché is based on a fact. The reason for it is that, as a country and as a nation, we began experiencing life with civil relations in the constitutionalist period. If you look at the fate of the Constitutional Revolution, you see that, because of the underlying wrangling and because of the Constitutional Revolution's fundamental weaknesses—part of which had to do with the Constitutional Revolution's ideas—the revolution ultimately led to a phenomenon known as Reza Shah. Reza Shah is a paradox in Iran's history. On the one hand, you meet a large number of people who love Reza Shah and who say, "These are the handiworks of Reza Shah." And it's really true. You can see Reza Shah's handiworks in every nook and cranny in Iran. He built railroads. He built universities. There are countless examples of infrastructural works and services relating to urban life which were built in Reza Shah's time. Whereas people don't say this about the reign of [his son,] Mohammad Reza Shah.[58] So in this sense, you can really say that Reza Shah fulfilled what the Iranian people had hoped to achieve through the Constitutional Revolution, which was to step into modern life. But, on the other hand, Reza Shah was opposed to all the civil institutions that were necessary for modern life. In other words, with the appearance of the phenomenon of Reza Shah, Iran went forward in terms of modernization, but modernity suffered a reverse. Life in the West has shown that these two always go together. In Iran, the process remained incomplete. This is why, when Reza Shah left and his son, Mohammad Reza Shah, took over, we found ourselves faced with another substandard specimen. So in the years when we could have experienced civil

58 Mohammad Reza Shah was Reza Shah's son and the last Shah of Iran.

life again, we experienced the outward appearances of it. We could travel abroad or see many things from afar, but civil institutions did not exist in Iran. We didn't have a real parliament. We didn't have the real tools with which the people could exercise their will. In Mohammad Reza Shah's time, they used to say, "We have the Rastākhiz [Resurrection] Party; anyone who wants to join can join and anyone who doesn't want to join can come and pick up their passport and we'll pay for their ticket and they can leave!" So the idea that we have no experience of democracy is true.

After the revolution, that is to say, from 1979 onward, I believe that more has been done for us to reach these notions, at least in the realm of theory. You know better than I do that civil life begins with "I" and with "the individual." In Iran, we've never had individuals! If you examine the efforts that were made to actualize and consummate the individual here, you will see that they began in our modern literature. I mean, it was in literature that Nimā[59] said for the first time to a second person singular: "Look at the world!" And he gave this advice to his imaginary friend: "When you're on the road and you stop at the tea house, look at that tree! Look at that turtle!" Hedāyat was the same. This is, in fact, the consummation of modern thinking, where you have an "I." And it takes shape in the realm of theory. But, since we haven't had a political movement based on civil life in conjunction with this, all these things remain incomplete. But it all burst into view in the 1979 revolution.

---

59 Nimā Yushij (1896–1960) is known as the father of modern Persian poetry and blank verse.

S.R. Do you mean to say that intellectuals closed the gap with the people or is there still a distance between the two?

H.M. The 1979 revolution was, in fact, a manifestation of all the contradictions of the Iranian nation. I mean, although we wanted modern life, we were opposed to the West! Although we were intellectuals, we opposed democracy. I mean, even in 1979, we, as Iranian intellectuals, did not recognize the importance of democratic slogans. Why? Iranian intellectuals convinced themselves that, for various reasons, they could do without freedom for now. That is to say, they could forego freedom in order to achieve some other aims! But we saw that the other aims were not fulfilled, because all these things were meant to move forward together.

What happened in 1979 and its subsequent results brought about changes in the country's economic structures. A new stratum, a so-called bourgeoisie, came into being, but it was not necessarily linked to political power. The question of power is worth studying in Iran. In the past, in Britain for example, there used to be families that had been in power for three hundred years. I mean, alongside the political authority, there were other powers that had a share in things and could affect the power structure. But this hasn't been the case in Iran. When the Qajars came to power, they crushed Karim-Khān Zand's bones under their boots. I mean, power has always consisted of a very steep pyramid. Since the revolution, this situation is changing. At the same time, we've arrived at a better understanding of democracy. And, of course, I believe that international developments have been another helpful factor. Now, what has happened in the international arena is that the Soviet system has vanished and the intellectual models of justice have vanished. And in Iran, too, we have had our own experiences, so that these debates are now taking place.

S.R. To what extent have Iranian intellectuals, thinkers, and writers fulfilled their mission to inform the people? Do you think that the people are more informed? And is it even possible to talk about the people in this way, as an indistinguishable mass?

H.M. Let me quote Nimā. He said: "Knowing isn't enough; or saying isn't enough." We know many things and we say many things, but to what extent have these things turned into matters of conscience for us? This is something that requires a life process. We've been deprived of this life process. We inevitably mimic many things. Many people have gone abroad and have studied at university. But their underlying way of thinking is the same old, worn-out ancestral way of thinking. Part of the mistakes of the intellectual movement in Iran stemmed from these same contradictions.

S.R. Do you think there have been fewer such mistakes since the 1979 revolution?

H.M. The only useful thing about the 1979 revolution was that it brought these contradictions right under the spotlight. For example, look at the work of religious intellectuals in Iran after the 1980s. Religious intellectuals have played a very prominent role in

Iran for at least the past hundred years. And throughout this time, they maintained that "if what we're saying is realized, all the country's problems will be solved!" Mr. Mehdi Bāzargān was one of the most active religious intellectuals. Toward the end of his life, he said, "We were fighting for something all our lives; now, we realize that implementing it is a calamity!" In other words, the revolution gave them the opportunity to bring all their contradictions right under the spotlight. When they saw that what they had imagined did not correspond to the way things had turned out, when they saw that modern life requires its own tools and its own ideas, it forced both us and them to reconsider.

The amount of research that has been carried out over the past thirty years in Iran into the history of our culture exceeds that of the preceding one hundred years. None of this amounts to a return to the past or to the official culture that the government propagates. The Iranian nation has developed the urge to figure out how it got to where it is today and to understand how those who thought they were on the threshold of a golden civilization ended up in this strange crisis. This crisis and the person who, regardless of his motives, left us in this mess has compelled us to think and our thinking has become less hemmed-in. Of course, we still lack a political philosophy and, in fact, we don't have a philosophical system of thinking. The same goes for our literary criticism. The same goes for many other fields too. We are an inward-looking nation. We aren't a wise, wisdom-oriented nation. These years and these experiences have brought us to a point where we've started having doubts about our experiences, and we want to find other meanings for them. This is why, today, religious intellectuals aren't shutting their minds to the views of Western thinkers. For example, twenty years ago, if you'd mentioned Karl Popper to an Iranian intellectual, he might have become agitated and said: "Surely, you can't expect me to read Popper!" Popper is a philosopher who has, on occasion, had fascist and very reactionary views. For example, during the Persian Gulf War, he had a very fascist view (which is, in my view, unexpected in a philosopher). But, today, we read Popper. We believe that part of the truth of Western thinking and civilization is to be found in Popper. In the past, we looked at Marx as a taboo. But, now, for us, Marx's teachings are part of European humanist knowledge. Why did we turn Marx into a rite and a religion, which led to rigid thinking in a segment of our intellectuals? These are some of the gains that we've made over these years and no one has handed them to us on a platter.

In recent years, we've turned to deliberating and studying our past. I think it may well be that the presence of this state has, in a way, induced us to discover our identity. Because, before the revolution, our intellectuals were living with a bunch of theories and the society they were living in was alien to them. But, after the revolution, they started grappling with the people and with society in a very tangible way. And it occurred to them that they should get to know their society, although even the intellectuals in our society are still tied to tradition. They may say modern things too, but, in practice, they haven't been able to free themselves from tradition yet.

S.R. In the West, some analysts call the Iranian revolution "the Iranian experiment." What they mean by this expression is the synthesis of modernity and religion. Do you think this synthesis is feasible? And has Iran had any success in reconciling religion with modernity? This question is based on the fact that there has always been a movement to this end in Iran, since the time of the constitutionalists, to Mossadegh and the national-religious forces, to today. The motivation has always been to create a united front against Western or Eastern imperialism by relying on the rule of justice and religion, on the one hand, and European reason, on the other. Do you think that the Iranian experiment has been successful in this respect? And, finally, do you think that the reconciliation of religion and modernism is a modern phenomenon or a return to the past for Iran, or even, in the words of some Westerners, a return to the Middle Ages?

H.M. Westerners are mistaken in their analysis of the revolution in Iran, because they assess things on the basis of their own models. The analysis that contemporary scholars and analysts offer of our revolution stems from the experience of modernity in the West. Recently, I read an article by a contemporary Western thinker who said that human beings were religion-oriented at one time. Then, in the age of reason, they pulled God down from the sky, in Nietzsche's words! People in the West, or even philosophers in the West, make the inference that, when human beings reached Auschwitz—that is to say, killing on the most massive scale in history—they came to the conclusion that we had lost something in the past and that that something was meaning or spirituality. This tendency may see the Iranian revolution as a kind of return to this meaning or spirituality, but this is not true at all! I mean, if you look at the declarations and statements that were made in 1978 by these same religious leaders that we have in Iran today, you'll see that their emphasis was largely on social justice. They didn't come onto the scene with a promise to create meaning and spirituality. When you look at our religious leaders' speeches, you see that they always revolve around the idea that "they're pillaging our oil," "they're doing this," and "they're doing that."

So we see that the Iranian revolution was not a spiritual revolution. Western analysts make the mistake of thinking that it was a revolution for spirituality! If this tendency emerged in a Western society, where they enjoy prosperity, it could be aimed at achieving meaning and spirituality, but, in the Iranian revolution, "meaning" was not an issue. All the slogans of the religious movement itself were bent on saying: "We'll bring prosperity for the people; we'll set up a democracy for them." They kept saying that the nation's rights had been infringed, and so on and so forth.

Clerics in Iran did not come on to the stage as heralds of new meaning and spirituality (because people already had meaning and religious beliefs). The people didn't carry out a revolution in order to gain religious meaning. The people were under pressure. Intellectuals wanted freedom, which was lacking. There were sharp class differences in Iran. And so on and so forth. This is where the revolution's causes lie: here, in Iran.

S.R. So can we understand the Iranian revolution through the classic Marxist perspective? Can we see it as a historical necessity?

H.M. Although the Iranian revolution's leaders were clerics, it did not take place for the sake of religion. It wasn't for the sake of proving our identity either. Analyzing the Iranian revolution has its own particular complexities, like any other social phenomenon. The Iranian revolution resulted from the incompatibility of the structure of the Shah's state with the realities of modern life. Look, you have to investigate the process through which modernity suffered a reversal in Iran. During Mohammad Reza Shah's time, we had roads, we had freeways, and there were refrigerators in people's homes, so to speak. And people watched television too. We'll set aside, for now, the use to which it was put, culturally speaking. We had all these things. But, the political structure was a very backward structure.

During the reign of the Pahlavis,[60] some strata gained prominence. Universities were being built and some of these people were graduating each year. Iran was producing its own intellectuals. Thanks to oil revenues, some people were coming into money too. But none of the people who were emerging from this system, so to speak, had social or civil rights. I mean, as long as a university professor sang the monarchy's praises, he could continue, but if he put a foot wrong, he'd be dealt with. There wasn't a structure that allowed anyone to speak out. Democracy in the realm of the

---

60   Dynastic name of the last two Shahs of Iran, Reza Shah and Mohammad Reza Shah.

press was being crushed with unyielding, harsh laws. It was the same in the realm of day-to-day life.

Setting Tehran aside, in Iran's villages, people were living in poverty and hardship. I think that if we go back to general analyses and theories, we can, in fact, place the Iranian revolution in the context of Marxist analyses too—if we don't take Marxism to mean some unyielding and rigid law. In other words, a state has appeared and brought along various strata. When you create a factory—for example, Iran Khodro or Iran National,[61] with about twelve hundred workers—the workers gradually lose their rural social mindset and acquire an urban social mindset, and this affects their cultural life. Their kids come into the streets, go to cinemas, etc. The so-called political structure of the Shah's state did not measure up to this infrastructure; it was at odds with it. This can be explained using sociological analyses, which stem from Marx's ideas to a large extent. But the context in which these developments unfolded was a religious context. That is to say, religion has always been and continues to be an inextricable part of the Iranian people's culture. If an Iranian intellectual wants to think about his society today, he has to bear religion in mind as an element of the national culture. But I don't agree with the analysis of Westerners, who say that this was a revolution for spirituality.

S.R. So as many neo-Marxists or post-Marxists are suggesting today, wasn't it a result of economic colonialism or psychologi-

---

61   Iran's biggest carmaker was originally called Iran National; the name was later changed to Iran Khodro (meaning, Iran Automobile).

cal colonialism or cultural colonialism? Didn't we pay the price for being a neighbor of the Soviet Union? Didn't we become a victim of the Cold War—like many other "peripheral" countries—because of Westerners' fear that Iran would be infiltrated by communism?

H.M. Maybe it was a combination of all of these things. In a Marxist analysis, you have to see what factor makes the two structures incompatible. I think that the incompatibility was between the structure of the people's lives and the political structure. In other words, the type of life that that same state—with all its modernization—created for us wasn't compatible with the state's dictatorial structure. We didn't have political parties. There were no civil institutions. And all of these things, in a country that's ruled dictatorially, leads to a revolt. And if the revolt triumphs by using religion as a lever, this doesn't mean that the people revolted for the sake of religion.

S.R. Do you think the 1979 revolution was good for us? For self-knowledge and for constructing our identity?

H.M. This takes us into the realm of value judgments. I think that what happened was beyond our control. We have to analyze it. Declaring it good or bad won't solve anything.

S.R. Is it taking us forward or backward?

H.M. I think that society as a whole is moving forward.

S.R. So we can sum up this movement in one word: paradox. We're living in a historical anomaly or paradox. That is to say, under an absolutist regime, we're becoming democratic. Women are gaining more rights although the suppression of women is part of the state's everyday policies and laws. And political parties are multiplying although suppression is an everyday affair for them too. Newspapers are multiplying although they're constantly being banned.

The question is, what's the role of Iranian writers and artists in such a society? Can we say that these divides that have come about in Iran—these norms and these abnormalities, these paradoxes—have created fertile ground for Iranian writers? How do literary activities now compare with literary activities before the revolution? Especially in view of the fact that, when we go to bookshops, we find that they're full of books, although print runs are small. Why is it that many people feel as if a literary and artistic explosion is taking place in Iran?

H.M. This subject came up once when a number of European writers were at Mr. Javād Mojābi's house, and I was there too. They said: "We envy your situation, because, in your society, intellectuals play a more prominent role." Although I'm happy to learn that they envy Iranian intellectuals, it has to be said that there is a kind of misunderstanding involved in all this! The argument that they were making was that, as long as the Soviet Union existed, with that state, dissident intellectuals played a prominent role, but, now, they've vanished. In other words, literature follows from politics: it's in opposition to the state. In other words, we have to imagine that literature is somewhere within the circle of power.

S.R. So based on this viewpoint, when there's no freedom, literature is more fertile? And freedom is, basically, detrimental to literature, because the bigger your wall, the more windows to freedom you can put in it?

H.M. I think this is a very backward idea. It doesn't hold at all in the real world. Art and literature basically flourish when there's freedom. The idea that the more the hardship, the more productive the literature is incorrect. I mean it turns literature into an element of suffering. Literature is an element for liberating people.

S.R. They say that an individual has to be a captive in order to be liberated.

H.M. No, because freedom is relative. Freedom and justice aren't things that are standing still somewhere, waiting for us to approach them. In fact, they're goals that become more distant the more we move toward them. Anyway, the blossoming of European and American literature over the past century is a strong counterargument to the viewpoint that imagines that literature needs captivity and tyranny to blossom.

S.R. So you think that the politicization of literature is not a necessity?

H.M. Artists don't take their orders from politics. Artists take their orders from life. And political life is part of it. I think it has an impact on the underlying layers of a society's culture. I think that Nimā has a beautiful example in this regard. In the circumstances by which Iran was entering the experience of modern life, Nimā told us that we're a nation that's not very good at looking. Nimā tried to change the way we look at life. Nimā told us to look carefully at the objects around us and to pay attention to the world outside our minds. Isn't this the route that modernity has followed? Nimā turned this into an artistic structure and, in this way, he had an impact on our culture. Today, too, I'm of the view that, if you look, you'll see the reflections of our social life in our art. In our movies, poems, and stories. But if what you mean is that artists turn into political megaphones, then, no, artists have their own political views and artists undoubtedly have their own particular social views. But art isn't about turning into a political megaphone.

S.R. In the West, they say that, when you live in a closed, censorship-ridden system, your literature is richer. Mr. Enzensberger even cites Saadi, Hāfez, and Rumi as examples. He says, look at how subtle their poetry was and how rich their language, and this was because they couldn't say everything openly. Do you agree?

H.M. If that's the case, then, compare T. S. Eliot or Octavio Paz to their contemporaries in Iran. Since these ones were living under a dictatorial state, they should have produced much bigger masterpieces than they did. If that were the case, then, no more artistic masterpieces ought to be created in countries that don't have our kinds of problems, because they're not enduring hardship and misery!

S.R. But your position—as poets, thinkers, and writers—is more important in Iran than that of your colleagues over in the West. One of the examples that Mr. Muschg, the Austrian writer, gives is: "In Iran, when a poet gives a public reading, he can fill a ten-thousand-seat stadium; but we'd hardly be able to draw three hundred people at best!"

H.M. Our social conditions create a particular responsibility. Look at Western intellectuals in France, for example, during the time of Sartre and Simone de Beauvoir. They would initiate a movement in support of something, whether domestic or European or international. Then, a huge intellectual movement would take shape in support of various revolutions, in support of countries that had national demands, and so on.

Iranian intellectuals are, without a doubt, living in particular social conditions, in a society that lacks a democratic or party structure. And because they have a platform, which cannot be easily taken away, they have a particular role to play. I mean, intellectuals have a platform, one way or the other. Their platform is their pen. Their platform is their camera. They have some tools, at any rate. They have a medium at their disposal. This puts them in a special position. But this doesn't determine much in terms of literary or artistic value. I mean, it's not necessarily the case that we should be happy that we live in a less free or more dictatorial or undemocratic society because we can produce fantastic works.

In circumstances where there is pressure, sometimes you have to think of ways to get around it. A few years ago, ten years ago, I saw a play. I think it was something by Brecht, performed by a semi-amateur theatre group. In the play, there was a love scene between a young woman and a young man. Since there are restrictions on love scenes here, the director had had the idea of using fingers instead of the two human beings! That is to say, they were backstage and the two lovers—in the form of a finger dressed as a women and finger dressed as a man—displayed all the erotic moves. This creativity could only have emerged in these particular circumstances. But this isn't a basic principle. We can't say: the more the repression, the more art will flourish. This is a dangerous idea in my view.

The enthusiasm shown for artists in Iran is a mixture of politics and art. It's true that Shāmlu's funeral procession[62] can be seen as an amazing event that was an exception. Shāmlu, on his own, encapsulated all the tendencies of Iranian intellectuals, whether cultural or political, as well as various modes of life. All of this gave Shāmlu a particular historical position, a sensitive, special

---

62   The funeral procession drew a large crowd.

position, which may be unattainable for a Western intellectual. But Shāmlu can't be judged by his funeral procession; he has to be judged by his poetry.

S.R. Finally, in your view—as a poet—isn't writing novels a difficult thing to do here, given the fact that this land has always viewed itself in the mirror of poetry? Europeans see the novel as a phenomenon that is unique to their culture, a culture that has progressed from the Middle Ages to the Renaissance to modernity to postmodernity. In his *Henry Corbin*, Dariush Shāyegān writes that, since we did not become modern and we did not acquire the mind-body or soul-body division that the Europeans did, we didn't need the novel to fill the division. In a place where you have "unity of being," composing poetry is like a revelation from God. Don't you think that it's difficult to write novels in a land where there is illuminationism and mysticism?

H.M. Mr. Shāyegān's analysis is correct. Our literature has been a universalist literature. The novel is the product of modern society, in which the individual plays a fundamental role. In other words, in the novel, it is the individual who speaks. In song and poetry, before modernity, you don't hear the voice of the individual, you hear the voice of the collective. In this sense, poetry has played a central part in our culture. But with the advent of modern life, we see that novels have come into being too. That is to say, since the Constitutionalist Movement, we've gradually started having novelists.

I think that what you said is correct. A subject that's being discussed now in our literary criticism is the question of polyphony or multiple voices. Novel writing is a multivocal art. I mean, if you write a novel with a single voice, it turns into an ancient tale; whereas in a novel, Anna Karenina is supposed to speak for herself. You can't make a pitiless judgment about Anna Karenina before the end of the book and dismiss her out of hand. When you read *Madame Bovary*, you can't fail to sympathize with her now and again, because you can hear Madame Bovary's voice too. Madame Bovary's voice hasn't vanished in a universal, moral judgment. This is how a novel works. This is why the novel was born in Western society, a society that gives priority to individual experience. I think that the enthusiasm shown for novels in Iran in recent years is because we are entering this phase in our social life. This doesn't mean that the same can't be said of our poetry too. The level of enthusiasm for novels has grown, but poetry hasn't been left behind either. That is to say, the same thing has happened in our poetry too. If you cast a general glance at recent poetry, you'll see that the angle from which poets look at society and the subjects they're writing about—this angle has changed. Poets don't speak about things as if they are know-it-alls; they allow everything to appear with its own voice.

Moniru Ravānipur

Born in Bushehr in 1954, her short story collections and novels include *Sanghā-ye Sheytān* (Satan's Stones), *Kanizu* (Kanizu), *Ahl-e Gharq* (The Drowned), *Del-e Fulād* (Heart of Steel), and *Kowli Kenār Ātash* (Gypsy by the Fire). Her works in the field of children's literature and drama include *Rostam az Shāhnāmeh-e Raft* (Rostam Leaves the Shāhnāmeh). She wrote the script for the controversial film *Vākonesh-e Panjom* (The Fifth Reaction) jointly with the film's director, Tahmineh Milāni.

MONIRU RAVĀNIPUR

Ravānipur believes that, after the revolution, literature has been more restricted, not just because of official censorship but also because of a cultural censorship that's characteristic of Iran. She doesn't believe that this phenomenon stems from the Islamic Revolution alone, but also attributes it to the "raped soul" of Iranians, with their invasion-filled history. Despite this constraint, she believes that, on the whole, the experience of the revolution has been of undeniable importance for the development of Persian literature, because the Islamic Revolution has been a boon for Iranian society's self-knowledge and for stripping away religious and traditional delusions. And the fact that writers have had to grapple with society's revolutionary situation has contributed to contemporary literature's progress. She is of the view that possibly the revolution's most important service to Persian literature was that it freed good literature from being "politics-ridden." That is to say, writers and poets are now learning to express their political and social commitment in a literary form without falling into the trap of sloganeering (as was the case before the revolution). At the same time, Ravānipur is certain that contemporary Iranian literature will pull a revolution-stricken society out of the identity crisis from which it has been suffering over the past twenty-five years and help Iranians gradually to construct their true identity.

Ravānipur is of the view that the new developments in Iranian society have helped the growth of the novel, to the point where it can boldly be said that the novel has replaced poetry as society's "mirror" for self-reflection. She believes that this is because Iranian society is throwing away the "reveries" on which Persian poetry has relied for hundreds of years and is looking at itself and its own position in the world with a "realistic" eye. This is why Ravānipur does not consider herself an artistic outcast at all—i.e., in her capacity as the writer of works within an imported genre—and she describes the novel as a global and an Iranian phenomenon.

For Ravānipur, as a writer, being a woman is important, but now, with the passage of time, it has become less important. She sees her writing like "a child growing up," a child who, thanks to an accumulation of experiences, has learned to distance herself from her emotions and to write "easier." But Ravānipur still considers it pivotal to write from a child's perspective in as much as she wants to show social issues to the reader in a new light, to use this technique to make the ordinary seem extraordinary. For Ravānipur, writing is basically a way of being committed on social issues, and this is why she thinks that writing is like having hope. She sees hope especially in writing of "love," not of mystical and celestial love, but of earthly love, between a woman and a man.

SHIVA RAHBARAN: The first question is a general question about democracy in Iran. What impression do Iranians have of democracy? Do they think that it is a good form of government? Are they aware of the dangers of populism—like the dangers of the referendum at Hitler's time that led to dictatorship? And have Iranian thinkers performed their mission in terms of explaining democracy and its highs and lows? And, finally, a related general question: many people think that, in view of Iranians' rites, traditions, and history, democracy is basically not suited to them. What do you think?

MONIRU RAVĀNIPUR: I think that if we consider our own intellectuals, they've been under so much pressure that they don't think of the dangers of democracy anymore! That's one point. Then, there's the fact that we're the sort of people who like to solve the problem that we've got without thinking about the problems that will follow. That's the second point. But what's a populist regime going to do to people anyway? Strangle them? Jail them? Maybe prevent them from publishing their books? We've experienced all of these things! The only thing that we haven't experienced is democracy. We want to experience that too, to get a taste of it!

Well, many of our friends were being persecuted by the authorities in 1998 and, as I'm sure you know, some of them were done away with.[63] The points that you made are for a society that has experienced many things, that has had years of democracy. Although amassing power is possible in any system, each in a different way. Everyone, regardless of what they say and regardless of their ideology, comes with the aim of hammering in a nail and ends up chopping off a head. History is full of these things. They've come to power with many claims and then ev-

---

63   See Note 46 under Ali Ashraf Darvishiān, page 126.

eryone gasps at their behavior! They haven't let anyone breathe. The thing that's clear to me as a writer is that individual freedom should be respected. No one should meddle in anyone else's private life. People shouldn't be considered guilty first and then be proven innocent. We should assume that everyone is innocent. If someone does something wrong and if what they did was harmful to society, only then should we put them on trial. We're faced with a bunch of people in this country—and we always have been (they're far fewer at the moment of course)—who think that everyone is guilty, unless proven otherwise!

It goes without saying that what you, in Europe, have in mind when you speak of sexual freedom, for example, is not what we have in mind. Because we—and everyone who is striving for freedom here—are traditionalists in a way, deep down inside. This stems from our general culture. We have nothing against democracy. What I want is for young people to be able to speak to each other very easily in the streets. And I don't think there's anything wrong with them being friends. But I don't by any means want to see, here, the sort of things that come out of democracy—which I've seen in Europe. And I don't pretend otherwise. I don't want to be such a broad-minded intellectual as to say that this is a stable and everyone can do whatever they like! Those sex shops and those cabarets and so on. As an intellectual who grew up in this country, my starting point is that I take a dim view of that sort of thing. But I'd like coffee shops to be free enough so that, instead of buying heroin, people can sit in coffee shops and enjoy each other's company and chat! I want Europe's culture and civilization, not the things that come from opening the window. When you open the window, you get both dirt and dust, and fresh air. I want fresh air. But we have to pay the price in terms of dirt and dust too.

Another thing is that we writers are very sensitive to everything around us! As a writer, I'm in a better position to know what's what, especially because of the kind of life I've led. I'm in contact with people constantly and I see the pressure on them and I see its psychological consequences. What I'm saying is this: how long must this furtiveness continue? I want everything to be in the open. I don't want to see people have two lives, a day life and a night life. Things should be simple. When you're constrained, when you're being controlled, you have to hide some things. This way, people become complicated. I think a human being is like a narcissus. They should be what they are. They shouldn't have to hide things and be forced to spend energy on some aspects of their life. For example, I write stories. It's really stupid if I have to go to someone who knows nothing about story writing and hear them tell me to take out this paragraph, put in that paragraph!

We use swear words in our dialogues, in everyday conversations. But the official censorship eliminates these dialogues. We say, "Your mother is a whore"; "Your sister is a cunt!" We can't write these things. But how can you expect a society not to have these things? These expressions, these words, they've been created and they've entered the language over a period of years and years. Are we supposed to throw them away?! Can't be done! So they're writing these things in secret. They stash them in a corner, so that they can publish them one day. This is the simplest form of what I'm talking about. There are worse ones. This is why I think that we've done what we could, we writers of this land—within the scope of what we know.

We tend to rely on our own experiences, rather than on global knowledge. Speaking for myself, I'm fighting because of my own experiences, not because of global knowledge. Because, for quite some time, we had no contacts with the world. Fortunately, more recently—with the onslaught of published books, translations, the different ideas of Europe and East and West—we're reading things. I have no problem with this. I like to breathe in fresh air and I'm fighting for us to gain freedom and democracy. But the kind of democracy that we need is different. This is natural. The world isn't a hen coop! We blend, produce, and mix our own culture into everything, and it becomes something new. We like to see the merging of these ideas benefit the Iranian human being who lives on this earth, who has the right to live well, and who has the right not to be subjected to inquisitions all the time. This is one side of it. And the other side of it is that we don't just face official censorship. We also face a very private, insidious, cultural censorship, all of which, in my view, arises from the reactions that we see among our own people. This is because we have a soul that has been raped. Iran was raped over many, many years. This nation and our history are riven with invasions. We've had to develop cultural intricacies. We've had to have traditions and tricks in order to survive, in order to preserve ourselves. Now, we have to learn that, in a free society, people don't have to play so many tricks to stay alive. I want to see a society in which people don't have to use any tricks in order to stay alive, to stand up, to breathe.

S.R. This takes us to the history of this raped soul, this injured mind that has to act in this way. Over the past hundred years, one of the methods that we've always used to try to prevent the assaults by colonialist foreign powers and their attempts to sow dissension in Iran—as well as to unify people—is to try to join up religion and modernity. I'm thinking of the Constitutional Revolution, Mossadegh and the National Front, other national-religious movements, and the 1979 revolution. In the West, some analysts describe this kind of movement and revolution as "the Iranian experiment" and they consider it an "anomaly" or "paradox." Do you think that this synthesis is feasible? Have we had any luck to this end over the past hundred years?

M.R. Let me tell you that you can measure someone's kindness, but you can't measure someone's savagery. When someone wants to turn savage, when power is without limits or bounds, when power is not controlled by laws and is based on total obedience, this will inevitably have consequences. So it seems to me that religion has manifested itself in movements against this [absolute power] and against the obstacles that human beings have faced for many, many years. It has been a step forward, a kind of rebellion. Then, some people come and want to stake a claim to this heritage and, without any creative thinking, they want to take a society forward in the twenty-first century [using religion]. This can't be done! Everything has its own ways and means.

My mother and father are Muslims, and they were born in a Shiite country. As for myself, I believe in God in many moments of my life. I have my own particular beliefs—the beliefs that are particular to southern Iran. I have all of these things. All of these things must serve the human being. When an ideology becomes an impediment to human beings' progress and when it doesn't serve anyone, then you have to doubt it! You have to think: well, religion is something that concerns my inward life, me and my God. What, for example, does religion have to say about the highway code? This is something that demands modern laws, laws that are particular to driving in the modern world.

Religion has given us some things, some general things. Very good. Many of these things are right to some extent for human beings' survival. For example, be kind—I'm talking about Christianity. Don't be violent. Now, what happens when a priest in the Middle Ages burns a woman thinker as a witch and wants to impose his own belief on the people? We have to protest. Any writer or thinker has to protest.

I think that, in order to take a country forward, in order to have democracy, we have to use other countries' experiences. The same goes for our scientists. And, with creative thinking and bearing in mind our own correct traditions and correct beliefs, we have to create a framework that strives to merge all these things to the benefit of Iranian human beings—or to the benefit of human beings in whichever region they may be living.

S.R. So in your view, has this synthesis of religion and the state been a step forward, despite all the harms, or have we gone backward?

M.R. No, I think this has been a step forward. Don't look at superficial appearances. We were suffering from delusions ourselves. We were suffering from superstitions in a way. When the revolution happened, women threw their lipstick and blush into the streets and said, "We're not going to wear makeup." Anyway, they've realized that beauty isn't a bad thing. If this hadn't happened, we wouldn't have realized that beauty isn't a bad thing! Also, for example, women want a lock or two of their hair to show despite the fact that they're wearing headscarves, whereas before, they were just tying an ugly square piece of cloth on their heads and that was that. Now, if things become open and free again, all these women may go back under the chador, because all these sorts of things are just counterreactions. This was a difficult experience for us, but it was a good experience. We've found ourselves. We've found our essence, our roots.

I remember, in the early days after the revolution, I was in Bushehr. Everyone was excited and they were saying, "Pull out the grass and plant vegetables!" This stemmed from the Chinese revolution. So they pulled out the grass, but they didn't plant anything! Now, there's a crater there, full of flies. These are childish emotions. I think we've put our childish emotions behind us now. We've reached a kind of maturity from within and we needed this. We hadn't had this experience before.

S.R. How do artists and thinkers view their role in Iranian society today? Also, how do they view themselves now in view of the fact that the former regime's policies made it very difficult for artists to work in Iran?

M.R. We've fought hard to obtain what we have. It's thanks to our own efforts that libraries are full of books. We paid with our own blood to win these facilities. Some of us were killed. There were members of the Writers' Association who were strangled. We were under the worst kind of pressure, but we kept working and we won what we have today. Nobody gave them to us on a platter. The other side has realized after twenty years that it, too, has changed now. You know, when slabs of rock break off a mountain, they keep rolling down until they finally become round and fall into the river. This is how it was with us. In fact, all of us, all the people who you're interviewing now, had their clenched fists raised in the air during the revolution. But I don't think there's anyone in this group who would go and raise their clenched fists for no reason now! We've put that historical experience behind us. We've learned that shouting and raising clenched fists in the air and chanting slogans doesn't lead anywhere. Don't tire yourself out! And the fist may turn around and punch you in the face!

It's thanks to our own efforts that we've gained what we have. And the other side, too, kept advancing through a process of trial and error. They kept stumbling and getting back up. They caused their own errors, because they're sincere people! We have a lot of people who went forward sincerely and fought in the war. I mean they weren't motivated by greed and love of power. And they weren't that young either. These people went to the fronts for the love of God and they lost their lives. And some people survived with their love of God and became aware of the errors they'd made. Until we got to where we are today, when the books you see are being published. Never in our history have we had so many books being published. Even professional writers can't keep up with it all. A vast army of women is writing books. And they're writing so well that it's amazing. And there's a huge army of young people who want to make films. A huge army of young people want to paint. The reason for this is that we don't have those political reveries anymore. A segment of the population has set political reveries aside. And the ones who are still seeking the reveries of the past with the hope of following some leader or other—I think there are very few of them.

S.R. So we can say that the divides and anomalies of Iranian society today have created fertile ground for Iranian literature.

M.R. Possibly. Literature mainly comes into being in hardship, confinement, and wretchedness. Of course, it's much better if you're free to do as you like. But the fact of the matter is that we've always written on the basis of reactions and problems. I remember I had a psychology professor who always used to say: "Life is solving problems." I'm an adventurous person; I don't know about others. I said in an interview once: "I don't like straight roads at all! You fall asleep at the wheel!" A road should have lots of twists and turns. You're alert. You have a challenge with yourself and with your surroundings. The challenge shouldn't be beyond your endurance. It should be something that, if you get the better of it, you can get a taste of victory. When it's so bad that it's unendurable, it destroys you. In the same way that it can destroy you, it can also give you wings. I like artists who, despite all these obstacles and despite all the chaos all around them, can remain strong, fight, and take their work forward. In *Man's Search for Meaning*, by the writer-psychologist Frankl, he says that the ones who had suffered hardship were better able to endure things at Auschwitz. They were more likely to survive than the ones who had always had their breakfast and lunch prepared for them, and who used to go for strolls in the countryside with Mummy and Daddy! These ones couldn't endure the suffering.

A friend of mine called me and said that the World Trade Center towers had been blown up. I said, We've endured no end of bombings and missile attacks. Why are they so scared just because they've hit these buildings! When five thousand people were attacked with chemical weapons at Halabjah, the whole world played deaf and dumb. Now, what do you expect me to do?! Of course, the blowing up of the New York towers was a sad story. But I've read so many stories like it. I told my friend: It's as if it's the first time you're hearing about something being blown up somewhere!

S.R. Is the suffering that you're talking about—the suffering that leads to creativity—the heritage of Iranian poets and writers? Have you inherited this responsibility?

M.R. We have a cultural heritage of resistance. This has become a model for Iranian thinkers, for Iranian writers: this heritage of resistance.

S.R. Doesn't resistance make art politicized?

M.R. Yes, up to now. If we hadn't had the experience of the Islamic Republic, we'd be making the same mistakes in our literary works; I mean being overexcited, politics-ridden, revolution-loving. Fortunately, the experience of the past twenty years threw us all together and brought us face to face with reality. We can touch it. Because we can see our roots. And, when we see our roots, like it or not, we think differently. Of course, this isn't the whole story. If this experience also connects with the global experience, then we can do something really impressive. I mean, once we're familiar with global literature too. Artistic work can be political but not be politics-ridden.

S.R. Some people believe that writing novels is very difficult in a land that has always looked at itself in the mirror of poetry. The Europeans see the novel as a phenomenon that's unique to their culture, a culture that has moved from the Middle Ages to the Renaissance to modernity to postmodernity. Dariush Shāyegān has written, in his book *Henry Corbin*, that the novel was born in the division between the mind and the body that came about within Europeans from the Renaissance onward. So the novel tries to close this divide and to reach a kind of "unity of being." But here, where we have illuminationism and mysticism, there's no divide within Iranians and it is as if poetry is a revelation from God. So this makes things difficult for the novel. Don't you think that writing novels is difficult in such a mystical land?

M.R. I think all that stuff is dead and buried! This is why people are turning to novels. Because now the body is important for people. People used to be in outer space and they'd write: "I care nothing for my body!" These are reveries woven in outer space. They're dreams that didn't turn into reality. Heavenly dreams. Reveries. When we hit a wall (until we do, we don't think about it), when our skulls hit a wall, then we can't separate mind and body and say, "We're doing these things for our minds." I think this sort of thinking is nearing its expiration date. It's on its last gasps. When someone comes on TV and talks about spirituality, a few youngsters are sitting there and watching. I think that when the program is over, they'll go out, light up their cigarettes, and commit their first offense in the next street! I mean I think the time for pretty, lifeless sentences that just dangle in midair is finished in this country! We've come face to face with so many bitter realities, we've had so much misfortune dumped on our heads that I couldn't even begin to add it all up. There's a whole army of women writing right now and none of them are writing about spirituality.

S.R. So what about a poet like Rumi?

M.R. Rumi stays where he is. Rumi did what he had to do in his own age, in the historical and cultural circumstances of his day. When I go on a trip and I get a mosquito bite and my face swells up, "We're from above and thence we'll return" doesn't cut it with me! First, we have to teach this mosquito a lesson it won't soon forget. Then, if we don't have any mosquitoes left, we can sit and read Rumi's poetry! It's good for when we're sitting quietly at home. It's good for people who've got everything they need! They can listen to it in America. I can tell you, a lot of people in our country are against this sort of thing. They can listen to it in America. They can cross their legs and listen to Madonna sing! It's not for me. I do enjoy it, but when there are so many problems here, when a bunch of university students come and tell me, "We want to make a film but we don't have any money; find a producer for us," I really want to go and find a producer for them instead of reading Rumi!

S.R. So as a novelist, you don't consider yourself an artistic outcast in Iran?

M.R. No. Why should I? Everyone around me is grappling with the same realities now. Not many people in this country go for the mystical states that you're talking about. I don't think there are many of them. It's over on the other side that they're going on about mysticism or playing at being dervishes.

S.R. I think it's because of the identity crisis that Iranians are suffering in "exile" abroad.

M.R. In fact, we used to suffer from an identity crisis. Now, we're finding it. Now, we're sensing it with our flesh and blood. We're gradually shaping our identity. What they were giving us as an identity in the past was a fantasy. We're constructing our real identity now.

S.R. Through literature?

M.R. Whether through literature or through existence and being there.

S.R. Do you feel that the novel form belongs to you? I mean, do you not feel that the novel is something that has been imposed on you by the West?

M.R. The shirt I'm wearing is European, but it doesn't look bad on me. But the long coat and headscarf that they've given me here look terrible on me! It's true that I've got my own shirts too. I'm from the south and I have my own beautiful clothes. I wear them and I look very pretty in them! But the fact of the matter is that you can't wear these clothes in the cold in Tehran or in the cold in Munich! Come on now, the earth is perfectly round these days. Don't you know?! The earth has become small! No, things aren't like that. I want to show you lots of things in Europe that were being used a long time ago in Iran. The straw that you put in your glasses to sip your drinks, Darius and Xerxes, the Achaemenid kings, used to sip their water through it! Human beings give each other their experiences. Land borders are being done away with! Then, they say that that story isn't ours, it belongs to someone else! Who knows who it belongs to? Have you read *The Thousand and*

One Nights or *Sinbad*? Many of those films, images, and serials were based on Sinbad. The main theme of *The Thousand and One Nights* appears in many Western stories, novels, and films. If we share our experiences, the world will become beautiful.

S.R. Aren't you afraid of this doing away with borders? Of the possibility that someone may lose their culture in this universal homeland?

M.R. No, cultures won't be destroyed because artistic human beings are creative. They take beautiful things and reconstruct them. They constantly construct things. When I lived in the south, we had these tales, and the tales were made up by the people there. They're making up tales now too, but they're a bit different from the tales of the past.

Look, when it has to, anything that has to cease to exist ceases to exist. I can't wear this dress in Munich, but I can wear it on a special occasion! Some things are destined to cease to exist. Cultures don't cease to exist; they merge. They take new shapes. For example, we only have a name left of the Sumerians and the Chaldeans now. But how do you know, maybe one of your actions or gestures now is Sumerian. You can't separate things. In a way, a human being is the product of past human beings' intellectual and cultural struggles and their struggle for survival. Whether it is Dante writing in Italy, Toni Morrison writing in America, or Isabel Allende. Now, since we have closer relations, because of mass media, well, the impact is quicker.

If a day comes when all the flowers in the world are the same color, then all of humanity will have a single culture. It's totally impossible! People have different temperaments. They construct cultures, they construct tales, they construct beliefs.

S.R. Don't you worry about cultural exploitation?

M.R. No, these fears are senseless and baseless. There's no such thing as cultural exploitation. This sort of talk is outdated. I take anything that I like. Come on! This nation likes films! You prevent them. A guy holds his wife's hand, you prevent it! Well, then, they go and watch a pornographic film in their own home! So are you to blame for the [West's] cultural onslaught or are they?! If you made it easy for people to see the films they like, then this wouldn't happen.

S.R. I get the impression that being a woman is very important to you. Don't you think that this kind of focus on a writer or poet's gender harms their art? Some people think that a focus on gender reduces their creative power.

M.R. Yes, my writing was like a growing child. At first, I was shouting, "They're raping women." But now, if you read my most recent work, *Frankfurt Airport*, you'll see that there's nothing about women being raped and so on. I did my shouting! Like a toddler walking on all fours. Now, I'm walking like a grownup. Now, I can see that injustice is always injustice, regardless of the circumstances. You can't say, "Why is there injustice against women but not against men?"

As a woman, I like being a mother. I love my child. A woman is capable of becoming a mother. A woman is capable of loving others and is, basically, less violent. I like these traits and characteristics. Well, now I've moved away from the rage that I originally started writing with. I can write more easily now.

S.R. You mean you feel that you've crossed the gender boundary in your writing?

M.R. Yes.

S.R. The first time I read *Kanizu*, I was devastated. Before coming here, I read it again and I found it just as delicate. It becomes stronger if anything when you reread it. You have a very delicate and strange sensitivity toward people who have been treated unjustly; here, it is women who have been treated unjustly. It is women who have been defeated, who wanted to become free and find their feet but didn't succeed. Do you think there's no hope that people who have been wronged will find their feet?

M.R. Yes, there is. When I write, there's hope. When a writer writes about these people, there's hope. Someone somewhere is paying attention to them. There's hope. Definitely. And I'm writing about this hope.

S.R. It seems as if writing from the perspective of children is an important technique for you.

M.R. Let the child see these things and find them strange. As grown-ups, what we do is ordinary for us. We don't hear the sound of the sea anymore. All these things are ordinary for us. I write from the perspective of children because they're not "used to" seeing things; they're still discovering the world.

Sometimes I see street walkers who are very young, fourteen or fifteen years old and with so much makeup on. It makes my heart ache. There's no sex education here; no one talks about it. And the fact that there's no sex education leads to its own horrors. This sort of thing happens a lot in Afghanistan now. They sell their children, their daughters. I think it's happening a lot less in Iran. Maybe it doesn't happen at all and anyone who talks about it is talking about the distant past. Because I visit villages too and, now, girls in villages prefer to run away and come to Tehran. Well, of course; they've found a way out.

You find this kind of thing in Europe too. I was visiting Paris and in the city there's an area where these kinds of women stand on the sidewalk. The face of one of them still sticks in my mind. I'm sure she'd come from Eastern Europe and was doing what she was doing because she didn't have any choice. I didn't talk to her but the anxiety, the sordidness, and the suffering that I saw in her face—in the heart of Paris—made me turn around for a second glance at that Mary-like face. And there was a black woman next to her who was standing there with pride! She was just practicing her profession and it didn't worry her at all. You could tell from her gestures that she was made for the job and she didn't give a fuck about anything! Basically, she behaved just like a man. I don't feel sorry for those women. She likes doing this. But the ones who do it with suffering, it really makes me feel sorry.

S.R. When I read contemporary Iranian literature—and when I discuss it with a lot of people—I feel as if there's very little space for love.

M.R. Read my *Kowli Kenār Ātash* (Gypsy by the Fire) and see what love is! All the woman's troubles are because she's in love with a man. Because in this society, they've lumped her in with the gypsies. She's a gypsy girl. One day, someone who is visiting the area over the New Year vacation meets the man, falls in love with him, and escapes with him. The gypsy woman spends her whole life looking for him and then she finds herself.

S.R. When you show these things and when you talk about a woman's stubborn love, do you see yourself as an iconoclast?

M.R. Sure. I don't accept many traditions. I say that a woman who's not in love is completely useless! Human life hangs on love. Can you picture it? Not celestial love. Earthly love. The love of a man for a woman. Bed! You have to go and "love in bed!" [Ravānipur says "love in bed" in English.] That's love. Sighing behind a window and playing at Layli and Majnun! It's been done so many times.

So has Khosrow and Shirin.[64] Seven or eight hundred years have passed since then and no one does that sort of thing any more. They just talk about it. I mean, our society has a night version and a day version now. No one falls in love in this country at all! This is our misfortune. Everyone does "love in bed," but they do "love in bed" without love. This is bad. I say, love! And love leads to that. It leads to you taking the hand of the man or the woman you love and going together to a coffee shop. Going for a stroll. And maybe you'll give yourself to him. It's so sordid when two people who didn't know each other until yesterday go and sleep together! Unless they're so screwed up in their minds that they're greedy for sex. It needs to have a tender psychological prelude. Can you imagine sleeping with just anyone that easily?!

S.R. Why can't you explain this "love in bed" in a literary form, whereas you can describe the bad aspects of being in bed? For example, when a young woman is destroyed on her wedding night. I mean, why is showing lovemaking in bed harder than showing rape? Is it because of the official censorship or our society's taboos?

M.R. Where's the woman who was at ease in bed? She's always been forced. Her father found her a husband, or her clan. Who chooses for herself?

S.R. But it's not like that today.

---

64   Layli and Majnun, and Khosrow and Shirin are Eastern literature's equivalents of Romeo and Juliet.

M.R. We know it's happened recently.

S.R. You mean the practice hasn't been done away with despite the Islamic Revolution?

M.R. I'm sorry to have to tell you: people don't fall in love. This means that love no longer exists. You don't know this.

S.R. Hasn't this absence of love and that intensification of sexuality among the young led to a kind of emancipation for girls and women? I mean, hasn't the old fear of male sexuality diminished because of all the furtiveness and the absence of love?

M.R. This is another matter. It has a totally sociological and psychological basis, which would require a very lengthy argument. But I'm prepared to argue over it with you. A nine-year-old girl can learn about sexual violence in one of two ways: Either like Golpar[65] or like most kids in Europe. Where has the sexual freedom in Europe taken people? When I go there, I see that they have

---

65   A character in "The Long Night" by Ravānipur published in an anthology of Persian fiction (in translation) entitled *Stories from Iran: An Anthology of Persian Short Fiction from 1921–1991* (Mage Publishers, 1992). The following is a passage from a review of the book: "In 'The Long Night,' an Iranian village lies awake, terrorized, as it listens to the sounds of a young girl's screaming. Trying to escape the sound, the villagers close their doors and their shutters, and command their children to sleep. But for a whole week, the screaming has not stopped, and now children are begging their mothers to help their friend. There has been a wedding. Golpar, the child bride, has been given away by her mother to a much older man, her own Uncle Ebrahim, in return for a few bracelets, a headscarf, and two pairs of shoes . . ." (*Los Angeles Times*, July 19, 1992)

a problem too. They have a problem. They're lonely in a way. How can you get to know someone at night? This ends up as a kind of loneliness. We don't want to reach that loneliness. We have a lot of things that have to do with love in our literature. We have a lot of love poems. What I'm saying is that we have to merge this love into a means to sexuality. I mean we should love someone. Not just spend the night. And when you wake up the next morning you feel terrible! Because your loneliness is still there.

We have certain beliefs in our subconscious. You experience constant recriminations and become totally mental because you're hiding something. And no one loves you and you don't love anyone! People don't live to have sexual relations; people live to love someone. Here, too, it's become like that. They get into bed and then they say: "Bye-bye!" First, you have to be friends.

S.R. You mean you see a kind of cultural schizophrenia?

M.R. Yes, totally.

S.R. You spoke earlier of the schizophrenia of society and the revolution, and now you've arrived at mental schizophrenia. It seems as if this sense of split (or multiple) personalities has been fruitful for Iranian art and literature.

M.R. No, we haven't got there yet. The stages that we've been experiencing in recent years, since the war, haven't matured for us yet. But they'll appear in our literature in the future.

S.R. Maybe it's because of censorship that we don't talk about it?

M.R. No, it hasn't become accepted practice yet. It's still a shock.

S.R. We're still in a state of shock?

M.R. No; it's a shock for me as an artist. I grew up with something that said: First, love, then bed. Now, we see that a culture is very slyly growing under the surface that says: First, bed, then bed, then bed! In other words, something is changing. We have to get used to it. It will take time before we get used to it. Of course, I've written it in *Kowli Kenār Ātash*. I refer to three women, who are prostitutes, and the *Kowli* (gypsy) goes with them. She's effectively selling her body, but she does it under a religious cover. Each day, she gets into a temporary marriage contract with someone.

S.R. Don't social taboos and self-censorship play a big role here?

M.R. They do. We've grown up in a culture that makes self-censorship part of our being. Why do you insist that I can't write about bed or "love in bed" properly? My mind censors itself subconsciously. They've told me, "Don't say it, don't say it!" It'll take a long time before we're rid of this. Of course, there are some people [who are exceptions], like Mandanipour. In *Del va Deldādegi* (The Courage of Love), he presents some very beautiful ideas about war. The guy is a pederast! He's taken a soldier and is servicing him, at the battlefront.

S.R. But it's still very oblique.

M.R. That's right; it's still oblique. Sometimes I think that Hāfez said things much more explicitly than we do. Or Rumi, for example; there are points at which he's said things that they hardly allow to be published today. He names the sexual organ!

For example, I have a scene where a couple sleeps together. In fact, it's a man and a woman's wedding night. My protagonist marries. Well, I can't show them in bed. And I don't know how to anyway! I put them at sea, where there's fishing. He's fishing. He moves the oars and this is their lovemaking, at sea. There's just the fisherman and his boat. That's it. I've described the lovemaking from start to finish. The breathing, the moans; I've said everything. This is how you take language into your own hands. We're clever enough to take our own language in our own hands!

S.R. Do you consider yourself to be one of Forough Farrokhzād's children?

M.R. No, not at all. She was someone and I'm someone else. What does Forough Farrokhzād's children mean anyway? My life started somewhere which had absolutely nothing to do with her. This corpse-loving, single-god nation always latches on to someone, but, while they're alive, they couldn't give a fuck about them!

S.R. Now, I'm going to ask you a question that I was asked myself. Some people see the study of (contemporary) Persian literature—

especially by people who come from the West—as a kind of tool for exploiting this culture again. They even see it as redoubled colonialism in as much as this type of research takes the Iranian soul hostage as well. Do you see it like this too?

M.R. This is the kind of thinking that imagines that everyone is a spy. No one should do any research in this country because it would benefit the British! Well, pull up your socks. Wipe your nose. Mind your own chickens! What nonsense. You can't close off one part of the world from the rest of the world. We shouldn't speak because it might benefit someone? What for? To preserve what? So that they flog us a bit less? Come on. I'm opposed to flogging, to jailing, to torture, to all of these things. Should I keep quiet and pretend they don't exist? (Although, of course, it's much less now, but it does exist.)

If the Westerners hadn't come, we would have remained untouched. We'd be living in tents. And you'd have fifty children hanging on your shirttail. And one of them would have trachoma, for example. Another would have diarrhea. Yesterday, on TV, they showed a scene from Afghanistan where they were inoculating children against polio. Weren't the Taliban natives of Afghanistan? They used to gather people in the football stadium and execute them. Their leisure activity had become watching executions! What sort of exploitation is that and what sort of independence is this?! We shouldn't talk about East and West. We should say, an accomplishment of human culture. How can you expect a human being who lives on planet Earth not to use the accomplishments of human culture?

This country's officials have a closed, Iranian outlook. This means that anyone who wants to carry out research doesn't have a positive outlook! Come on. This way of looking at people is suspiciousness to the point of illness. We're constantly hearing this sort of thing on radio and TV. Just take a blond person to a village and they'll say that he's a spy! Unfortunately, it's become a cultural thing. In the TV series "Dear Uncle Napoleon"[66] there's a character who keeps saying, "It's the work of the British! It's the work of the British!" Whatever happens, he says, "It's the work of the British!"

We suffer more at our own hands than at the hands of others. The one who leads us to perdition is not outside; it's us. The flight from freedom is within our own being, not outside. No one comes to instill the flight from freedom into us.

S.R. Maybe they come and stoke the flame?

M.R. It has to exist for them to be able to stoke the flame. Why can't they stoke in Sweden? This doesn't happen in Sweden. There's fertile ground for it here.

Why can't the Taliban come to power in Iran? Why? Because we know better now. Until the time when we know better, everyone can use us. If someone is a donkey, people will ride him, one way or the other.

---

66 Based on a very popular, satirical novel by Iraj Pezeshkzad. The novel is now available in English as *My Uncle Napoleon*, trans. Dick Davis (Washington, DC: Mage Publishers, 2000).

We shouldn't make contact with the world because they'll come and spy on us?! What are they going to take that they haven't taken already? Anything that's weak dies. This is a necessity in a biological organism. All weak things die. If you're a man and you have something to say, you have to step into the ring and defend what you've got, not hide away at home. This hiding is a kind of Eastern narcissism, which is obsessed with what it already has. The business of exchanging experiences doesn't reach us here.

We have a shared world. Our artists and thinkers have a shared psyche. This is why Chomsky exists in America too. It's not just Bush, saying we'll do this to you and we'll do that to you! Chomsky remembers how his country was built. It's up to us to remind governments what being human means.

SHAHRIĀR MANDANIPOUR

Born in Shiraz in 1957, his short story collections and novels include *Sāyehhā-ye Ghār* (Shadows of the Cave), *Hashtomin Ruz-e Zamin* (The Earth's Eighth Day), *Mumiā va Asal* (The Mummy and Honey), *Del va Deldādegi* (The Courage of Love, a novel in two volumes), *Māh-e Nimruz* (Midday Moon), *Abi-ye Māvarā-ye Bahār* (Ultramarine Blue), and *Sharq-e Banafsheh* (Violet Orient).

Arvāheh Shahrzād (Shahrzad's Ghosts) is his latest work in the field of literary criticism.

[Mandanipour has been living in the USA in recent years and a book of his, *Censoring an Iranian Love Story*, has been published recently in an English translation by Sara Khalili (New York: Vintage Books, 2010). —Trans.]

SHAHRIĀR MANDANIPOUR

Mandanipour believes that the 1979 revolution was a historical necessity that should have occurred a hundred years ago, at the time of the Constitutionalist Movement, but instead triumphed much later, on the threshold of the twenty-first century. This historical delay also reflects Iran's socio-literary delay in entering the age of modernity. Be that as it may, Mandanipour sees the Islamic Revolution as a necessary phenomenon which, one way or the other, helped take Iranian society and literature forward. He is of the view that, after the reversal that the Iranian nation suffered in the coup against Mossadegh, the current experience is the only opportunity for contemporary literature to attain a kind of Iranian—as opposed to imported and assembled—modernism.

One of the most important effects of the Islamic Revolution on contemporary literature is that today's young writers avoid producing politics-ridden works. Mandanipour has nothing against a poet being politically and socially committed, but he believes that the good poet is one who refrains from "sloganeering" under the guise of literature.

He believes that another of the Islamic Revolution's main effects in the realm of literature is the phenomenon of censorship from on high. He is aware that, over the bulk of Iranian history, the poet and the writer have been burdened with censorship, but, since the Islamic Revolution, this phenomenon has taken on bizarre forms, which are very detrimental to literature. Nonetheless,

Mandanipour does not reject literary restrictions altogether, because restrictions also contribute to intricate literary forms and the attainment of meaning. Mandanipour believes that literature's maneuverings between these restrictions and the various aspects of censorship open up a space for creativity in artistic works, as well as creating a space for thinking in the reader's mind, thereby helping society achieve freedom and progress. He attributes the unprecedented growth of Persian literature over the past two and a half decades to the success of these maneuverings.

Mandanipour does not agree with the idea that since the novel was originally a European phenomenon, it takes second place to poetry in Iran. He, too, like Dowlatābādi, points to Persian romances, such as *Samak Ayyār* and *Eskandarnāmeh*,[67] and maintains that modern Persian literature and modern Western literature largely rest on a similar foundation. Of course, he acknowledges that the fact that Iranian society fell behind Europe in attaining the products of modernity, such as the complex demography of urban life, democracy, and industrialism, left the Persian novel weaker than the European one, because these phenomena produced factors such as realism, polyphony, and multifaceted composition, which are necessary for writing a good novel and which are hard to find in contemporary Persian

---

67   There are a number of works by this name in Persian. The earliest *Eskandarnāmeh* was roughly based on *Alexander Romance* by pseudo-Callisthenes which consisted of tales about Alexander the Great. The Persian work also included stories from the Koran and Iranian tales, and is thought to have been written in the eleventh century. (For *Samak Ayyār*, see Note 11 under Mahmoud Dowlatābādi, page 24.)

novels. But Mandanipour believes that the main reason for the backwardness of the contemporary Persian novel, as well as poetry, lies elsewhere. He attributes it to "the slumber of the Persian language," which started in the fifteenth century and reached its lowest point under the Qajar Dynasty.

Mandanipour sees himself as an iconoclast in the Persian sense of the word. He believes that iconoclasm, in the sense of throwing away tradition, has been impossible in Iran so far, and modernity and tradition have come to a kind of understanding or compromise. Mandanipour strives to write "Iranian novels," novels that convey the complicated situation of Iranian society, which has one foot in *The Thousand and One Nights* and one foot in the third millennium on the Christian calendar. To this end, he uses the events of Iran's contemporary history—especially the ruinous Iran-Iraq war—and the country's old legends. In this way, his novels can be said to be a midway point between historical novels and surrealist novels.

SHIVA RAHBARAN: The first question is a general question about democracy in Iran. What impression do Iranians have of democracy? Do they think that it is a good form of government? Are they aware of the dangers of populism—like the dangers of the referendum at Hitler's time that led to dictatorship? And have Iranian intellectuals and thinkers performed their mission in terms of explaining democracy's highs and lows to the people? And, finally, a related general question: many people think that, in view of Iranians' rites, traditions, and history, democracy is basically not suited to them. What do you think?

SHAHRIĀR MANDANIPOUR: I think that we have an elementary and idealistic impression of democracy. Unfortunately, we've never had the historical opportunity to experience democracy and to understand it. The most suitable opportunities have been taken away from us, or we've failed to rise to the occasion, or historical circumstances have not been in our favor, for example, because of the element of foreign interference, which has altered the natural processes of our growth and our experiences. The Constitutional Revolution was a historical opportunity when democracy could have been established and practiced in this land, so that we could have become acquainted with the methods of rational-mindedness and tolerance, learned to channel our contradictions, and started playing chess by the rules. Our most recent opportunity—and maybe our last opportunity globally—was during the time of Mossadegh. Unfortunately, it was taken away from us. Of course, we shouldn't put all the blame on foreign interference. Nor should we put all the blame on ourselves. Nor, for example, on a single political party. We have all played and still play a role in our backwardness and in our historical failure. One way or the other, in our private relationships, in our relations with the state, in the family, in our neighborhoods, in towns and cities, and even in our relationship with the dead, we're totally unacquainted with democracy, tolerating one another, and believing in the existence of the Other. To see this absence of tolerance we only have to look at our intellectuals. So in these circumstances, the facts change a great deal and I believe that many historical models will be ineffective for analyzing our situation in Iran.

As for some people believing that democracy is not suited to Iran, I strongly disagree. Yes, some kinds of democracy—imported models or absolute imitations—may be unable to regulate our interpersonal relations and our relations with the state, but a democracy that arises from our hearts, from our demands, from our will, from our culture, and from our national, historical presence would appear to be our only way out.

S.R. Even though you say that the Iranian people have had no practice in democracy?

S.M. We have no choice but to practice democracy, bit by bit, so that, little by little, it becomes institutionalized in our land. This kind of democracy can't be achieved without paying the cost. We Iranians expect to reach the best system of government in the world without bringing about any change in ourselves, without throwing away our high level of self-importance and our low level of knowledge. We don't want to accept that even the West has paid many costs to achieve its democracy, such as it is.

Various historical experiences have shown that, for the time being, humanity is unable to put into effect any better system than democracy. There are many ideals, aspirations, and ideologies to choose from. They've all been tested in various circumstances and it would appear that they've all failed. So far, democracy has been the only system that, despite all its flaws, has caused relatively less harm to human beings than the alternatives.

I believe that, now, when we're finally starting to look at democracy realistically and demanding it, the global conditions for systems of government have changed. The golden age of democracy and, at least, the Western form of social democracy no longer exist. This world is a postmodern world. And, in this world, democracy is being emptied of its contents even in Western countries. We are more or less familiar with its critics and even its postmodern critics. But what about Iran now? I wouldn't be so presumptuous as to offer a blueprint! But I feel that, whichever direction we choose to take, whichever direction our historical destiny takes us, we must unavoidably have democratic institutions. We have to practice democracy and tolerance and learn to accept the presence of the Other, whether at the broader level of the country or the narrower level of the family or the relationship between two people. We really need this kind of practice, so that we internalize these things or at least respect them outwardly in the way that we accept social contracts and step beyond our individual selves.

Just over these past few years, when we have, in a way, experienced elections and the presence of interest groups and parties in Iran, we have seen some good aspirations. We have been practicing this outside the realm of ideals, away from our aspirations and dreams, and in the realm of reality and realism. For example, we can see that the people have sensed what a powerful factor voting can be. This, by itself, has been a very important lesson for our country. We've had voting in our country since the Constitutional Revolution, but at no time before—apart from 1950 and 1951—

had the Iranian people sensed, to this extent, the power of voting and the determining power of their votes. Given the disappointing conditions of the world, this was a positive experience.

It depresses me when I talk in this way about minimal things and take heart from them, but I sense the enormity of the bitter reality outside my mind. You spoke of populist systems. Yes, we had to go through the experience of these years, all the blood and all the feuding, in order to understand that the conception that we had of the majority and the people was very idealistic. Only now are we beginning to understand the meaning of, for example, a play like Ibsen's *An Enemy of the People*. And it was written back in 1882!

S.R. Has our revolution and the so-called "Iranian experiment" been a step toward modernity or a leap back?

S.M. That's a very difficult question. All the things that we've been through over the past twenty or twenty-five years have been over this question and have attempted to find an answer to it. I belong to the generation that, before the revolution, was tempted by the third way or what you called the Iranian experiment. The dream of experiencing a third way—I mean a way other than socialism and liberalism—wasn't extinguished in the hearts of many of our intellectuals even after the reversal suffered by the Third Force of Khalil Maleki and Jalāl Āl-e Ahmad.[68] In those days, religious

---

68   Khalil Maleki and Jalāl Āl-e Ahmad were originally members of Iran's now-defunct communist party, the Tudeh Party, but broke away from it because it was too subservient to the Soviet Union. In the early 1950s, Khalil Maleki formed the Third Force, a left-wing group that supported Mossadegh.

intellectuals still harbored an amalgamation of religion and democracy on their aspirational horizon. And secular intellectuals harbored a combination of socialism and liberalism in their minds. But all these aspirations had remained at the elementary stage of hopes and dreams. No group had any specific, detailed program, any specific analysis of Iran's conditions, or any practical ways and means of achieving its aims.

As to whether the experience of these past years has been a step back, I can tell you resolutely that, over the course of history, there has never, ever been any such thing as a step back. It may happen, in some circumstances, that forces and factors that have been held back and crushed in the past may become actualized at a given moment. But, even in a time machine, moving toward the historical past is, in fact, a forward movement.

Let me approach this question from another angle. We have an unproven and clichéd assumption that Iran entered the flow of modernity in the early decades of the twentieth century. But I've started to doubt this over the last few years. The doubt first started niggling at me when I was preparing an article about the confrontation between tradition and modernity in Iranian literature for a literary festival in the Norwegian city of Stavanger. Well, as usual and as everyone always does, I intended to write that Iranian literature entered the course of modernism with Sādegh Hedāyat and continued until today, when the "third generation" of our writers has taken up this process. Midway in my work, I felt a niggling doubt. On the basis of what documented evidence and what well-thought-out analysis was I repeating this hackneyed theory? Had I ever asked myself whether these verdicts were correct or not? And so my doubt persisted. My constant observations of our society only compounded the doubt. We can all see constantly that there are many modern objects and modern instruments and tools all around us, but we can also all see that, in many instances, we don't have the culture for using these tools correctly and in a modern way. Anyhow, I finally came to the conclusion that, in Iran, modernism and tradition have reached a peculiar kind of coexistence. Contrary to the West, where modernism and tradition engaged in a long, heated conflict, brimming with sublime ideas, views, criticisms, and conclusions—and brimming with bloody wars— in Iran, modernism and tradition only fired the occasional shot at one another's edges and never aimed at one another's hearts.

It has often been said that Iran's modernization started before the revolution thanks to oil money. But did importing cars, telephones, televisions, modern fashion, and pop music amount to a real, internal process of modernization? I can speak better and more confidently about literature, which is my area of expertise. In the article I wrote on this subject, I showed that even in the big and important works of geniuses such as Hedāyat and Nimā, who began the modernist trends in our literature, we find a Janus-like quality. That is to say, when we approach these works with modern methods of assessment, they give us modern answers and, when we analyze them using traditional systems and criteria, they give us traditional answers. What I mean to say is that many of our great literary works have a dualistic structure. They are an intricate, organic blend of the peaceful coexistence of tradition and modernism, albeit with some outward signs of conflict. Of course, I don't want to follow the Iranian habit of issuing an imposing, definitive verdict. I believe that we also have some literary works that are modern in the true sense. But most of our apparently modern works also have a hidden, traditional face. I didn't just rely on *The Blind Owl* or Nimā's poetry to prove this theory. I went back to a work known as *Siāhatnāmeh-ye Ebrāhim-Beyg*[69] (Ebrāhim-Beyg's Travelogue); a novel-like travelogue that features an Iranian-style intellectual. In this work, the narrator is an Iranian intellectual who lives outside Iran and has become familiar with the West's progress and the leaps and bounds that the West has taken to outstrip the East. He continually, again and again, expresses the hope that Iran, too, like the West, can emerge from the inequities of backwardness and move toward industrial development, knowledge, and democracy. In order to fulfill this aspiration, he sets off for Iran, in the hope of playing an effective part in raising the awareness—or so he imagines—of Iran's backward, trachoma-ridden society, crushed as it was under the thumb of colonialists and autocrats. In other words, he was seeking exactly what most Iranian intellectuals seek. This man enters Iran with his aspirations and dreams.

---

69   Published in three volumes in the early twentieth century (in the years of the Constitutional Revolution), the first volume did not carry the name of the author, Hāij Zeynolābedin Marāghe'i. Several people were wrongly arrested on the suspicion that they may have written it. The book contained such bitter social observation and satire that it was banned at the time in Iran, but some copies were smuggled in by travelers coming back from Russia. It was only the third volume that bore the author's name.

Again and again he emphasizes that Iran should follow the course taken by Western states. They have reached modernism, progress, and development, but we have stayed behind. His journey is, incidentally, a novelistic travelogue. He presents very dark images of Iranian society: people's backwardness, horrific poverty, wretchedness—that is to say, people being crushed under all this oppression—ignorance, diseases, etc., etc. Finally, Ebrāhim-Beyg arrives at the Qajar Court, meets this or that prince, and explains all these maladies to him in the hope that his interlocutor will be moved and set out forthwith to carry out reforms. Instead, the prince orders his footmen to give Ebrāhim-Beyg a thorough thrashing and to throw him out! Ebrāhim-Beyg goes back home and dies of grief. I mean he grieves so much that he dies. This is a representation and a model of Iranian intellectuals' destiny, which keeps repeating itself: being very idealistic and harboring lofty dreams for their homeland and for themselves, on the one hand, and giving up and dying of despair, on the other.

Taking this travelogue itself, we see that, if we look at it from a modern standpoint, it appears to us as a modern work. But if we look at it from a traditional standpoint, it is a traditional work. What I'm trying to say is that, in our country, in our culture, and in our social aspect, we have a kind of duality: one visage faces toward modernity and another visage is totally traditional. For example, take this travelogue. At the time when it was written, there was no sign of modern literature in Iran. But we know that the Western novel evolved out of travelogue-like novels, such as *Don Quixote* or other picaresque novels. Well, here, too, we have a travelogue-novel based on the plot of a journey. But when we study the text and look at it from a traditional standpoint, we see that it is a traditional work too. For example, at one point in the text, the narrator reaches a village in the Azerbaijan region. A woman comes out of her house and goes into the house next door. The narrator turns to his guide and says angrily: "What on earth do you call this? Why did that woman come out in that state of undress? Why was she so scantily clad?" On the one hand, the narrator dreams of progress and modernization for the people, and, on the other hand, when he sees this woman, he reacts in a more fanatical and reactionary way than the villagers and the local culture!

You can see this Janus-like quality in the works of Hedāyat, Nimā, and many of our country's artists. Modern objects have entered our society, but when we look at them—take the computer, for example, are we using this object in the true sense? Look at the Internet or the mobile phone, for example. Because of its industrial and social needs (in the first instance), the West's industrialized society was driven to create a means for quick communication. In other words, it has arrived at a point where the seconds count in the fate of its capital and its industrial, social, political, and scientific activities. But there are many occasions when we use the mobile phone for killing time in Iran. I mean, just look at this telling expression that we have and use constantly: "killing time"!

What I'm trying to say is that, in the West, phenomena, and new objects and institutions, emerge in the natural context of growth. But, in our country, uneven growth and the coexistence of tradition and modernity, which have never aimed a shot at one another's hearts, have created major problems. The point I'm trying to make is that we must never forget how complicated a human society is and especially how complicated Iranian society is.

S.R. You used the image of technology to explain how our intellectuals think: on the one hand, modern, and on the other hand, traditional. So there's a kind of cultural schizophrenia in Iran which carries a big destructive force. But this is an approach that Iranian intellectuals have always used in order to create a strong front, which can withstand the "duality" of tradition and modernity. This is how it's always been, from the time of the Constitutional Revolution to Mossadegh to the Islamic Revolution. So how can there be any hope of Iranian intellectuals performing their mission in terms of raising people's consciousness?

S.M. Well, I'll follow up your question with another question. In a world that's in its postmodern stage, do we have to view intellectuals as saviors and prophets? Do we have to give them such a big role as to expect them to determine the direction that a country takes?

S.R. But intellectuals are responsible for generating ideas. So they influence the direction that their country takes.

S.M. But have Iranian intellectuals reached the stage of generating ideas at all?

S.R. So they, too, are assemblers?

S.M. I can't deny that we have exceptions. We have thinkers who generate ideas for enlightenment and hopes of progress. But are they a group or a trend? No. Have Iranian intellectuals been able to generate a well-thought-out process of enlightenment like Western intellectuals—like the members of the Encyclopedia in France, for example?

Obviously, if a trend or trends for generating ideas comes about in Iran, it will emerge from the essence and elements of this land. And it will naturally lock into the conditions and structures of the forces that exist here and bring movements and institutions into being. But we've rarely seen such a generation of ideas. On the one hand, we've had the idea of Western liberalism and democracy and, on the other hand, we've had the Marxist ideology, which is also an import. And, now and then, we've been tempted by third ways! I mean the propagation of something in this guise. One of these third ways is the system that we're experiencing now. Another third way was that of Khalil Maleki and Jalāl Āl-e Ahmad, who had in mind an amalgamation of Western democracy and socialism. But when we look at them all again, we see that they have, unfortunately, remained at the level of intentions. They haven't generated the ideas that would have allowed them to say: "Look, when we come to power, we'll proceed like this and like that. Our economic program will be based on this or that corresponding theory, which our economists have formulated over the past five or ten years. We have programs and proposals for political parties, etc. etc." We've never had groups or trends of this kind. We've constantly either shouted hurrah and "Long live . . ." with fanatical fervor or, the reverse, sought to topple someone or something with cries of "Death to this" and "Death to that." And we've sacrificed so many people, so much blood, and so many opportunities in the process. And the latest example of this is the current "reformist" trend. Here, too, we've created a shining Seyyed [Mohammad Khatami] and put him on a pedestal, so that we can subsequently grieve his defeat. This is something that we love to do. I mean to praise the West's progress and to speak at great length and with great pleasure about their latest inventions, whilst also wallowing in sorrow and despair at our own failures. But it never occurs to us that, in the age of the information explosion and at a time when there is such a boundless appetite for the quickest possible accumulation of endless information, we can't expect to achieve very much with print runs of three thousand. It's obvious that in such a wilderness of low readership and low scholarship, ideas that can solve our problems are unlikely to emerge and circulate. We've always tried to achieve felicity, prosperity, and progress by means of revolutions or reforms from above. It has never occurred to us that we must also carry out revolutions and reforms within ourselves. Through an average of twenty minutes of productive work per day, a handful of pages read per year, endless hours spent watching TV serials, and endless hours spent grumbling, the typical Iranian wants to achieve the same progress as the Japanese. Well, this being the case, we're always bound to be wallowing in sorrow and laments.

S.R. So was this Iranian experiment or this Iranian revolution, which is also afflicted with a Janus-like quality, a historical necessity?

S.M. It seems as if it was. I think that something that should really have started to happen during the Constitutional period was delayed, again because of interference by colonialists and the conditions within Iran itself. I mean, if we look at things carefully, we will see that religion has always been moving toward politics in Iran. It is worth remembering that Islam is possibly the only religion in which the Prophet had a plan for a movement. This trend was suppressed during the Constitutional Revolution with the execution of Sheikh Fazlollah Noori. It was repeated in 1963,[70] when it was suppressed again. Until, finally, it triumphed in 1979.

S.R. Now, let's turn to the role of the writer and the poet in Iran today. How do poets and writers view their role since the Islamic Revolution? I'm asking this bearing in mind that the previous regime stifled artistic activity too.

S.M. As a humble writer of fiction, I may have a very poor understanding of politics. I mean, there isn't any rule or definition that says that an artist has to be able to propose socio-political ideas, theories, and ways and means. My most important duty and task as a writer is, in the first instance, to try to write good short stories

---

70   There were anti-Shah protests in Qom in June 1963, led by Ayatollah Ruhollah Khomeini. The Shah sent Khomeini into exile at the time, but he returned to Iran triumphantly in February 1979.

and novels. This is an artist's mission. But, well, it goes without saying that a writer has socio-political power and responsibility too, like everyone else.

A novel that's a good love story is much more valuable than a bad political novel, because, in an artistic novel, the reader experiences and understands the existence of a number of different individuals. This stretches the reader's thinking to beyond the world of legends, epics, and monophonic autocrats. This amounts to understanding an Other, with other thoughts and an other personality, whose rights must be recognized. This is a lesson in tolerance and democracy.

Let's look at a good example of a politically committed writer by the name of Jalāl Āl-e Ahmad. I try to criticize Āl-e Ahmad out of respect, not because it's fashionable nowadays. Āl-e Ahmad always had the aim, the credo, and the conduct of a committed, political writer. He started off from religion. He reached the socialism of the Tudeh Party. Then he broke away from it and set his hopes on a third way. Then he arrived back at religion. And throughout all these stages, he was utterly resolute and passionate. The Western equivalent is Orwell or Koestler. How great the distance, after all, from a fervent defense of the Soviet Union to a fervent turning-away from it to suicide?! So many contradictions gathered in one place! Or, for example, let's compare the relative merits of Jack London's *Call of the Wild* and his *Iron Will*. I don't want to advocate seclusion and inactivity. On the contrary, I want to say that the socio-political value of an artistic, outwardly non-political novel is greater than that of a contrived political novel. I want to raise the issue of specialization and the idea that the artist is always afflicted with tragic doubt and the exploration of relativity.

S.R. So on this basis, have the divides and anomalies of Iranian society provided fertile ground for your art and literature, or have they made things more difficult for you—because these conditions can lead to the politicization of art without the artist wanting it?

S.M. A bit of both. For example, at Columbia University, in New York, I tried to enumerate—for the benefit of the Iranians who live there—the conditions, members, and characteristics of the generation of fiction writers that has become known as the "third generation." I explained that one of their characteristics is that the "third-generation" writer is not politics-ridden.

S.R. By the "third generation," you mean from the 1980s onward?

S.M. Yes. In general, the generation after Golshiri and Dowlatābādi; people my own age. Of course, "third-generation" is a general label. It's not a precise, rigorous classification. Anyway, when I said that this generation is not politics-ridden, I didn't mean that it's not political. But, in the usual way with us Iranians, instead of listening carefully to what I was saying, some people began preparing their responses in their own minds and I met with strong reactions. The first criticism was: You're looking forward to literature not being committed anymore! You want a literature that's opposed to politics! You're advertising ivory-tower literature! But that's not what I was saying. What I'm saying is that a writer may write a story about a tree, but it can still be an absolutely political story. I was talking about writing that's politics-ridden and inartistic. In the generation that preceded us, many of our best writers were destroyed by this blight. Someone like Bozorg-e Alavi had shown that he was a skilled writer. But when he made himself write to publicize an ideology or to turn the admirable sacrifices of a group of militants into a political report instead of a novel, then he didn't produce any more artistic works. And even the people who were promoting committed and political literature didn't read his works very much after that.

Before the revolution, we had writers whose works were very much talked about, as they were themselves. But their works were politics-ridden, and not even political. Now, hardly anyone reads their works. Readers say: "These works are very elementary; they're sloganeering." So what's happened? It means that we've reached the understanding that artistic creativity is different from me putting a piece of paper in front of myself and deciding in advance that I must definitely write about the heroic deeds of a political man in order to encourage other people to follow in his footsteps. Nowadays, we have, after much effort, come to the conclusion that, whatever else these kinds of works may be, they aren't art.

I think that when a writer goes out into society, he can be a man of politics. He can become the leader of a political party. He can become a guerrilla. He can do whatever he likes! Vote or shoot!

But when he writes, he has no choice but to be committed to art and creativity. Even if he is writing about a political campaigner, he should show the campaigner with all his human strengths and weaknesses, not base him on an ideology's formula of a hero. I think that this is one of the lessons that we've learned during this period—and we've learned many lessons over these past twenty years. I mean, our writers have sensed deep down that they should try to do their own work well and not expect to bring about a revolution or political reforms through their works of fiction.

The interesting point is that before 2 Khordad,[71] we had a period during which writers were viewed as "politicos"; a view that aroused the protest of 134 writers.[72] But, after 2 Khordad, with the proliferation of newspapers and political groups, political journalists and political thinkers had a chance to surface. This gave writers of fiction something of a breather. I mean, everyone could fall into their own place and do what they were meant to be doing. This is something that rarely happens in Iran. But now that so many newspapers have been banned, it seems that we've gone back to the old vicious circle again.

S.R. Not just you but all the writers I've spoken to have constantly expressed the wish that the burden of political problems be kept off their shoulders. This brings us to the next question, a question

---

71   Date on the Iranian calendar corresponding to 23 May; election date on which Mohammad Khatami unexpectedly beat the establishment candidate to become president in 1997.

72   Reference to a letter against censorship signed by 134 Iranian writers and sent to the Islamic Guidance and Culture Ministry in October 1994.

about your literary heritage. When we look at Iranian literature—even when we look at Hāfez—we sense that all of life's burdens, ranging from politics to relationships and love to economic issues, have fallen on the shoulders of writers. I mean, Iranian literature has always tried to take everything—the expected and the unexpected, the normal and the abnormal—together (toward a "unity of being"). Does your work differ in this sense from the works of Hāfez, Saadi, or Rumi?

S.M. I think that Hāfez is a good example of an artist who was committed to his own art in his own day. Just as he wrote about love, Hāfez also wrote about the socio-political conditions of his day, within the constraints of censorship. In other words, he was an active artist, an active thinker, and an aggregate of the active sentiments of his day. A good contemporary example is Houshang Golshiri. He isn't a politics-ridden writer. But he has written stories that are political in the true sense. For example, those in his short-story collection *Namāzkhaneh-ye Khuchak-e Man* (My Little Prayer House). In these stories, he exposes the inner depths of our social structures, antiquated complexes, and old characteristics in fictional form. In other words, what he does is similar to a deconstruction.

At any rate, it goes without saying that a true artist is influenced by the events and developments of his own land. In fact, the sensitive, unshielded feelings of a true artist absorb despair and sorrow and hope and joy into the heart and the mind more quickly than others, and, naturally, they will, sooner or later, surface in his work. Otherwise, he would be nothing but a potato! A device for rousing fans!

S.R. I imagine you heard that when a number of Western writers, such as Mr. Muschg and Mr. Enzensberger, visited Shiraz a while ago, they said that they were very envious of Iranian writers. In the West, many writers envy, to some extent, not just the position of Iranian writers but the position of all third-world writers or writers who live under dictatorships, because (based on Henry James's idea that every novel is a window in the house of fiction) they think that the lack of freedom makes writers and their works more creative and meaningful. Is it true that the more walls you have, the more the opportunities to put in windows? Are we to conclude on this basis that freedom is bad for art?

S.M. No. This is a general verdict. It may happen that, in some specific conditions, constraints may lead to creativity in the mind of a specific writer. But we always have to bear in mind that freedom makes a society flourish and, when society flourishes, art and the artist will flourish too.

At that session in Shiraz, we (Messrs Dowlatābādi, Ātashi, and I) spoke to Messrs Muschg and Enzensberger for seven or eight hours. It was a very interesting discussion. And when it got to the point where we were speaking in an informal way about our feelings about writing and our problems, aims, and values, they said something which suggested envy for the position of Iranian writers. I don't know to what extent what they said was heartfelt. Maybe they just wanted to make us feel better. Or maybe, because life in the West is on an even keel and has fewer ups and downs, what they said was an expression of longing for excitement and dynamism.

Once, when we were visiting the Norwegian Authors' Union in Oslo, they told us that every time a writer's book is borrowed from a public library in Norway, a sum amounting to more than the price of the book is paid into the account of the Authors' Union, which, in turn, gives it to the writer. I found this really interesting. Apart from the financial aspect, what amazing concern for the rights of writers and the value of their works! I suppose that I, in turn, have felt envy for the kinds of advantages, freedoms, and peace of mind that writers have in the West. I mean, it seems as if the envy is a two-way street. But, at any rate, words and their shadings are different for an Eastern/Iranian writer than for the Western writer. In Iran, writing is like life in a way. It is birth. It is a reason to go on living. And it is death. Whereas, in the West, for some writers, it is just a job.

Yes, for me, as a writer, the war was an important event, an event that was brimming with things to write about. As was the tragedy of the earthquake.[73] But I'd never want a war to destroy my country and to blow its best young people to smithereens, nor for an earthquake to level several towns so that I could have good material for a novel. I'd rather never write another story and have my pen die of boredom for lack of material and instead, see our people lead prosperous and happy lives. Have you ever felt the

---

73   A reference to the earthquake on 26 December 2003 that destroyed the town of Bam. The official death toll was over 26,000.

insatiability of the camera lenses of foreign reporters when they're covering the quarrels and misfortunes of us Easterners? The photographers are eager to photograph the dead bodies lying in the streets; eager to capture artistic photographs of the strange and unparalleled shapes that they find in ruins; and eager to hunt the moments of weeping, the moments of flesh being torn apart in explosions and exchanges of fire. I don't want to suggest that they feel no human sympathy or, God forbid, suffer from some kind of journalistic sadism and are looking for disturbing scenes, but this is one side of the story anyway: our suffering fills their newspapers and their books. Western writers may view Eastern writers in a similar way and with similar interest. But this was just a small aside, a kind of parenthetical sentence. The main, beautiful part of it is the sincere discussion and understanding between several writers—which is universal and knows no East or West. This is why I think we have to thank Messrs Muschg and Enzensberger for their interest in Iranian writers and for the fact that, from a great distance, they have discovered a nice and important aspect of Iranian writers' lives. Yes, it's something to be proud of: the passion and the faith of writing, the selflessness of writing, and the authors' unity with their work that we experience in Iran.

S.R. So what about the problem of censorship? Is censorship good for creativity or not?

S.M. We have to examine this issue in a general way too. Censorship may, in some circumstances, lead to creativity, much like the form of a story. I describe form in art as a framework or a frame, which we choose voluntarily for our work. In other words, a form imposes limitations, rules, and boundaries of a kind on a work of art. And although it robs the artist of some freedoms, by the same token, it forces the artist to think of creative ways to work within those limitations. It is like the rules of soccer, for example. We decide that the ball shouldn't be hit with the players' hands. But, as a result, the players are forced to be more creative with their feet than they could have been with their hands. But in this case, the harm that censorship causes is greater than these kinds of benefits.

The important point is that, in examining censorship in a rigorous way, we should separate its impact on society from its impact on art. The more complicated the problem of censorship has become and the more complicated and strange its effects, the more simplistically we've tended to view it. Look at the difference: despite all the freedom of speech that they have, American writers, in this day and age, have chosen to write stories that are miles away from pornography and scurrilous material. And this seems to be a conscious reaction against pornography and indecency, even, in a way, against the work of Henry Miller and the like. But two novice Iranian writers, in their first work published in the West, have put pictures of themselves, naked from head to toe, on the cover of their book without it being relevant in any way to the contents of their work. This kind of behavior or reaction, of which there are many examples, arises directly from the dysfunctionality of censorship in our society, a dysfunctionality that doesn't only relate to recent years or recent decades but goes back many centuries. The Hāfez whom we're rightly presenting as one of the world's greatest poets was apparently so terrorized by this same censorship and its effects as to refrain from setting down, in his own handwriting, a single collection of his poetry in book form throughout his life.

The problem is that despite the fact that we've had censorship for so long and despite all that's been said in pained condemnation or joyous praise of it, no one has ever carried out a systematic and rigorous study into it. Maybe one of the reasons for this shortcoming and for the pervasiveness of censorship here is that we've never viewed writers' work as a productive profession. Every country tries to develop and export its productive capabilities. But we constantly restrict our artistic and literary products. Our officials attach far less value to the profession of writing than they do to some small cottage industry or handicraft industry in some far-flung village. For example, we're happy to display and promote clay vases produced in some unknown corner of the country as works of art, but we're so suspicious of our literary products that we think every word might be an act of sabotage or treachery.

Our society hasn't accepted that a writer's work, whether good or bad, is actual work and that we need systems and mechanisms that allow writers to practice their profession without having to work in a bank, without having to sweat in a factory to earn a living. An Iranian writer's dream is to be able to work as a professional writer. Professional writing and having writing accepted as a profession will help boost our literature. One of the reasons why our literature is weak is that our artists do not have much time to read nor the opportunity or energy to write.

S.R. But, then again, they're more in contact with reality; they aren't just sitting in ivory towers.

S.M. It's not a question of ivory towers. Yes, if, as a writer, I go and work in a factory for six months, I'll come into contact with many realities. But if I have to spend twenty years of my life in the factory just to make ends meet, then I'll be crushed, like any other worker. I have never been able to live off the royalties from my books, not even for two months! I always have to work. Maybe I've been lucky to have found a job in a library, which is close to my art, but I have many friends who work in banks, for example, or accountancy firms, or archives, even in restaurants. These jobs totally destroy art, and it's a miracle that these writers and poets are still writing stories and producing poems.

S.R. Europeans see the novel as unique to their own culture, a culture which, from the Renaissance onward, through the periods of modernism and postmodernism, has experienced a division in people's being. I mean the mind-body division. Dariush Shāyegān, has written in his *Henry Corbin* that the novel was born in this divide as a bid to achieve a kind of unity. But we've always had this unity in our land, with all its mysticism, or, at least, we've felt as if we do. So we've always viewed ourselves in the mirror of poetry because poetry is revealed to the poet like a revelation or inspiration. Can we say that the novel is weak in Iran for this reason?

S.M. Well, maybe we can also talk about the novel and the weakness of the Persian novel from this angle. But there are other reasons too. In the United States, in a program that we had with PEN in New York, we had a meeting that was attended by Susan Sontag, who is a great, majestic writer. But at this meeting, she said in a kind of high-handed way: "We wonder, how have you Iranians dealt with the phenomenon of the novel, which is a Western tradition?" Our guide went into overdrive talking about Hāfez, Saadi, and Khayyám, saying, well, we've had these poets instead. As is the norm. But the question drove me to investigate this issue: Is the novel really a Western tradition?

I answered by saying: When you use the word "tradition," it brings to mind something that goes back many centuries, whereas even in the West, the novel is only about three to four hundred years old. If we set aside the clichéd assumption, we see that, for a long time, literature in the East and the West advanced at the same pace and in a similar way, taking one step forward and one step back. The form of folkloric, popular, old wives' tales that we had also existed in the West. As did fairy tales or stories with animals as characters. Many Eastern countries have stories that are similar to Aesop's fables. And the West, too, had something similar to the Eastern tales that have a moral or teach a lesson. And, so, as we move forward in time, we reach the period of romances, which laid the groundwork for the novel. At this stage, too, there are examples of Iranian romances. In the West, they characterize romances as the amazing adventures of a chivalrous hero. Well, we have Iranian romances with these same characteristics: *Samak Ayyār, Eskandarnāmeh, Layli and Majnun*, etc. But, after this period, our language starts to stagnate and decay, and this is when we started to fall behind. The important point that I have to highlight here is that, when I say that, for a time, we advanced at the same pace as the West in the realm of literature, I don't by any means intend to put a brave face on things and to conceal our backwardness, because I know that we've overplayed and exaggerated our achievements. My intention is simply to shed light on the realities and facts of our past within the limits of my capabilities.

Anyway, the West became industrialized and, in the process of this evolution, the romance turned into the novel. And, within the novel, various schools emerged, one after the other. But the sociopolitical decay and moldiness of Iranian society manifested itself in the Persian language of that time. Decline and deterioration became pervasive in everything, even in our national character, from around the fifteenth century onward. The height of literature at the time was the works of Saadi and Hāfez. After them, our prose became artificial or, to use Bahār's expression, bureaucratic.[74] And our poetry mainly consisted of eulogies and ingratiating praise of kings and courtiers. There was hardly anything resembling the mystical brilliance and beauty of Rumi or Hāfez. Or if there was, they were the exceptions, which always exist. This

---

74 One of the classifications in Malekoshoarā Bahār's *Sabkshenāsi* (A Study of Styles; Tehran: Amir-Kabir Publications, 1958).

decline reached its lowest point under the Qajar Dynasty. I mean the decay of the language, the fatigue of the language, the stagnation of the language. When a language stagnates, it's not static; it stagnates! I call it "the slumber of the Persian language" or "the catnap of the Persian language." I mean, by the time we get to the nineteenth century, our Persian language has no vibrancy in the field of philosophical terminology, although it had displayed good dynamism in the past and was able to accommodate and articulate philosophical expressions so to speak. In the field of science, too, Persian became stale and barren. And this is a weakness from which we're still suffering.

It goes without saying that this decline continued in our literature too, until we came to the Constitutional Revolution. During this period, we see the emergence of a quest for linguistic freedom in the Persian language, a will to rid ourselves of old linguistic tyrannies, just as there was a quest and a will to achieve socio-political freedom and justice. And it is natural that Hedāyat should be the offspring of this movement. I totally disagree with the simplistic view that Hedāyat went abroad, became acquainted with modern fiction, and then returned to Iran and implemented the principles of modern fiction in Persian. There were others who had gone abroad before Hedāyat. Jamālzādeh, the short-story writer, too, was acquainted with Western literature. But none of them was able to write a modern story (or modern fiction in general). So what was it about Hedāyat? My answer is that, apart from Hedāyat's genius, in his day, the grounds for writing modern fiction had also come about in the Persian language. From the time of the constitutionalist period's quest for freedom, there was a liberating force in the Persian language too. This led to the falling-away of old linguistic structures and methods, paving the way for modern structures and methods. In the course of this process, various familiar approaches were done away with and, most importantly, a realist approach gained the upper hand, whereas before, Persian had been dominated by similes and figurative speech. Apart from these important changes, we see that, during the Constitutional Revolution and thereafter, empiricism began to come to life in our cognitive system. And this cognitive system, plus the changes that I enumerated, led writers to develop an eye for the particular. This eye for the particular and the trick of using the particular as a metaphor for the general guides a writer's language toward realism. Hedāyat, with his genius for storytelling and with the knowledge that he'd gained, sat at this table and created his works. This was the start of modern Iranian literature.

The next point is that we've made good progress in the field of short story writing so far. With some leaps and bounds, we've made up lost ground to some extent. So I can confidently say that we have about fifty or sixty good short stories that can hold their own internationally. And this is no mean capital for a literature that started off only about a hundred years ago. But we still have problems in the field of novel writing. The main cause of these problems is something to which we've paid little attention in Iran: composition. Composition creates the backdrop for a multivocal novel. The world's best novels are multifaceted and multivocal, and they have a strong composition. Our novels are weak in this respect. We're reasonably good at character, different types of narrative, construction of time and place, and even form, but most of our novels are not up to scratch on composition. If you think about it, our music has usually been monophonic. Multiple instruments, but only one voice and one melodic line. This is where our weakness lies. And the cause of this weakness is that, although our society may be industrial, we don't have industrial human beings and industrial thought.

We know that the novel is an urban phenomenon. When the city came into being in the West, the novel came into being too for the middle class. If we think about it, we'll see that, in the West, when their society was feudal, a story-loving princess or a story-loving count would sit in the castle or in a romantic gazebo on a summer evening and read romances. She or he didn't read novels. The novel didn't exist then. But when cities came into being and the middle class came into being, the novel came into being too.

A city in the true sense is not a big village. It is a complex structure, with a layout, and complex networks of water pipes and electricity lines, and communications networks. For better or for worse, one way or the other, it has networks, it covers a big expanse, and it has a varied demography. And this is where you find the industrial human being, a human being who is engaged in production. In a system of production, you have composition. It is not a single line. There are multiple assembly lines, which culminate in production. The industrial human being's mind is acquainted with layout. It is acquainted with a multiplicity of elements. But we are a very good example for Derrida. We see everything in black and white, as absolutes. This means an absence of composition. Our mind can't accept that several voices or several factors can exist in a phenomenon. For us Iranians, people are either white or black, saints or devils. This kind of thinking can't produce a successful novel.

Why are Iranian writers successful short story writers? Because in the short story they have one protagonist and one antagonist, and they take them and run with them, and they do it well. But in a novel, they have to have—let's say—five or six characters, each of whom has his or her own voice. And the writer has to allow them to speak in their own voices. The novelist—like a true democrat—has to allow each character to say what he or she has to say convincingly. But our writers often find it difficult to accept that five or six different voices can all have convincing things to say. This means that the novel is presenting five or six different lines of thought, which all ring true. This is why, in our country, a good novel helps people arrive at a better understanding of democracy. And it is because we don't have a very good understanding of democracy that we have few good novelists.

Your suggestion that we tend to look at the world from the perspective of poetry is correct, but there are also poetic novels in the world.

S.R. Do you consider yourself to be an iconoclastic novelist?

S.M. I think that you can behave in one of two ways when you come up against tradition. The first way is the one that modernism adopted in its heyday. That is to say, whenever it came up against a former, old, traditional phenomenon, it would move it out of the way, bulldozer-fashion, and destroy it. Or it would deny it, without any thought, reasoning, or justification—blindly and simply as a matter of dogma and attachment to modernity's first principle, which was opposition to tradition. But, later on, this principle itself turned into modernism's tradition.

I think that the second way—instead of stubborn hostility toward anything that's traditional and instead of shooting down any traditional phenomenon—made progress, development, and evolution its basic principle. And it used tradition as a springboard toward the future. Naturally, if a phenomenon or institution did or does prevent its progress, instead of reducing its identity and *raison d'être* to hostility toward that limitation, it has—by virtue of defining its identity in terms of progress and the future—unshackled itself from the limitation and left it behind; it has, in a sense, dissolved tradition in itself and gone beyond it. In the era of the rise of modernism, we saw how some works defined themselves and were talked about purely and simply in terms of their contrast with tradition or their difference with tradition or their hostile dialogue with tradition. And, now that this principle of antagonism with tradition has itself turned into a tradition, this kind of work has lost its attractiveness and its raison d'être.

I prefer the second way to the first way, which only gains its identity and meaning from a palpable and natural battle with the past. And it is interesting to see that postmodernism is now leveling justified criticisms at modernism, criticisms that mainly target precisely this modernist tradition.

I believe anyhow that a work that belongs to the past has lost its raison d'être and is out of keeping with the level of progress and evolution of the present day, and it is perforce condemned to extinction. And it goes without saying that a work of art that is forward-looking will inevitably negate such a burdensome past. But you mustn't confine yourself to this, because being forward-looking means having the past behind you, having the present within you, and also having the shoots and possibly the stems of the future within you. I have the impression that, conversely, modernism, in the first sense, is facing backward. That is to say, when a work of art is totally focused on the past and is doing everything it can to negate the past, then this work will inevitably become backward-looking. You must try to do the opposite. I mean whilst distancing yourself from things that are decayed and obscurantist, you must save the bulk of your energy for leaping forward.

So my main response to your question is that I've never concerned myself with whether I'm modern or postmodern or, stranger than strange, a traditionalist. I'm certain that if, over the course of my life, I try to keep in step with the train of progress; if freshness and the avoidance of repetition and decay beat at the heart of my being; if I don't confine myself to using modern tools in a superficial way; and if I've made my outlook and perspective as desirous of innovation as I can—in other words, if I'm forward-looking, not superficially, but down to my skin and bones—I will undoubtedly write things that aren't outdated. And my writing won't be attached to a specific period or to a passing theory in any way. I was never so fanatically modernist when it was the fashionable thing to be—like graphic tees—that I was tearing my hair out over it, nor, now that postmodernist notions, correct or incorrect, have entered Iran, do I want to abandon myself body and soul to this mode of thinking.

What I'm saying is that, in our efforts to reach art, which is not a destination that you can ever reach definitively, there are no eternal, everlasting rules and laws. Theories and viewpoints are simply the working knowledge, and they're only of some slight use when we view them with a critical and progressive eye. Otherwise we'll rapidly turn into a building that, as soon as it's built, stands in the way of future roads.

Apart from these ideas and, maybe, slogans, I believe that I shouldn't turn my back on this vacuum, drawn by the assumption that I'm marching into the future. As a writer, Persian literary tradition is a path or footsteps that I must tread; it isn't something that I must deny or destroy with unjustified opposition, leaving a void behind my back. If I need to, I won't by any means balk at using the narrative form of *The Thousand and One Nights*, but with modern-day thinking and with a new treatment. If I can and if I need to, I will even try to learn something from the surrealism of *Tazkirat al-Awliya* (Biographies of Saints).[75]

At any rate, to the same extent that I loathe favoring everything that's old and repetitious, imitating the past, and using habitual

---

75 The only prose work attributed to the twelfth-century Iranian poet and mystic Attar, it is about the lives and deeds of a number of notable Sufis.

forms and structures, I must also recognize the importance of my language's literary past. After all, with each Persian word that I use today, I have to be aware of its shadows and ghosts in all the texts of the past. If, in addition to treating the word in a new way, I can also assemble all its past ghosts in my text, I can claim to have done something.

S.R. Now, I'm going to ask you a question that I was asked myself. Some writers see the study of (contemporary) Persian literature— especially by people who come from the West—as a kind of means for renewed cultural colonialism and exploitation. Is this how you see it too?

S.M. No. I don't think this is true and it's never been true. This is an academic issue, about academic exchanges or "commerce," so to speak. Well, some people might abuse it too. I mean, the travelogues of the first foreigners who traveled to Iran may have been abused by colonialist powers. But this doesn't justify calling the whole thing into question. Or if there are now foundations that are engaged in Oriental studies, we mustn't view them all with suspicion and assume that they intend to resurrect colonialist interference in Iran, although an espionage organization may, in fact, use the information.

We're living in the age of the extraction, storage, and utilization of information. And the body that has the most information is the most powerful. What we can do, in turn, is to begin Occidental studies, which we've never done. Or joking apart, we can establish foundations for studying their Oriental studies. In other words, "a study of Oriental studies." We can research and analyze the way in which the West views the East in order to understand the structure of this viewpoint and the factors behind it, to utilize it, and, if we want, to correct it.

On the whole, I don't have that impression and I don't think that these studies are all that menacing and conspiratorial.

S.R. But even people like Edward Said or people who operate on the basis of Foucault's philosophy say that, when there is an imbalance of power—i.e. when the West is more powerful than the East—even if a particular individual wants to come and study the East with good intentions, their study will inevitably demean the invaded culture again. This is a viewpoint that some Western students subscribe to as well.

S.M. It goes without saying, because those who have power are making it so, by using or abusing the information. In other words, the problem lies in the existence of that power; otherwise, academic studies, Oriental studies, in itself, only provides unadulterated information or abstract information. It is that unequal, hoarded power that taints knowledge, just as it did with nuclear physics. They exploited it to make an atomic bomb.

Let's not forget that we're also benefiting from Oriental studies. Had it not been for people who came and deciphered our ancient writings, would we have had anyone, to this day, to carry out this task? To have the required knowledge, to climb rocks and hills, to make copies of the writings, and to do the arduous work of deciphering it? We've benefited from Orientalism. Take Edward Browne, for example. Browne may also have given some information to intelligence agencies—this part of it is reprehensible and I, too, can say that he did a very wicked thing. But Edward Browne had another side too. He left behind, in Iran, a way of looking at things, a Western individual's way of looking at our literature which, if it is studied carefully, will create a difference in the way an Iranian looks at our literature. And I think that this is beneficial for us.

S.R. Looking at the works of some contemporary writers and at your own work, I've sensed that the Iran-Iraq war has had a deep impact on contemporary Iranian literature. But when I spoke to some poets and writers, such as Mr. Sepānlu, they said that the view that holds that contemporary poets and writers have a kind of duty to write about the war has created a kind of artistic "dictatorship" and that concentrating on this subject prevents writers from tackling other important issues.

S.M. Yes, this is regrettable. An eight-year-long war has occurred in our country, a very big historical event, with the destructiveness that all wars entail, and with all the consequences that all countries suffer from after a war. I even see a kind of schizophrenia spreading and affecting individuals in our society. These things are the products of war. I see poverty. I see prostitution. And these things, too, are undoubtedly the results of war. So what are they saying? That writers and poets shouldn't see these things? That they should shut their eyes to these things? That they should flee a historical event that has happened within earshot?

Of course, no poet or writer should be told what to write about. Everyone is free to write about whatever subject they want. But fleeing the realities that exist all around you is something else. A writer or poet may write about a tree or a ladybird on a wheat stalk, but if their sensory apertures are open to the surrounding world and to the times, their work will undoubtedly reflect the events that are happening all around them. And if their sensory apertures are closed, whatever they write about, they won't produce any art.

Why did so many writers and poets fight in the Spanish Civil War? What was the result? The things that Malraux experienced, the things that, let's say, Orwell experienced, or Hemingway or Koestler, all led to the creation of first-class works. These are products that resulted from these writers taking part in the historical circumstances of their world. I'm not saying that everyone should throw themselves into terrible events, as these writers did; I'm saying that shutting your eyes and fleeing is wrong. I'm saying that, when a writer really lives in his own times, when his sensitivities haven't become callous, the joys and sorrows around him will, inevitably, affect him, and they will, inevitably, be reflected in his works. They will lend his story or poem life, blood, and sensory perception. This is the key. In contrast, there are poets and writers who have written for more than half a century and who have constantly advertised their name and their works, but you'd be hard pressed to find a single line of their works that has lasted or made the slightest impression on anyone's mind. And the reason for this is that the sensory apertures of these writers have been shut.

Take the war, for example. A sensitive presence in life doesn't only mean that the writer or poet should go to the front. The war cast a shadow over towns and cities too. The bombardments, the nightly fear, fleeing the missile attacks, grieving the dead, the sorrow over the destruction, the universal fear felt by the displaced, all the injured and disabled people, the poverty. If an artist has felt these things, the effects will also flow in the veins of his words, even when he writes about the chair in his bedroom, for example.

I think we should tackle the war more actively. This is something that I experienced myself. Well, when the war started, I'd finished university and, on the face of it, I should have set out to do my military service. I was in a position to arrange things so that I wouldn't go to the front. But I thought that that would be a mistake; if I want to be a writer, I shouldn't do that. I was on the western front for eighteen months of my two-year military service. I think that it was a very important period for me as a writer. I couldn't have acquired the way of looking at things that the war gave me anywhere else. It was the war that showed me how beautiful life is. It was the war that showed me what a great blessing it is, now and then, to stride through a street or an alleyway in peace and security. It was only when the best soldier in my platoon died as I held him, with his blood pouring over my hand, that I started to realize how valuable life is and was more grateful to be alive.

In my foxhole, in our defensive position, I used to write stories to pass the time. I could hear the sound of mortar shells being fired by the Iraqis. It would take a few seconds before the shell would land in the vicinity of my foxhole or on its roof. In these few seconds, I could write one or two words, and just these one or two words taught me how valuable language can be, how much life is hidden in a word. In fact it *was* my life; I mean I could have been just one word away from my death. I don't know. Others may have a different view, which is valuable in its own right and worth hearing.

My view is that we should have tackled the war more actively. Even as I was writing my novel, I came to a point where I had to choose: Should I eliminate the Basij forces who took part in the war or not?[76] I'm describing the forces that are on a particular front. There are regular armed forces there. There are also Basij forces. So I tried to put them to paper in exactly the way that I had experienced them—assuming that I had viewed and experienced things the right way. I thought that if I eliminated them, it would amount to censorship. It would, in fact, amount to a betrayal of a part of our country's history.

---

76   Basij means "mobilization." It was the name of a volunteer force affiliated to the Revolutionary Guards during the Iran–Iraq war. Iraq attacked Iran in 1980, when Iran's armed forces were in disarray because of the revolution. Many Iranian generals were in prison or had left the country. This is why the Revolutionary Guards were formed and this is why many Iranians who were prepared to fight but were too young or too old to join the regular armed forces or the Revolutionary Guards joined the "Basij." This volunteer force became increasingly controversial after the war because the authorities started using it as a militia for suppressing dissent and for suppressing student protests in particular.

The war had a huge impact one way or the other. It indirectly seeped into even the individuals who tried not to see it and who tried not to mention the war in their poems and stories. Assuming, of course, that their artistic soul was alive and that they sensed the suffering and sorrow in their world, even in the form of the color of blood, even in the form of explosions, or songs, or the anxiety that breathes within them, an anxiety that isn't born of the world; it is born of war and we lived through it.

S.R. I had the sense that, in this big novel, you put the realist style and the surrealist style cheek by jowl. I mean I had the sense that you'd turned the schizophrenia that you were talking about into the novel's form and mold. Bearing in mind that there is always an argument that maintains that Iran just assembles Western things, can we say that you've written an Iranian novel?

S.M. That's what I've tried to do. In my short stories, too, I think I'm trying to be rooted here. I see a traditional situation—I shouldn't say "tradition," it is a very broad term—I see an old situation, an antiquated situation, alongside and coexisting with a modern situation. For example, in Tehran, you see a high-rise building belonging to the third millennium and, next to it, something from *The Thousand and One Nights*. For example, there's a fortune-teller sitting at the foot of the high-rise. There's someone sitting there and selling Indian or Arab medicines. This same person was sitting in a Baghdad market in *The Thousand and One Nights*, or in a market in Neyshabur or Samarqand. This is our society's situation. I mean, in addition to having very modern phenomena, we also have very antiquated phenomena alongside them. I find a story in the contrast between them. This is what I try to do. Now, the same thing has happened in the novel's form. I mean that I use different narrative methods. It may be a narrative of the *Thousand and One Nights* variety or of the *Tazkirat al-Awliya* variety, alongside a kind of stream-of-consciousness narrative or a monologue narrative. In *Del va Deldādegi* (The Courage of Love), an earthquake's tremors have even had an impact on the chapter divisions; as has, for example, the trembling of the earth under the impact of mortar shells.

S.R. You mean to say that you use different narrative methods to convey different worldviews?

S.M. Not different worldviews, but different narrative methods and tricks. In other words, I haven't tried—from the outset—to determine a fixed form for my novel and to proceed loyally on that basis. I made the narrative method fluid, so that the narrative discourse could change depending on the atmosphere of events, moods, characters, and the nature of the conflicts and calamities.

Over the past quarter century, we've gone through a very compressed, rapid, and eventful period, to make up for centuries of historical and cultural lethargy. And all these experiences provide good material for fiction. All the highs and lows, all the diverse events and perspectives, all the political, social, and ideological earthquakes and their aftershocks have to be reflected in our works too. In order to record these twenty-five years, which have seen as many events and exploits, and as much sorrow, hardship, suffering, pride, and even joy as several centuries in the life of a European nation, we have to use all kinds of literary resources and tricks. It isn't without reason that in the writings of my generation, in comparison to the writings of the 1960s and 1970s, there is a greater diversity of characters, forms, styles, and use of language. In the works of new Iranian writers and even in the generations before my generation, you can easily see the diversity of approaches and methods, ranging from, for example, derivative or home-grown magic realism, to Kafkaesque, Western surrealism, to our own kind of mystical surrealism. Well, again, I think that this is the result of the events that have taken place over the past two decades. In the realm of literature, good books have been translated in Iran. I mean, starting even earlier than this, stretching from the time of Hedāyat to the present day. So we have, in a way, been in contact with a distinguished selection of the world's literature, via the good and sympathetic translators that we've had. But it has only been a selection. In other words, we haven't had deep and extensive contact with the vast ocean of material that exists beyond our borders, whether in Latin America or to the East, such as in India or China, or in Africa, Europe, and the United States, let's say. But it seems as if we're slowly realizing that the world's literature doesn't just consist of the one or two hundred novels that we've been reading! It's much more vast than this. The handful of innovations that we've experimented with in our short stories and novels aren't all that there is! Many of these may have been tried already, but we don't know about them.

Iranian intellectuals are starting to realize that there is more to the world's pool of knowledge than the four or five books that they've read or the two or three philosophers whom they've become acquainted with, possibly via anthologies or compilations of one kind or another. And this may be a much more important development for us, if it continues and if the conditions come about for us to have deeper and more extensive contacts with the West's culture—not the West's trash culture.

After the revolution, we drew a dam-like wall around Iran to prevent contact between our culture and the West's culture. Whether the West's culture is bent on invading us or not, it is spreading and becoming prevalent because of its latent power and force. Deliberately or not, Western culture is pressing against the wall, like a river against a dam. Bear in mind that it's always the scum and filth on the water's surface that tends to flow over the top of the dam first. This is what's happened to us. The West's rich, powerful, long-standing culture is stuck in the depths behind the dam and the light, filthy stuff is spilling into Iran over the top of the dam. This is why we've had no contact with the American or European short story writers of the past decade, and we know very little about them. But we know many of their lightweight, famous-for-a-day singers. The evolution and development of their classical music is stuck behind the dam, and it's only their hip-hop that has spilled over to our side. It's the same with many of the West's cultural and artistic phenomena. All kinds of worthless Western action films or even translations of crime novels and thrillers are available in Iran, but you'd be hard pressed to find a copy of *Mrs. Dalloway* by Virginia Woolf. Even if it exists, it's gathering dust in a neglected corner of a bookshop.

We've really strayed from the subject of our discussion. At any rate, I think that, in these postmodern times in the arts, borders and indigenous-national affiliations have taken on new meanings and have moved and are moving closer together at least. So the forms, elements, and tricks of the trade have also become universal.

Despite all of this, there's still so much that hasn't been said. I feel that there's a lot that I need to learn from all the things that haven't been said, in order to be able to say them. So, after talking far too much, it seems that the best thing is to be silent and learn, but not with a satisfied silence or a know-it-all silence, and not with the silence of surrender or despair.

And thanks very much for your time, patience, and hard work, until a day when someone, somewhere will tell you much better things, more clearly and more precisely, as a reward for all your efforts and hard work.

SHIVA RAHBARAN was born in 1970 in Tehran. She left Iran for Germany in 1984, where she studied literature and political science at the Heinrich-Heine-Universität Düsseldorf. She continued her studies at Oxford University, where she was granted a PhD in English literature.

NILOU MOBASSER is an Iranian translator and occasional contributor to the *Index on Censorship*, currently living in England.

FOR A FULL LIST OF PUBLICATIONS, VISIT:
www.dalkeyarchive.com

SELECTED DALKEY ARCHIVE PAPERBACKS

Man in the Holocene.
CARLOS FUENTES, *Christopher Unborn.*
Distant Relations.
Terra Nostra.
Where the Air Is Clear.
WILLIAM GADDIS, *J R.*
The Recognitions.
JANICE GALLOWAY, *Foreign Parts.*
The Trick Is to Keep Breathing.
WILLIAM H. GASS, *Cartesian Sonata and Other Novellas.*
Finding a Form.
A Temple of Texts.
The Tunnel.
Willie Masters' Lonesome Wife.
GÉRARD GAVARRY, *Hoppla! 1 2 3.*
Making a Novel.
ETIENNE GILSON,
The Arts of the Beautiful.
Forms and Substances in the Arts.
C. S. GISCOMBE, *Giscome Road.*
Here.
Prairie Style.
DOUGLAS GLOVER, *Bad News of the Heart.*
The Enamoured Knight.
WITOLD GOMBROWICZ,
A Kind of Testament.
KAREN ELIZABETH GORDON,
The Red Shoes.
GEORGI GOSPODINOV, *Natural Novel.*
JUAN GOYTISOLO, *Count Julian.*
Exiled from Almost Everywhere.
Juan the Landless.
Makbara.
Marks of Identity.
PATRICK GRAINVILLE, *The Cave of Heaven.*
HENRY GREEN, *Back.*
Blindness.
Concluding.
Doting.
Nothing.
JACK GREEN, *Fire the Bastards!*
JIŘÍ GRUŠA, *The Questionnaire.*
GABRIEL GUDDING,
Rhode Island Notebook.
MELA HARTWIG, *Am I a Redundant Human Being?*
JOHN HAWKES, *The Passion Artist.*
Whistlejacket.
ALEKSANDAR HEMON, ED.,
Best European Fiction.
AIDAN HIGGINS, *A Bestiary.*
Balcony of Europe.
Bornholm Night-Ferry.
Darkling Plain: Texts for the Air.
Flotsam and Jetsam.
Langrishe, Go Down.
Scenes from a Receding Past.
Windy Arbours.
KEIZO HINO, *Isle of Dreams.*
KAZUSHI HOSAKA, *Plainsong.*
ALDOUS HUXLEY, *Antic Hay.*
Crome Yellow.
Point Counter Point.
Those Barren Leaves.
Time Must Have a Stop.
NAOYUKI II, *The Shadow of a Blue Cat.*
MIKHAIL IOSSEL AND JEFF PARKER, EDS.,
Amerika: Russian Writers View the United States.
DRAGO JANČAR, *The Galley Slave.*
GERT JONKE, *The Distant Sound.*

Geometric Regional Novel.
Homage to Czerny.
The System of Vienna.
JACQUES JOUET, *Mountain R.*
Savage.
Upstaged.
CHARLES JULIET, *Conversations with Samuel Beckett and Bram van Velde.*
MIEKO KANAI, *The Word Book.*
YORAM KANIUK, *Life on Sandpaper.*
HUGH KENNER, *The Counterfeiters.*
Flaubert, Joyce and Beckett: The Stoic Comedians.
Joyce's Voices.
DANILO KIŠ, *Garden, Ashes.*
A Tomb for Boris Davidovich.
ANITA KONKKA, *A Fool's Paradise.*
GEORGE KONRÁD, *The City Builder.*
TADEUSZ KONWICKI, *A Minor Apocalypse.*
The Polish Complex.
MENIS KOUMANDAREAS, *Koula.*
ELAINE KRAF, *The Princess of 72nd Street.*
JIM KRUSOE, *Iceland.*
EWA KURYLUK, *Century 21.*
EMILIO LASCANO TEGUI, *On Elegance While Sleeping.*
ERIC LAURRENT, *Do Not Touch.*
HERVÉ LE TELLIER, *The Sextine Chapel.*
A Thousand Pearls (for a Thousand Pennies)
VIOLETTE LEDUC, *La Bâtarde.*
EDOUARD LEVÉ, *Autoportrait.*
Suicide.
SUZANNE JILL LEVINE, *The Subversive Scribe: Translating Latin American Fiction.*
DEBORAH LEVY, *Billy and Girl.*
Pillow Talk in Europe and Other Places.
JOSÉ LEZAMA LIMA, *Paradiso.*
ROSA LIKSOM, *Dark Paradise.*
OSMAN LINS, *Avalovara.*
The Queen of the Prisons of Greece.
ALF MAC LOCHLAINN,
The Corpus in the Library.
Out of Focus.
RON LOEWINSOHN, *Magnetic Field(s).*
MINA LOY, *Stories and Essays of Mina Loy.*
BRIAN LYNCH, *The Winner of Sorrow.*
D. KEITH MANO, *Take Five.*
MICHELINE AHARONIAN MARCOM,
The Mirror in the Well.
BEN MARCUS,
The Age of Wire and String.
WALLACE MARKFIELD,
Teitlebaum's Window.
To an Early Grave.
DAVID MARKSON, *Reader's Block.*
Springer's Progress.
Wittgenstein's Mistress.
CAROLE MASO, *AVA.*
LADISLAV MATEJKA AND KRYSTYNA POMORSKA, EDS.,
Readings in Russian Poetics: Formalist and Structuralist Views.
HARRY MATHEWS,
The Case of the Persevering Maltese: Collected Essays.
Cigarettes.
The Conversions.
The Human Country: New and

FOR A FULL LIST OF PUBLICATIONS, VISIT:
www.dalkeyarchive.com

Collected Stories.
The Journalist.
My Life in CIA.
Singular Pleasures.
The Sinking of the Odradek
    Stadium.
Tlooth.
20 Lines a Day.
JOSEPH MCELROY,
    Night Soul and Other Stories.
THOMAS MCGONIGLE,
    Going to Patchogue.
ROBERT L. MCLAUGHLIN, ED., Innovations:
    An Anthology of
    Modern & Contemporary Fiction.
ABDELWAHAB MEDDEB, Talismano.
GERHARD MEIER, Isle of the Dead.
HERMAN MELVILLE, The Confidence-Man.
AMANDA MICHALOPOULOU, I'd Like.
STEVEN MILLHAUSER,
    The Barnum Museum.
    In the Penny Arcade.
RALPH J. MILLS, JR.,
    Essays on Poetry.
MOMUS, The Book of Jokes.
CHRISTINE MONTALBETTI, Western.
OLIVE MOORE, Spleen.
NICHOLAS MOSLEY, Accident.
    Assassins.
    Catastrophe Practice.
    Children of Darkness and Light.
    Experience and Religion.
    God's Hazard.
    The Hesperides Tree.
    Hopeful Monsters.
    Imago Bird.
    Impossible Object.
    Inventing God.
    Judith.
    Look at the Dark.
    Natalie Natalia.
    Paradoxes of Peace.
    Serpent.
    Time at War.
    The Uses of Slime Mould:
        Essays of Four Decades.
WARREN MOTTE,
    Fables of the Novel: French Fiction
        since 1990.
    Fiction Now: The French Novel in
        the 21st Century.
    Oulipo: A Primer of Potential
        Literature.
GERALD MURNANE, Barley Patch.
YVES NAVARRE, Our Share of Time.
    Sweet Tooth.
DOROTHY NELSON, In Night's City.
    Tar and Feathers.
ESHKOL NEVO, Homesick.
WILFRIDO D. NOLLEDO, But for the Lovers.
FLANN O'BRIEN,
    At Swim-Two-Birds.
    At War.
    The Best of Myles.
    The Dalkey Archive.
    Further Cuttings.
    The Hard Life.
    The Poor Mouth.
    The Third Policeman.
CLAUDE OLLIER, The Mise-en-Scène.
    Wert and the Life Without End.
PATRIK OUŘEDNÍK, Europeana.

The Opportune Moment, 1855.
BORIS PAHOR, Necropolis.
FERNANDO DEL PASO,
    News from the Empire.
    Palinuro of Mexico.
ROBERT PINGET, The Inquisitory.
    Mahu or The Material.
    Trio.
A. G. PORTA, The No World Concerto.
MANUEL PUIG,
    Betrayed by Rita Hayworth.
    The Buenos Aires Affair.
    Heartbreak Tango.
RAYMOND QUENEAU, The Last Days.
    Odile.
    Pierrot Mon Ami.
    Saint Glinglin.
ANN QUIN, Berg.
    Passages.
    Three.
    Tripticks.
ISHMAEL REED,
    The Free-Lance Pallbearers.
    The Last Days of Louisiana Red.
    Ishmael Reed: The Plays.
    Juice!
    Reckless Eyeballing.
    The Terrible Threes.
    The Terrible Twos.
    Yellow Back Radio Broke-Down.
JOÃO UBALDO RIBEIRO, House of the
    Fortunate Buddhas.
JEAN RICARDOU, Place Names.
RAINER MARIA RILKE, The Notebooks of
    Malte Laurids Brigge.
JULIÁN RÍOS, The House of Ulysses.
    Larva: A Midsummer Night's Babel.
    Poundemonium.
    Procession of Shadows.
AUGUSTO ROA BASTOS, I the Supreme.
DANIËL ROBBERECHTS,
    Arriving in Avignon.
JEAN ROLIN, The Explosion of the
    Radiator Hose.
OLIVIER ROLIN, Hotel Crystal.
ALIX CLEO ROUBAUD, Alix's Journal.
JACQUES ROUBAUD, The Form of a
    City Changes Faster, Alas, Than
    the Human Heart.
    The Great Fire of London.
    Hortense in Exile.
    Hortense Is Abducted.
    The Loop.
    Mathématique:
    The Plurality of Worlds of Lewis.
    The Princess Hoppy.
    Some Thing Black.
LEON S. ROUDIEZ, French Fiction Revisited.
RAYMOND ROUSSEL, Impressions of Africa.
VEDRANA RUDAN, Night.
STIG SÆTERBAKKEN, Siamese.
LYDIE SALVAYRE, The Company of Ghosts.
    Everyday Life.
    The Lecture.
    Portrait of the Writer as a
        Domesticated Animal.
    The Power of Flies.
LUIS RAFAEL SÁNCHEZ,
    Macho Camacho's Beat.
SEVERO SARDUY, Cobra & Maitreya.
NATHALIE SARRAUTE,
    Do You Hear Them?

Martereau.
The Planetarium.
ARNO SCHMIDT, *Collected Novellas.*
Collected Stories.
Nobodaddy's Children.
Two Novels.
ASAF SCHURR, *Motti.*
CHRISTINE SCHUTT, *Nightwork.*
GAIL SCOTT, *My Paris.*
DAMION SEARLS, *What We Were Doing*
and Where We Were Going.
JUNE AKERS SEESE,
Is This What Other Women Feel Too?
What Waiting Really Means.
BERNARD SHARE, *Inish.*
Transit.
AURELIE SHEEHAN,
Jack Kerouac Is Pregnant.
VIKTOR SHKLOVSKY, *Bowstring.*
Knight's Move.
A Sentimental Journey:
Memoirs 1917–1922.
Energy of Delusion: A Book on Plot.
Literature and Cinematography.
Theory of Prose.
Third Factory.
Zoo, or Letters Not about Love.
CLAUDE SIMON, *The Invitation.*
PIERRE SINIAC, *The Collaborators.*
KJERSTI A. SKOMSVOLD, *The Faster I Walk,*
the Smaller I Am.
JOSEF ŠKVORECKÝ, *The Engineer of*
Human Souls.
GILBERT SORRENTINO,
Aberration of Starlight.
Blue Pastoral.
Crystal Vision.
Imaginative Qualities of Actual
Things.
Mulligan Stew.
Pack of Lies.
Red the Fiend.
The Sky Changes.
Something Said.
Splendide-Hôtel.
Steelwork.
Under the Shadow.
W. M. SPACKMAN,
The Complete Fiction.
ANDRZEJ STASIUK, *Dukla.*
Fado.
GERTRUDE STEIN,
Lucy Church Amiably.
The Making of Americans.
A Novel of Thank You.
LARS SVENDSEN, *A Philosophy of Evil.*
PIOTR SZEWC, *Annihilation.*
GONÇALO M. TAVARES, *Jerusalem.*
Joseph Walser's Machine.
Learning to Pray in the Age of
Technique.
LUCIAN DAN TEODOROVICI,
Our Circus Presents . . .
NIKANOR TERATOLOGEN, *Assisted Living.*
STEFAN THEMERSON, *Hobson's Island.*
The Mystery of the Sardine.
Tom Harris.
JOHN TOOMEY, *Sleepwalker.*
JEAN-PHILIPPE TOUSSAINT,
The Bathroom.
Camera.
Monsieur.

Running Away.
Self-Portrait Abroad.
Television.
The Truth about Marie.
DUMITRU TSEPENEAG,
Hotel Europa.
The Necessary Marriage.
Pigeon Post.
Vain Art of the Fugue.
ESTHER TUSQUETS, *Stranded.*
DUBRAVKA UGRESIC,
Lend Me Your Character.
Thank You for Not Reading.
MATI UNT, *Brecht at Night.*
Diary of a Blood Donor.
Things in the Night.
ÁLVARO URIBE AND OLIVIA SEARS, EDS.,
Best of Contemporary Mexican
Fiction.
ELOY URROZ, *Friction.*
The Obstacles.
LUISA VALENZUELA, *Dark Desires and*
the Others.
He Who Searches.
MARJA-LIISA VARTIO,
The Parson's Widow.
PAUL VERHAEGHEN, *Omega Minor.*
AGLAJA VETERANYI, *Why the Child Is*
Cooking in the Polenta.
BORIS VIAN, *Heartsnatcher.*
LLORENÇ VILLALONGA, *The Dolls' Room.*
ORNELA VORPSI, *The Country Where No*
One Ever Dies.
AUSTRYN WAINHOUSE, *Hedyphagetica.*
PAUL WEST,
Words for a Deaf Daughter & Gala.
CURTIS WHITE,
America's Magic Mountain.
The Idea of Home.
Memories of My Father Watching TV.
Monstrous Possibility: An Invitation
to Literary Politics.
Requiem.
DIANE WILLIAMS, *Excitability:*
Selected Stories.
Romancer Erector.
DOUGLAS WOOLF, *Wall to Wall.*
Ya! & John-Juan.
JAY WRIGHT, *Polynomials and Pollen.*
The Presentable Art of Reading
Absence.
PHILIP WYLIE, *Generation of Vipers.*
MARGUERITE YOUNG, *Angel in the Forest.*
Miss MacIntosh, My Darling.
REYOUNG, *Unbabbling.*
VLADO ŽABOT, *The Succubus.*
ZORAN ŽIVKOVIĆ, *Hidden Camera.*
LOUIS ZUKOFSKY, *Collected Fiction.*
VITOMIL ZUPAN, *Minuet for Guitar.*
SCOTT ZWIREN, *God Head.*